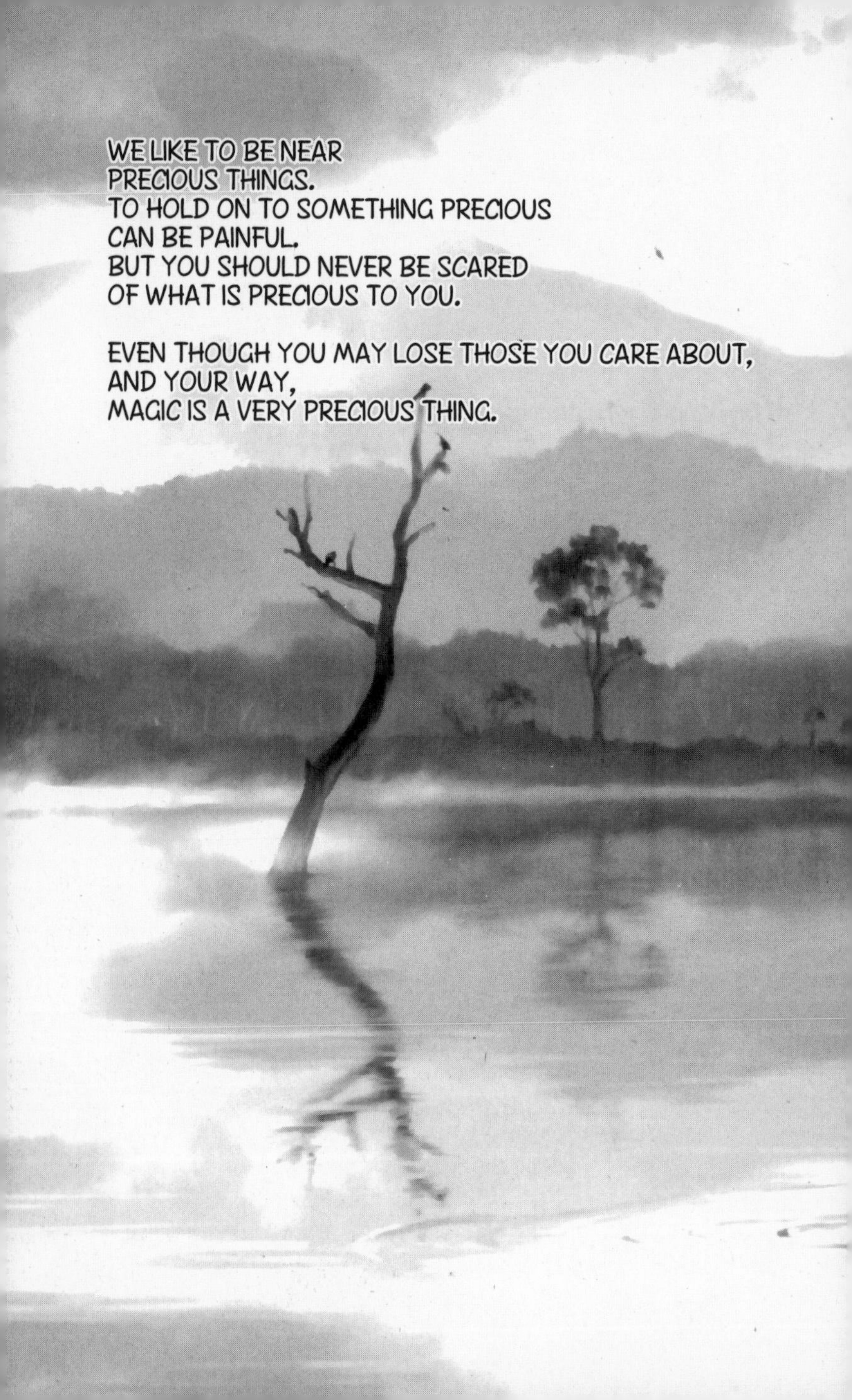
WE LIKE TO BE NEAR
PRECIOUS THINGS.
TO HOLD ON TO SOMETHING PRECIOUS
CAN BE PAINFUL.
BUT YOU SHOULD NEVER BE SCARED
OF WHAT IS PRECIOUS TO YOU.
EVEN THOUGH YOU MAY LOSE THOSE YOU CARE ABOUT,
AND YOUR WAY,
MAGIC IS A VERY PRECIOUS THING.

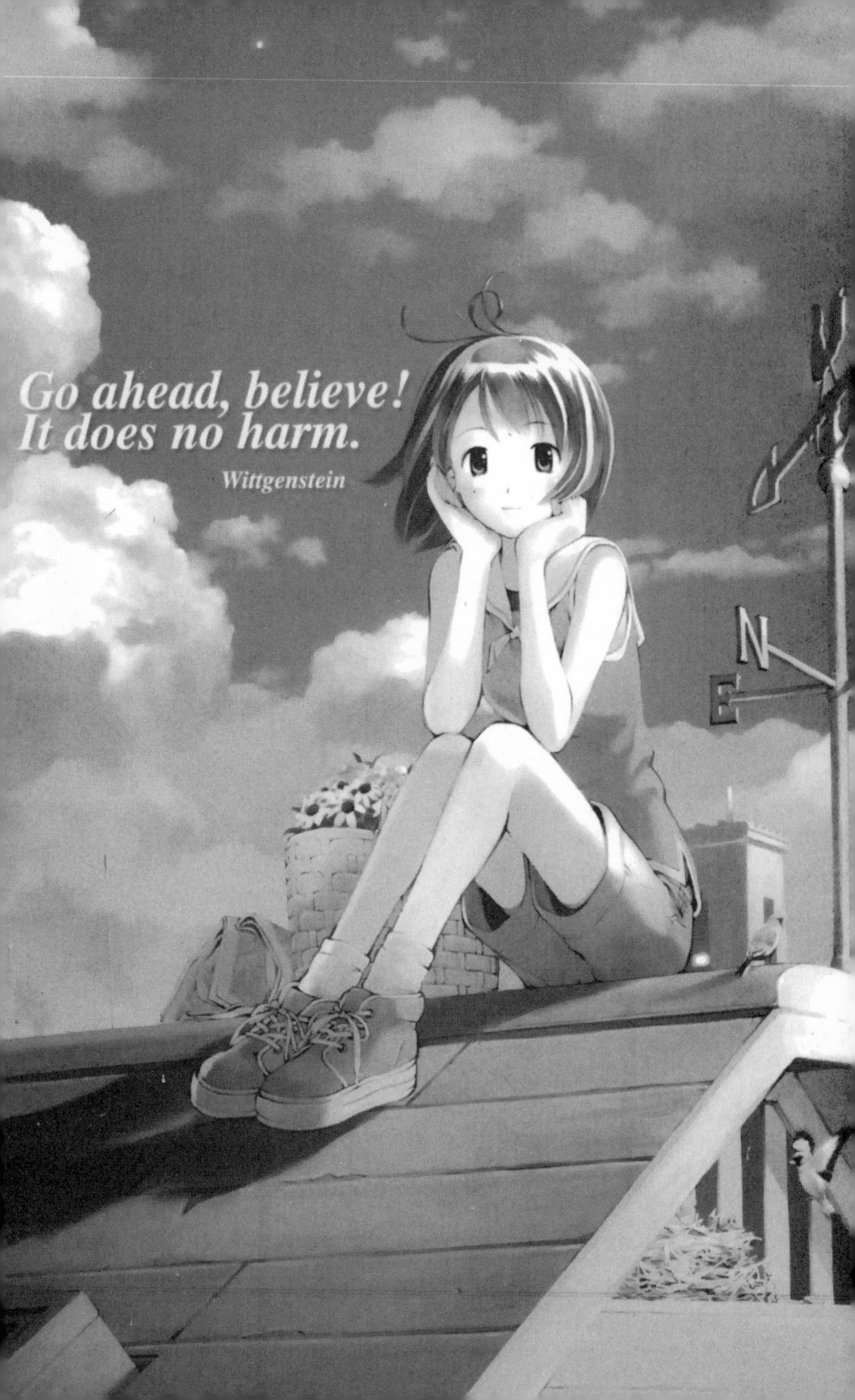
Go ahead, believe!
It does no harm.
Wittgenstein

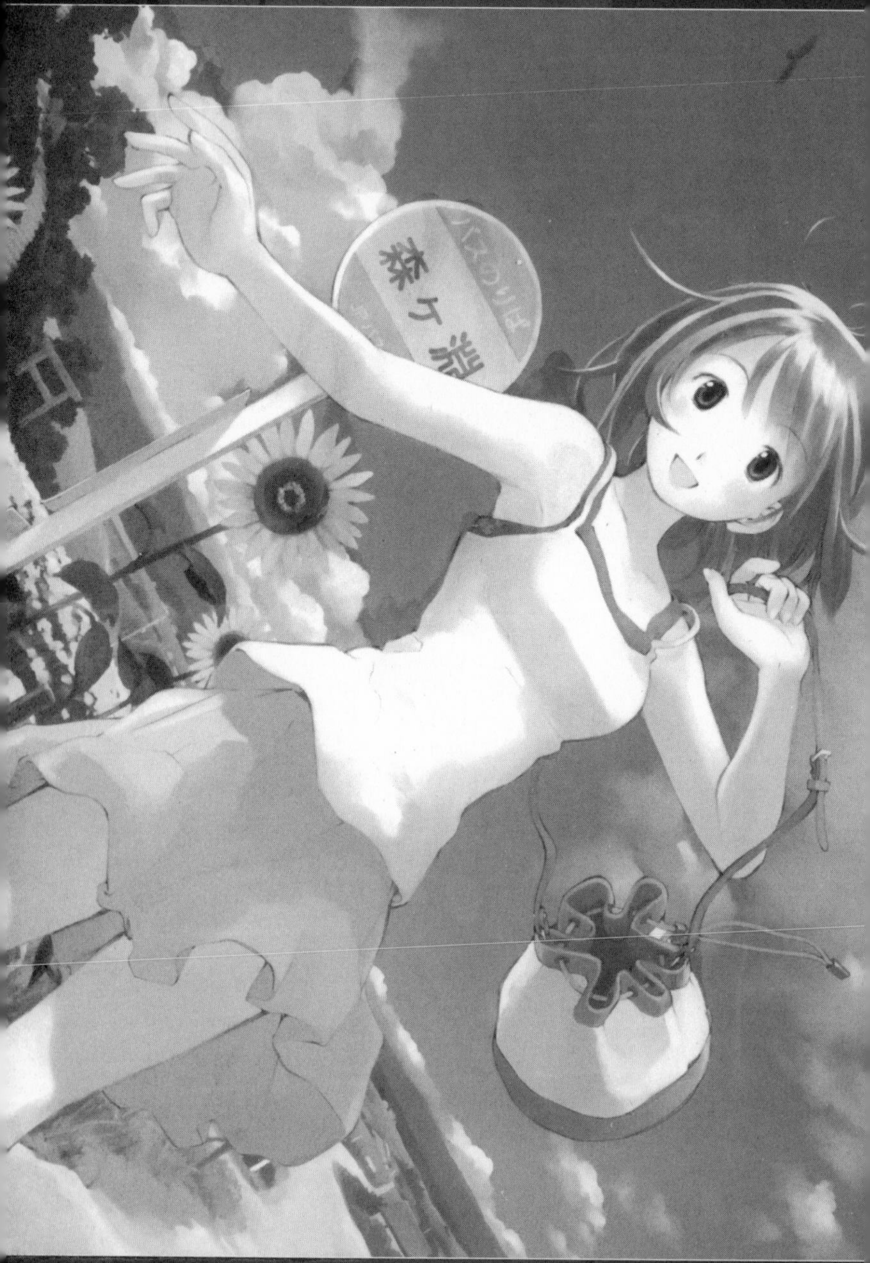
バスのりば
森ケ

Someday's Dreamers Vol. 2
Story by Norie Yamada
Art by Kumichi Yoshizuki

Translation - Jeremiah Bourque
English Adaptation - Hope Donovan
Copy Editor - Peter Ahlstrom
Retouch and Lettering - Creative Circle and Camellia Cox
Production Artist - Fawn Lau
Cover Design - Gary Shum

Editor - Paul Morrissey
Digital Imaging Manager - Chris Buford
Production Manager - Elisabeth Brizzi
Managing Editor - Lindsey Johnston
VP of Production - Ron Klamert
Editor-in-Chief - Rob Tokar
Publisher - Mike Kiley
President and C.O.O. - John Parker
C.E.O. and Chief Creative Officer - Stuart Levy

A  Manga

TOKYOPOP Inc.
5900 Wilshire Blvd. Suite 2000
Los Angeles, CA 90036

E-mail: info@TOKYOPOP.com
Come visit us online at www.TOKYOPOP.com

MAHOUTSUKAI NI TAISETSUNA KOTO Volume 2
© 2003 NORIE YAMADA/KUMICHI YOSHIZUKI
© NORIE YAMADA/KADOKAWA PICTURES/PNDTK/TV Asahi
First published in Japan in 2003 by
KADOKAWA SHOTEN PUBLISHING CO., LTD., Tokyo.
English Translation rights arranged with
KADOKAWA SHOTEN PUBLISHING CO., LTD., Tokyo
through TUTTLE-MORI AGENCY, INC., Tokyo.
English text copyright © 2006 TOKYOPOP Inc.

ISBN: 1-59816-179-2

First TOKYOPOP printing: July 2006
10 9 8 7 6 5 4 3 2 1
Printed in the USA

魔法遣いに大切なこと
SOMEDAY's DREAMERS

VOLUME 2

CREATED BY NORIE YAMADA

ART BY KUMICHI YOSHIZUKI

TOKYOPOP®

HAMBURG // LONDON // LOS ANGELES // TOKYO

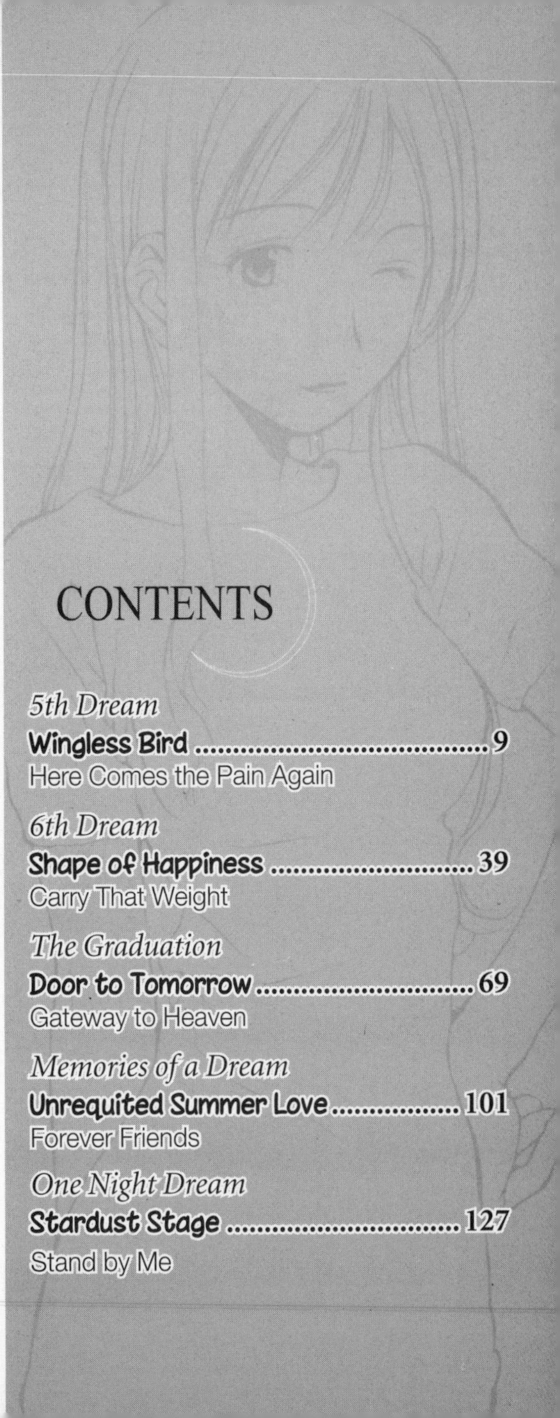

CONTENTS

IT'S OKAY. DON'T WORRY ABOUT IT.

I'M SORRY, SENSEI...

I CAN'T DO MAGIC TODAY, EITHER...

MAGIC ?!

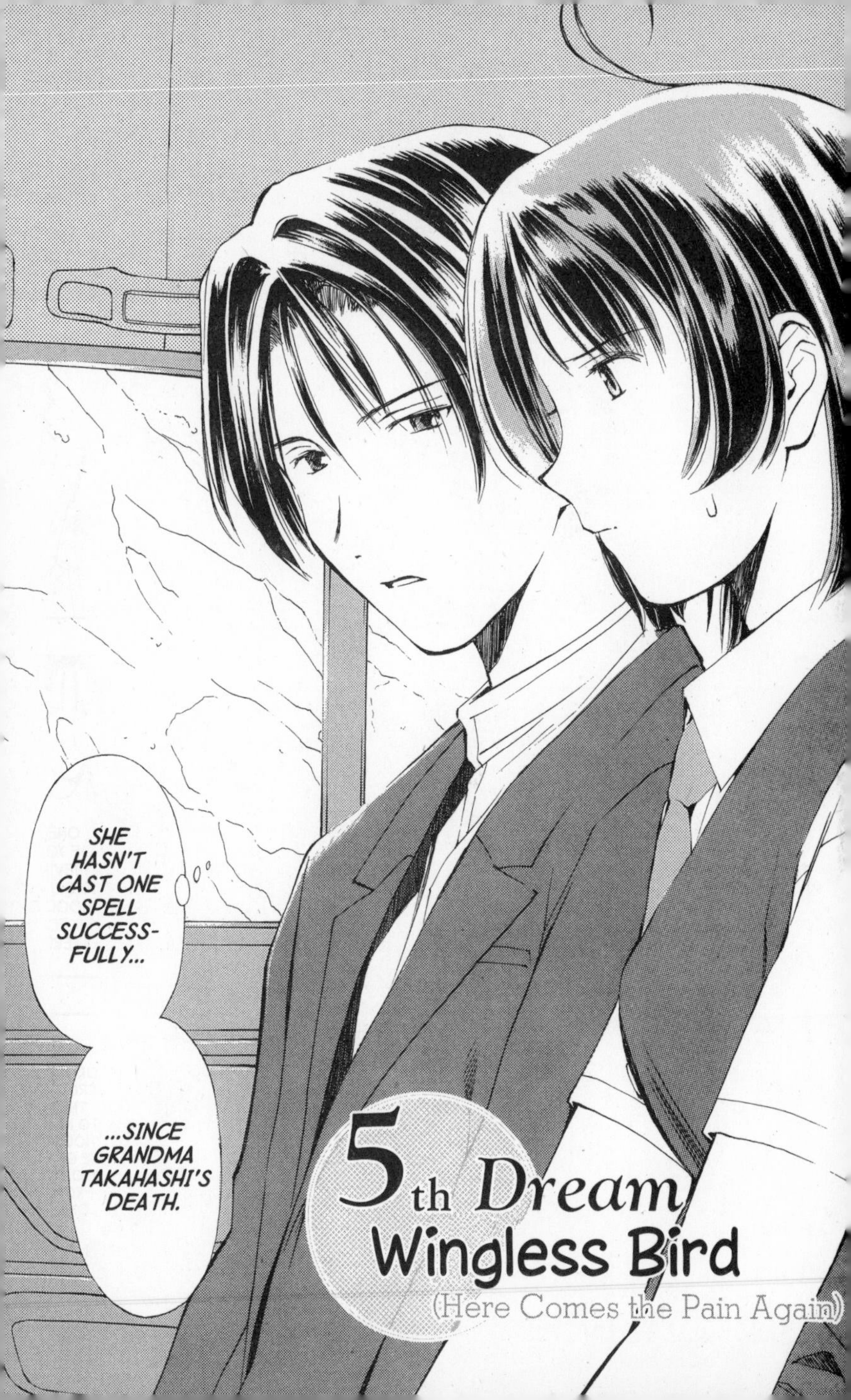
SHE HASN'T CAST ONE SPELL SUCCESS-FULLY...
...SINCE GRANDMA TAKAHASHI'S DEATH.
5th Dream
Wingless Bird
(Here Comes the Pain Again)

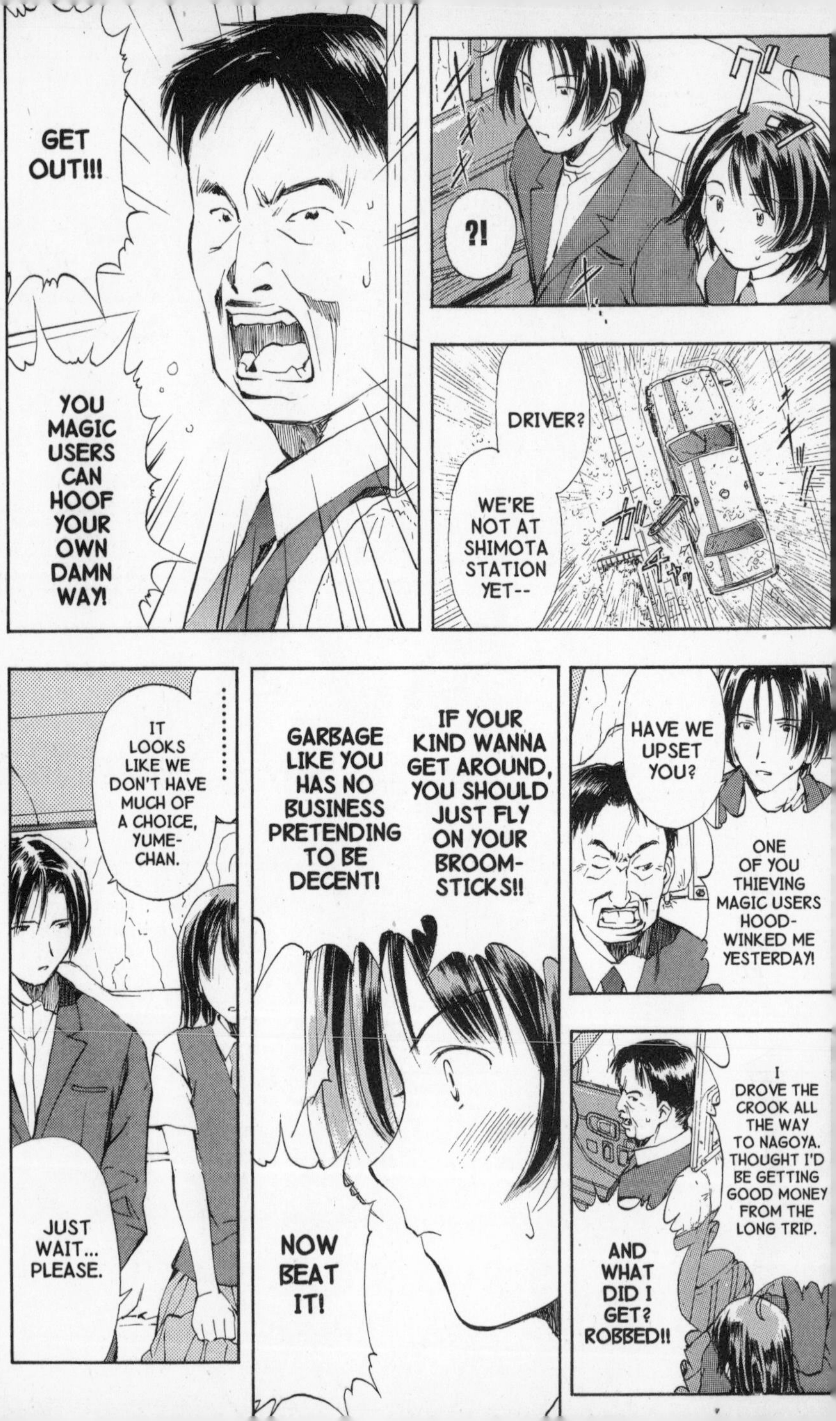
?!
DRIVER?
WE'RE NOT AT SHIMOTA STATION YET--
GET OUT!!!
YOU MAGIC USERS CAN HOOF YOUR OWN DAMN WAY!
HAVE WE UPSET YOU?
ONE OF YOU THIEVING MAGIC USERS HOOD-WINKED ME YESTERDAY!
I DROVE THE CROOK ALL THE WAY TO NAGOYA. THOUGHT I'D BE GETTING GOOD MONEY FROM THE LONG TRIP.
AND WHAT DID I GET? ROBBED!!
IF YOUR KIND WANNA GET AROUND, YOU SHOULD JUST FLY ON YOUR BROOM-STICKS!!
GARBAGE LIKE YOU HAS NO BUSINESS PRETENDING TO BE DECENT!
NOW BEAT IT!
....
IT LOOKS LIKE WE DON'T HAVE MUCH OF A CHOICE, YUME-CHAN.
JUST WAIT... PLEASE.

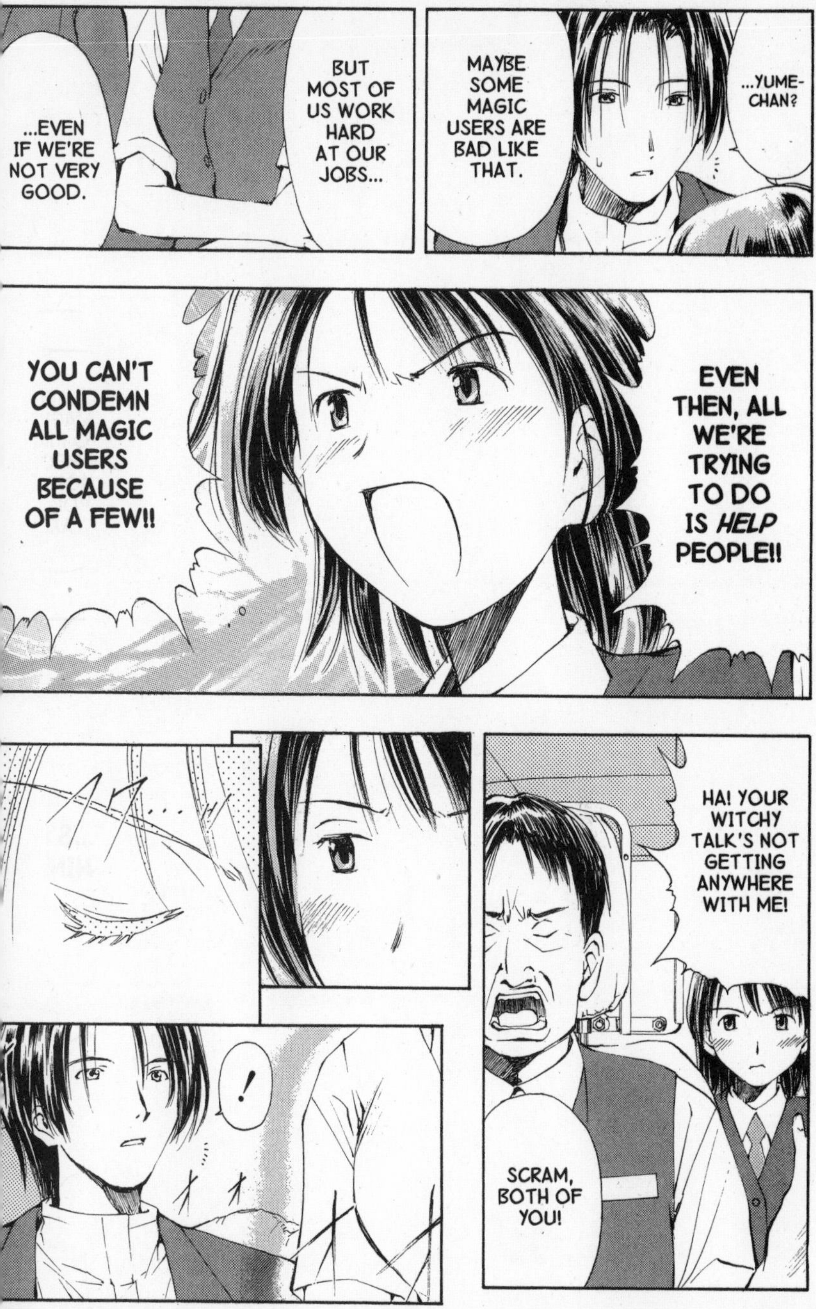

...YUME-CHAN?
MAYBE SOME MAGIC USERS ARE BAD LIKE THAT.
BUT MOST OF US WORK HARD AT OUR JOBS...
...EVEN IF WE'RE NOT VERY GOOD.
EVEN THEN, ALL WE'RE TRYING TO DO IS *HELP* PEOPLE!!
YOU CAN'T CONDEMN ALL MAGIC USERS BECAUSE OF A FEW!!
HA! YOUR WITCHY TALK'S NOT GETTING ANYWHERE WITH ME!
SCRAM, BOTH OF YOU!
!

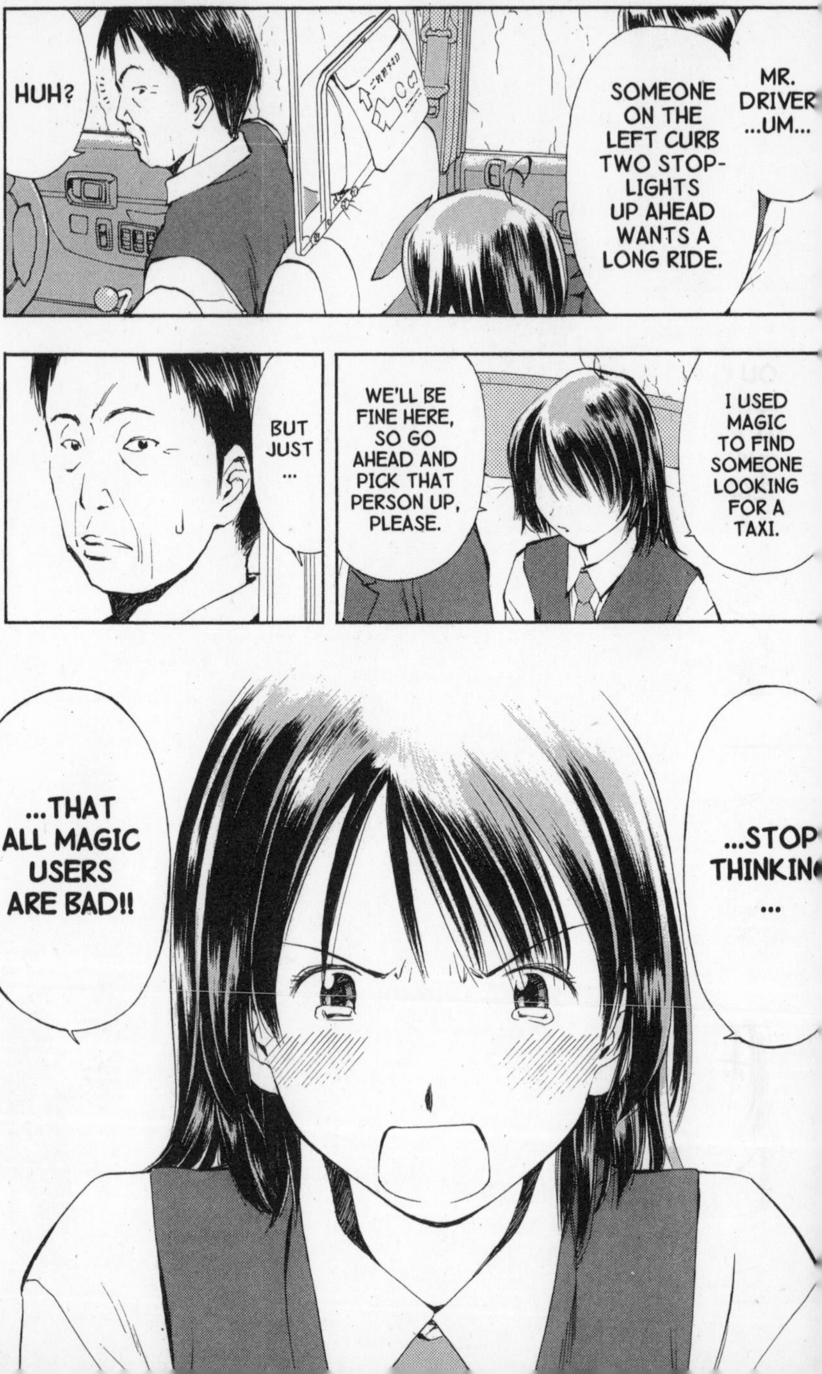
MR. DRIVER ...UM...
SOMEONE ON THE LEFT CURB TWO STOP-LIGHTS UP AHEAD WANTS A LONG RIDE.
HUH?
I USED MAGIC TO FIND SOMEONE LOOKING FOR A TAXI.
WE'LL BE FINE HERE, SO GO AHEAD AND PICK THAT PERSON UP, PLEASE.
BUT JUST ...
...STOP THINKIN ...
...THAT ALL MAGIC USERS ARE BAD!!

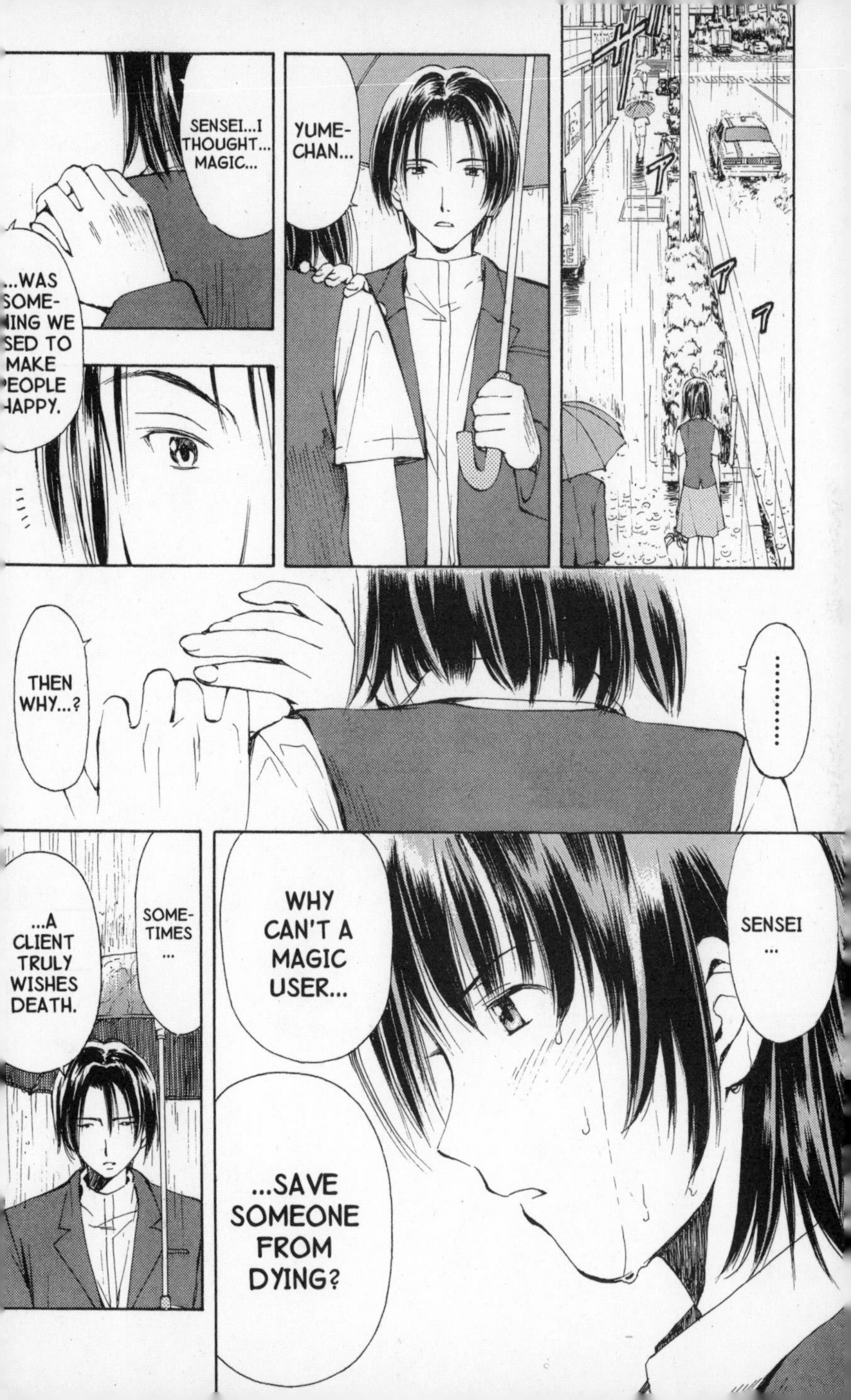
YUME-CHAN...
SENSEI...I THOUGHT... MAGIC...
...WAS SOME-ING WE SED TO MAKE EOPLE APPY.
......
THEN WHY...?
SENSEI ...
WHY CAN'T A MAGIC USER...
...SAVE SOMEONE FROM DYING?
SOME-TIMES ...
...A CLIENT TRULY WISHES DEATH.

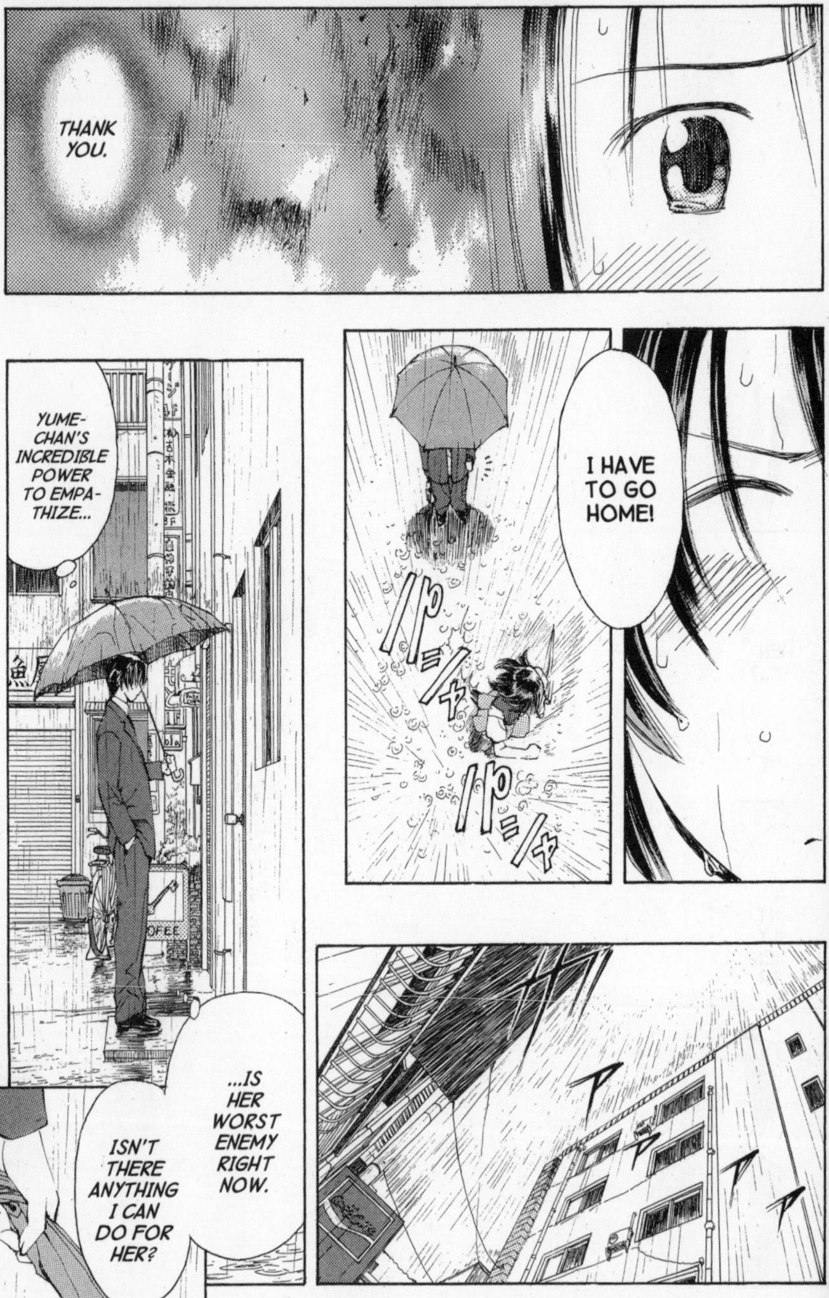
THANK YOU.
I HAVE TO GO HOME!
YUME-CHAN'S INCREDIBLE POWER TO EMPATHIZE...
...IS HER WORST ENEMY RIGHT NOW.
ISN'T THERE ANYTHING I CAN DO FOR HER?

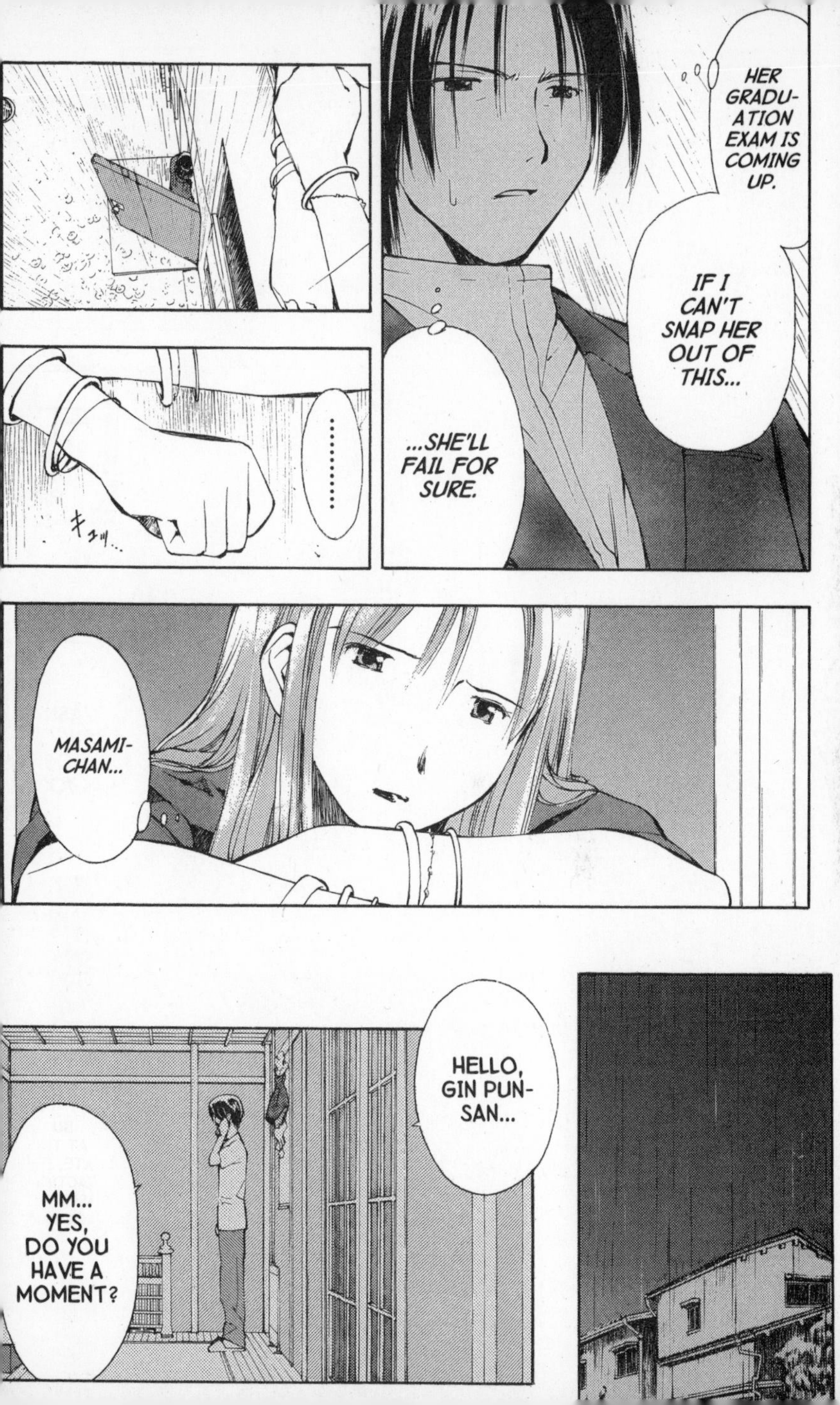
HER GRADU-ATION EXAM IS COMING UP.
IF I CAN'T SNAP HER OUT OF THIS...
...SHE'LL FAIL FOR SURE.
....
キュッ...
MASAMI-CHAN...
HELLO, GIN PUN-SAN...
MM... YES, DO YOU HAVE A MOMENT?

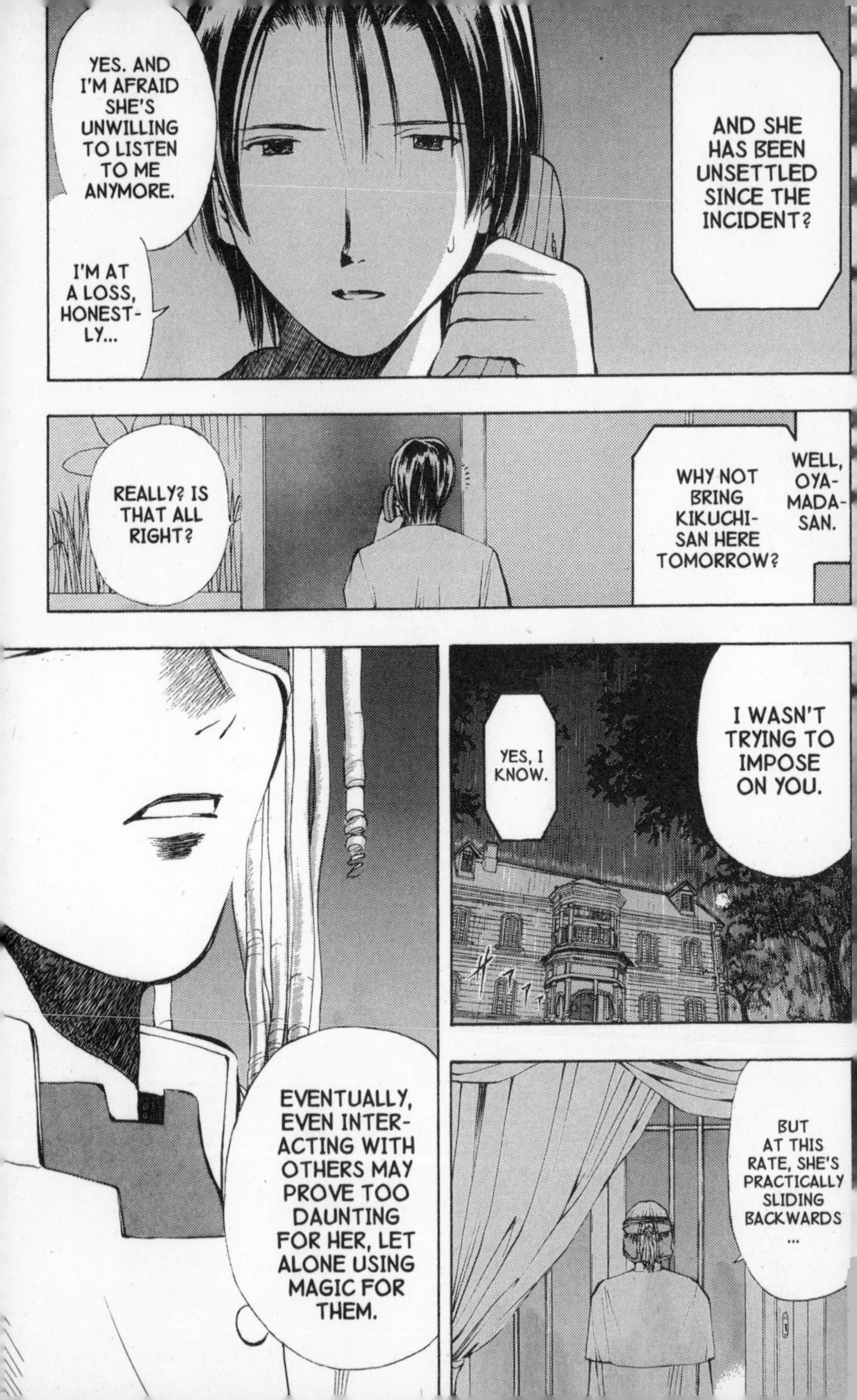
AND SHE HAS BEEN UNSETTLED SINCE THE INCIDENT?
YES. AND I'M AFRAID SHE'S UNWILLING TO LISTEN TO ME ANYMORE.
I'M AT A LOSS, HONESTLY...
WELL, OYAMADA-SAN.
WHY NOT BRING KIKUCHI-SAN HERE TOMORROW?
REALLY? IS THAT ALL RIGHT?
I WASN'T TRYING TO IMPOSE ON YOU.
YES, I KNOW.
BUT AT THIS RATE, SHE'S PRACTICALLY SLIDING BACKWARDS ...
EVENTUALLY, EVEN INTERACTING WITH OTHERS MAY PROVE TOO DAUNTING FOR HER, LET ALONE USING MAGIC FOR THEM.

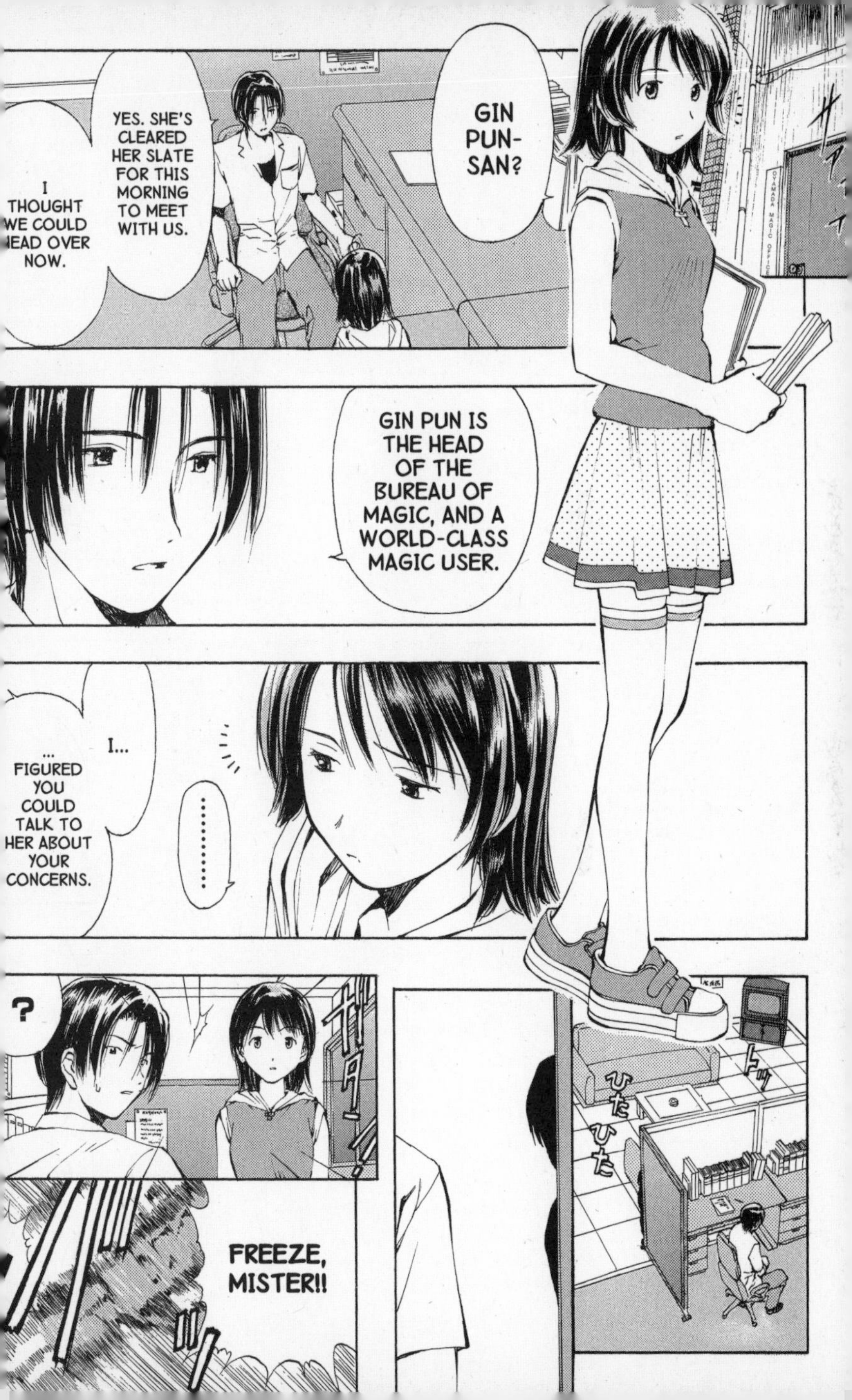
OYAMADA MAGIC OFFICE
GIN PUN-SAN?
YES. SHE'S CLEARED HER SLATE FOR THIS MORNING TO MEET WITH US.
I THOUGHT WE COULD HEAD OVER NOW.
GIN PUN IS THE HEAD OF THE BUREAU OF MAGIC, AND A WORLD-CLASS MAGIC USER.
....
I...
...FIGURED YOU COULD TALK TO HER ABOUT YOUR CONCERNS.
トッ
ひたひた
?
FREEZE, MISTER!!

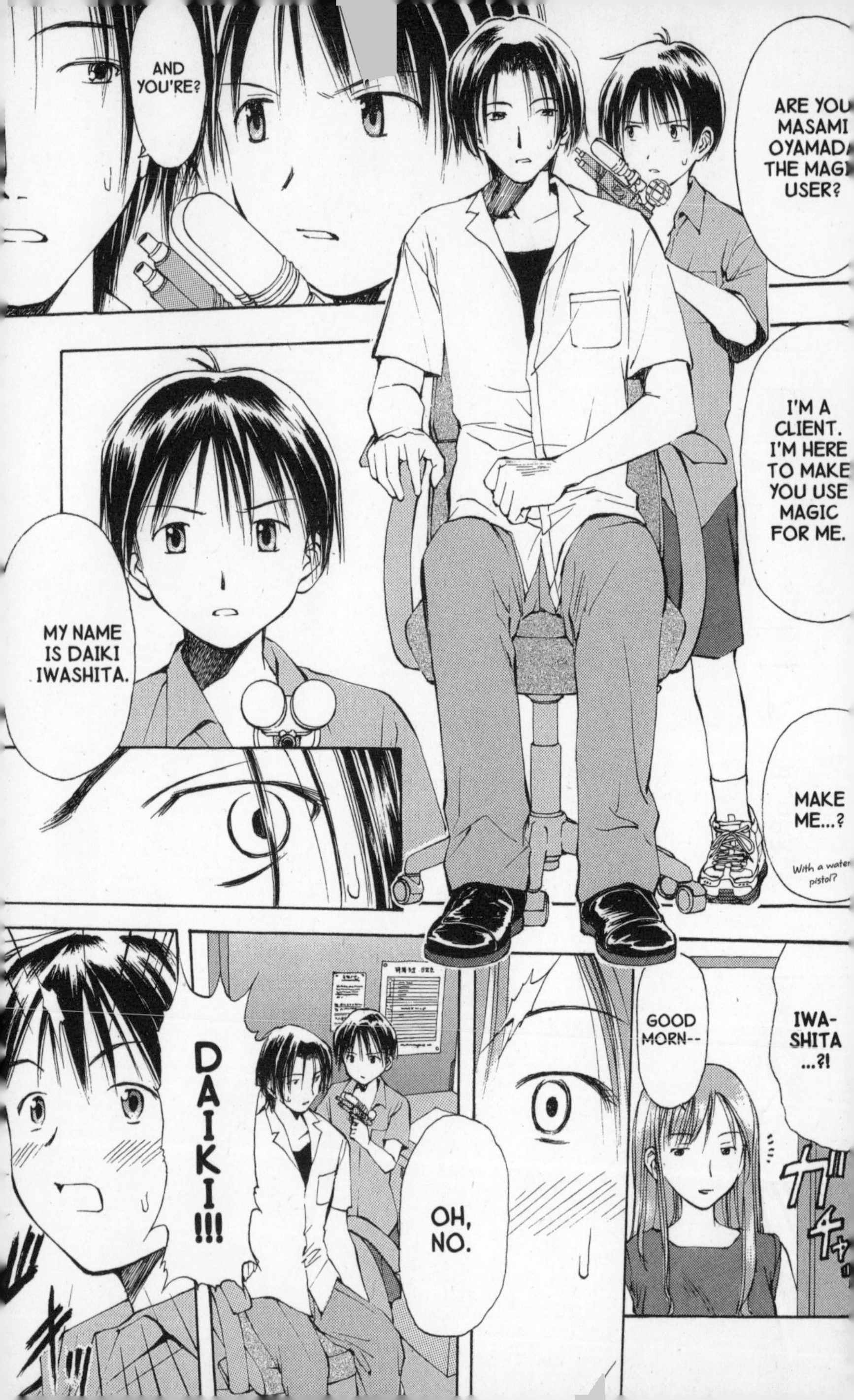
ARE YOU MASAMI OYAMADA THE MAGI USER?
AND YOU'RE?
MY NAME IS DAIKI IWASHITA.
I'M A CLIENT. I'M HERE TO MAKE YOU USE MAGIC FOR ME.
MAKE ME...?
With a water pistol?
IWA-SHITA ...?!
GOOD MORN--
OH, NO.
DAIKI!!!

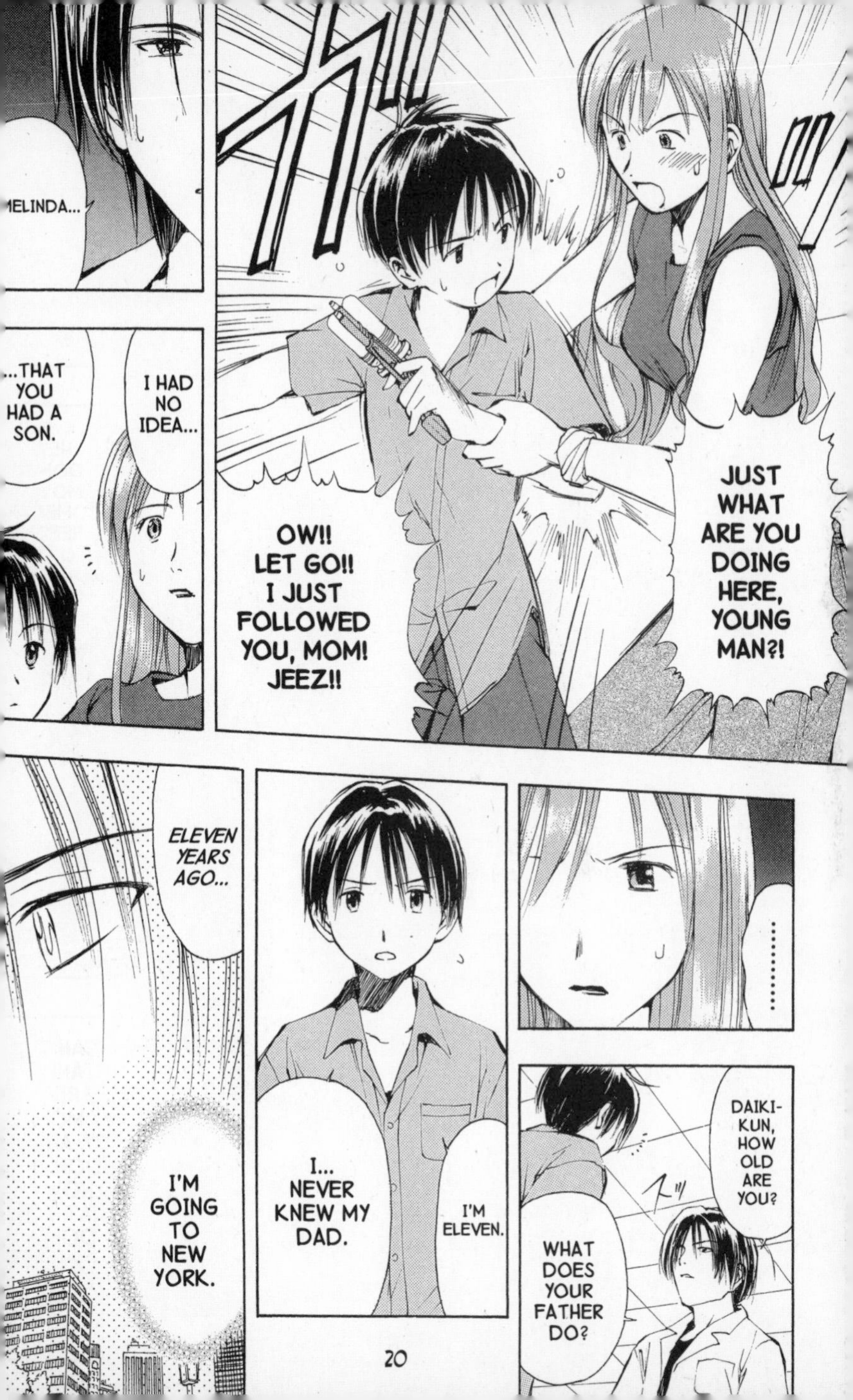
JUST WHAT ARE YOU DOING HERE, YOUNG MAN?!
OW!! LET GO!! I JUST FOLLOWED YOU, MOM! JEEZ!!
MELINDA...
I HAD NO IDEA...
...THAT YOU HAD A SON.
....
DAIKI-KUN, HOW OLD ARE YOU?
WHAT DOES YOUR FATHER DO?
I'M ELEVEN.
I... NEVER KNEW MY DAD.
ELEVEN YEARS AGO...
I'M GOING TO NEW YORK.

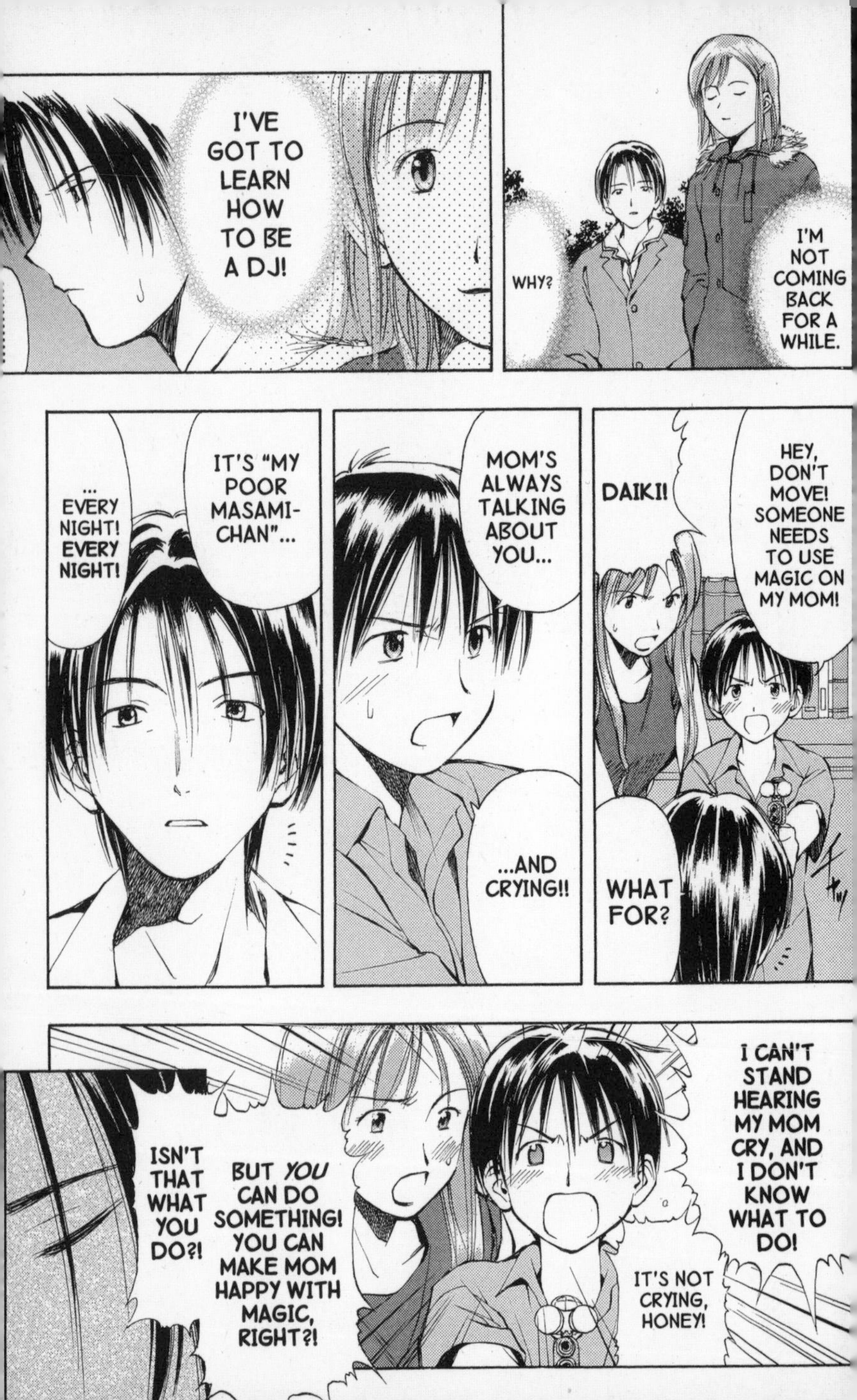
I'M NOT COMING BACK FOR A WHILE.
WHY?
I'VE GOT TO LEARN HOW TO BE A DJ!
HEY, DON'T MOVE! SOMEONE NEEDS TO USE MAGIC ON MY MOM!
DAIKI!
WHAT FOR?
MOM'S ALWAYS TALKING ABOUT YOU...
...AND CRYING!!
IT'S "MY POOR MASAMI-CHAN"...
... EVERY NIGHT! EVERY NIGHT!
I CAN'T STAND HEARING MY MOM CRY, AND I DON'T KNOW WHAT TO DO!
IT'S NOT CRYING, HONEY!
BUT *YOU* CAN DO SOMETHING! YOU CAN MAKE MOM HAPPY WITH MAGIC, RIGHT?!
ISN'T THAT WHAT YOU DO?!

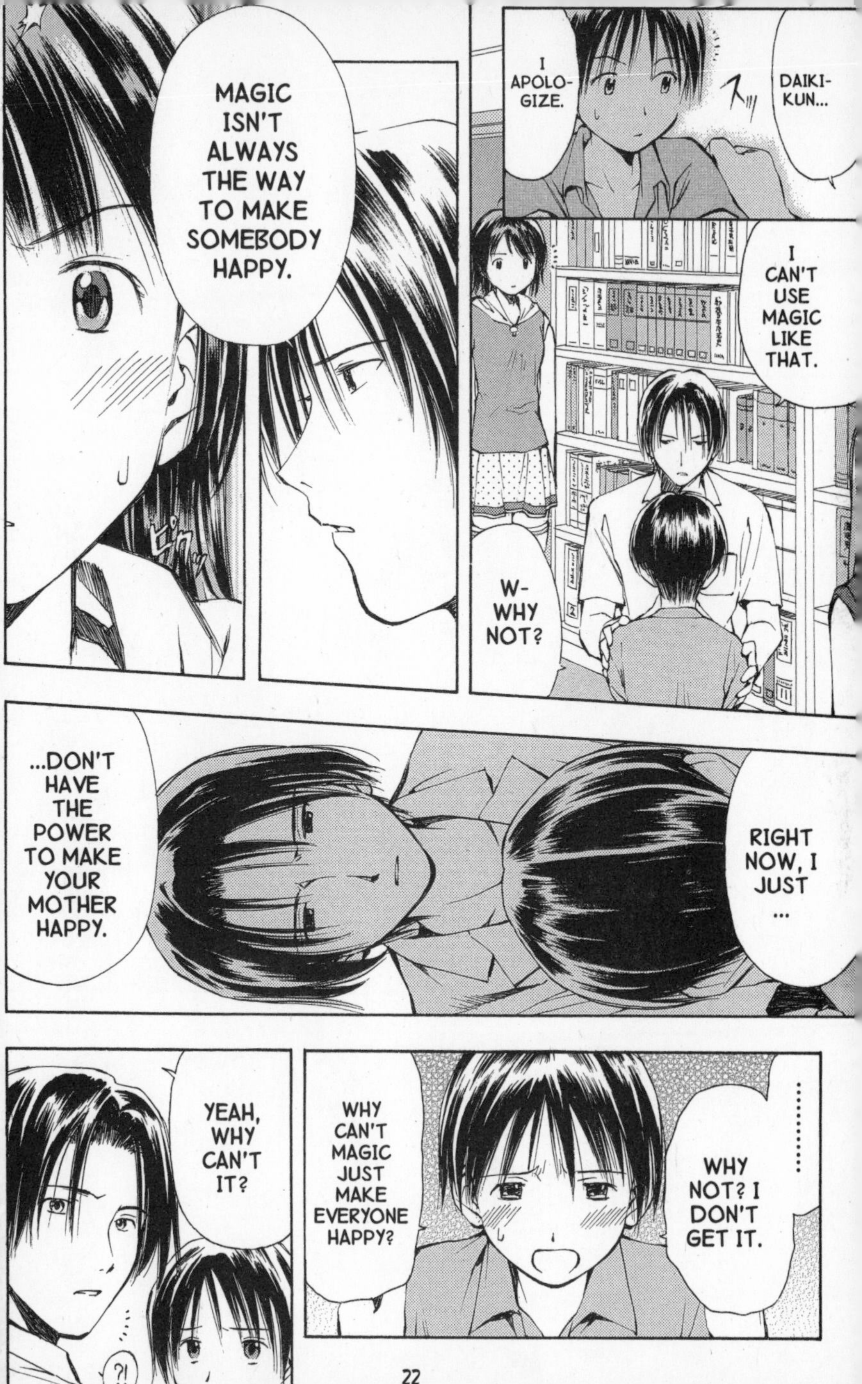
DAIKI-KUN...
I APOLOGIZE.
I CAN'T USE MAGIC LIKE THAT.
W-WHY NOT?
MAGIC ISN'T ALWAYS THE WAY TO MAKE SOMEBODY HAPPY.
RIGHT NOW, I JUST ...
...DON'T HAVE THE POWER TO MAKE YOUR MOTHER HAPPY.
......
WHY NOT? I DON'T GET IT.
WHY CAN'T MAGIC JUST MAKE EVERYONE HAPPY?
YEAH, WHY CAN'T IT?
?!

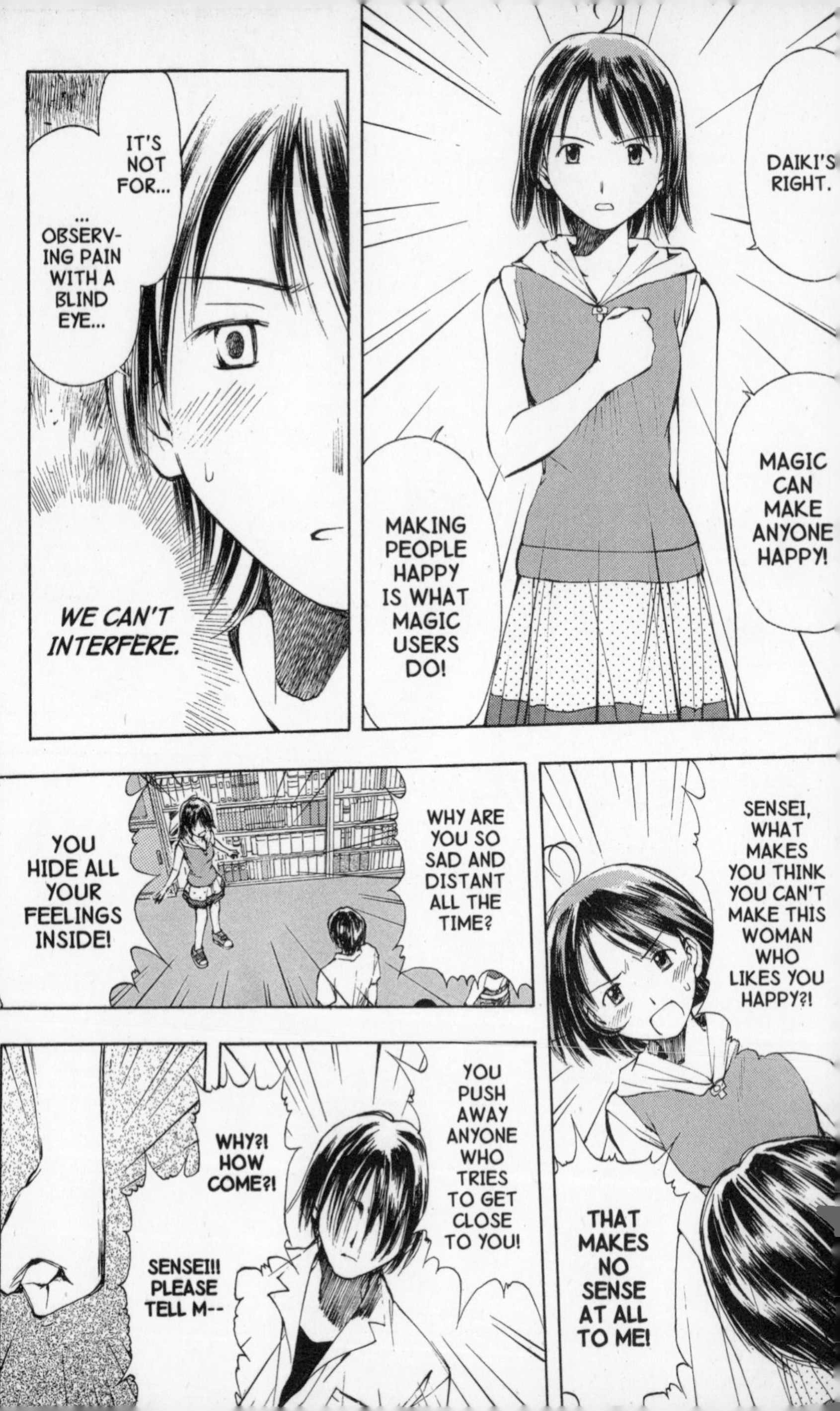
DAIKI'S RIGHT.
MAGIC CAN MAKE ANYONE HAPPY!
MAKING PEOPLE HAPPY IS WHAT MAGIC USERS DO!
IT'S NOT FOR...
... OBSERV-ING PAIN WITH A BLIND EYE...
WE CAN'T INTERFERE.
SENSEI, WHAT MAKES YOU THINK YOU CAN'T MAKE THIS WOMAN WHO LIKES YOU HAPPY?!
THAT MAKES NO SENSE AT ALL TO ME!
WHY ARE YOU SO SAD AND DISTANT ALL THE TIME?
YOU HIDE ALL YOUR FEELINGS INSIDE!
YOU PUSH AWAY ANYONE WHO TRIES TO GET CLOSE TO YOU!
WHY?! HOW COME?!
SENSEI!! PLEASE TELL M--

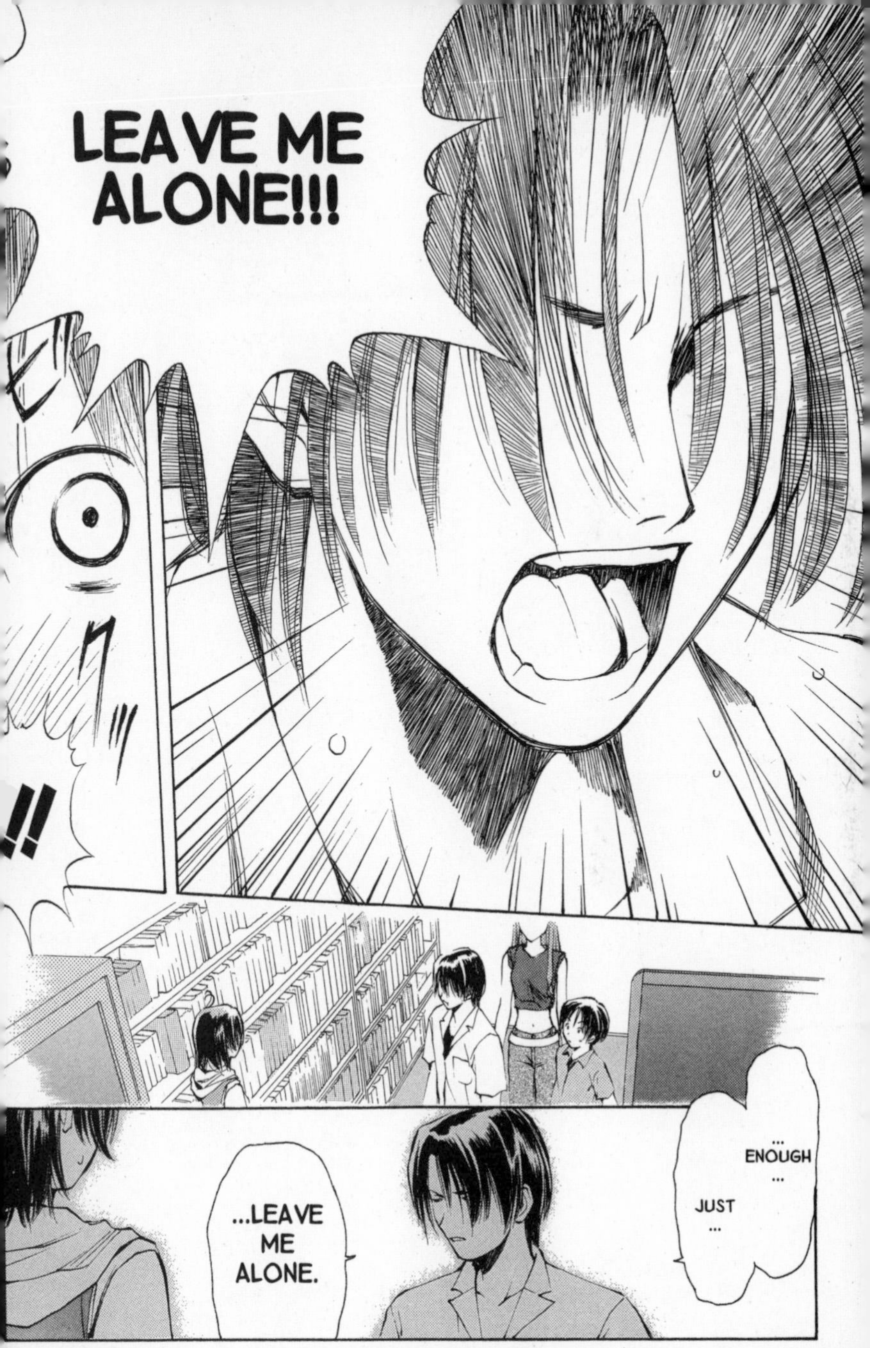

LEAVE ME ALONE!!!
!!
... ENOUGH ... JUST ...
...LEAVE ME ALONE.

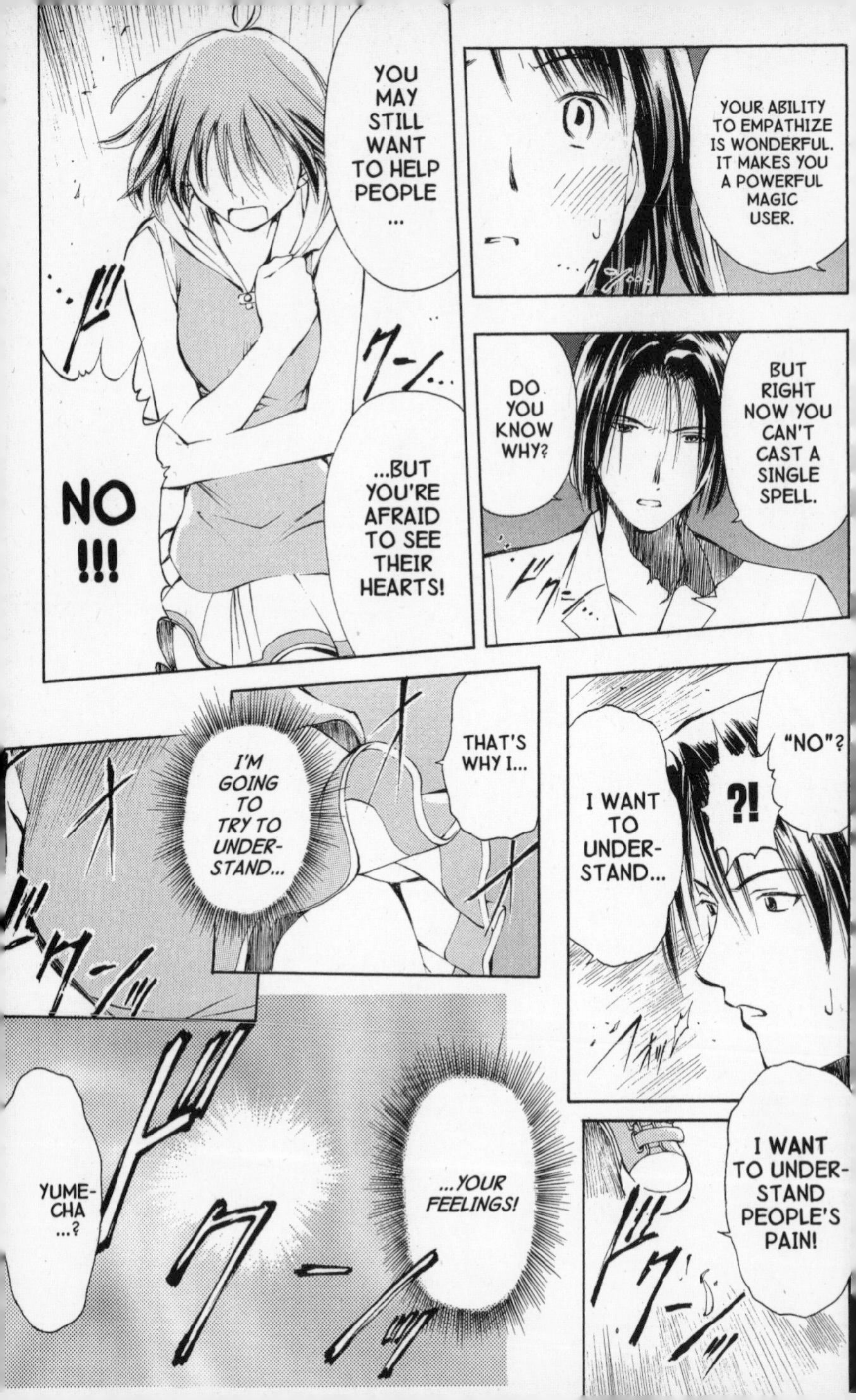
YOUR ABILITY TO EMPATHIZE IS WONDERFUL. IT MAKES YOU A POWERFUL MAGIC USER.
BUT RIGHT NOW YOU CAN'T CAST A SINGLE SPELL.
DO YOU KNOW WHY?
YOU MAY STILL WANT TO HELP PEOPLE ...
...BUT YOU'RE AFRAID TO SEE THEIR HEARTS!
NO !!!
"NO"?
?!
I WANT TO UNDER-STAND...
THAT'S WHY I...
I'M GOING TO TRY TO UNDER-STAND...
I WANT TO UNDER-STAND PEOPLE'S PAIN!
...YOUR FEELINGS!
YUME-CHA ...?

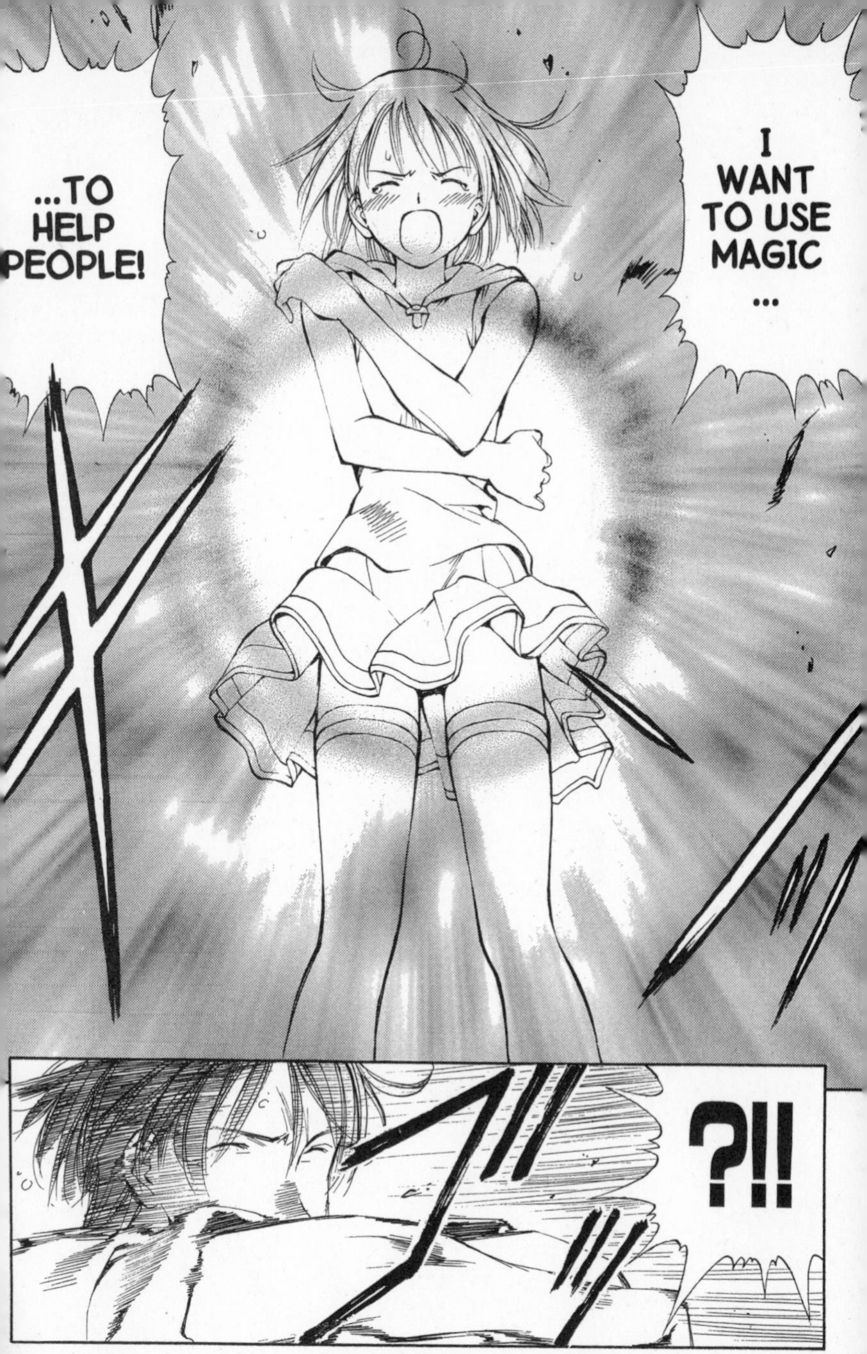
I WANT TO USE MAGIC ...
...TO HELP PEOPLE!
?!!

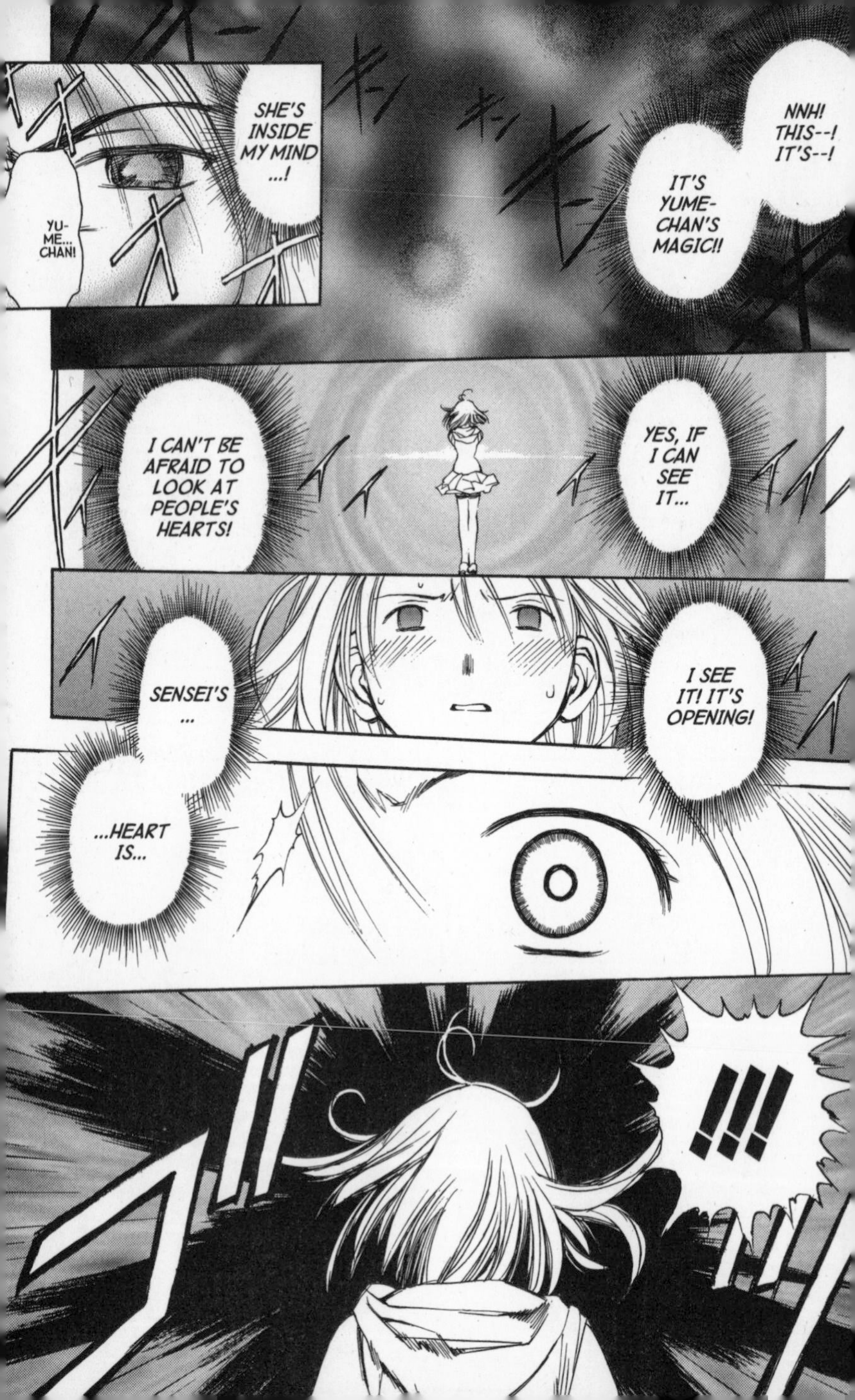
NNH! THIS--! IT'S--!
IT'S YUME-CHAN'S MAGIC!!
SHE'S INSIDE MY MIND ...!
YU-ME... CHAN!
YES, IF I CAN SEE IT...
I CAN'T BE AFRAID TO LOOK AT PEOPLE'S HEARTS!
I SEE IT! IT'S OPENING!
SENSEI'S ...
...HEART IS...
!!!

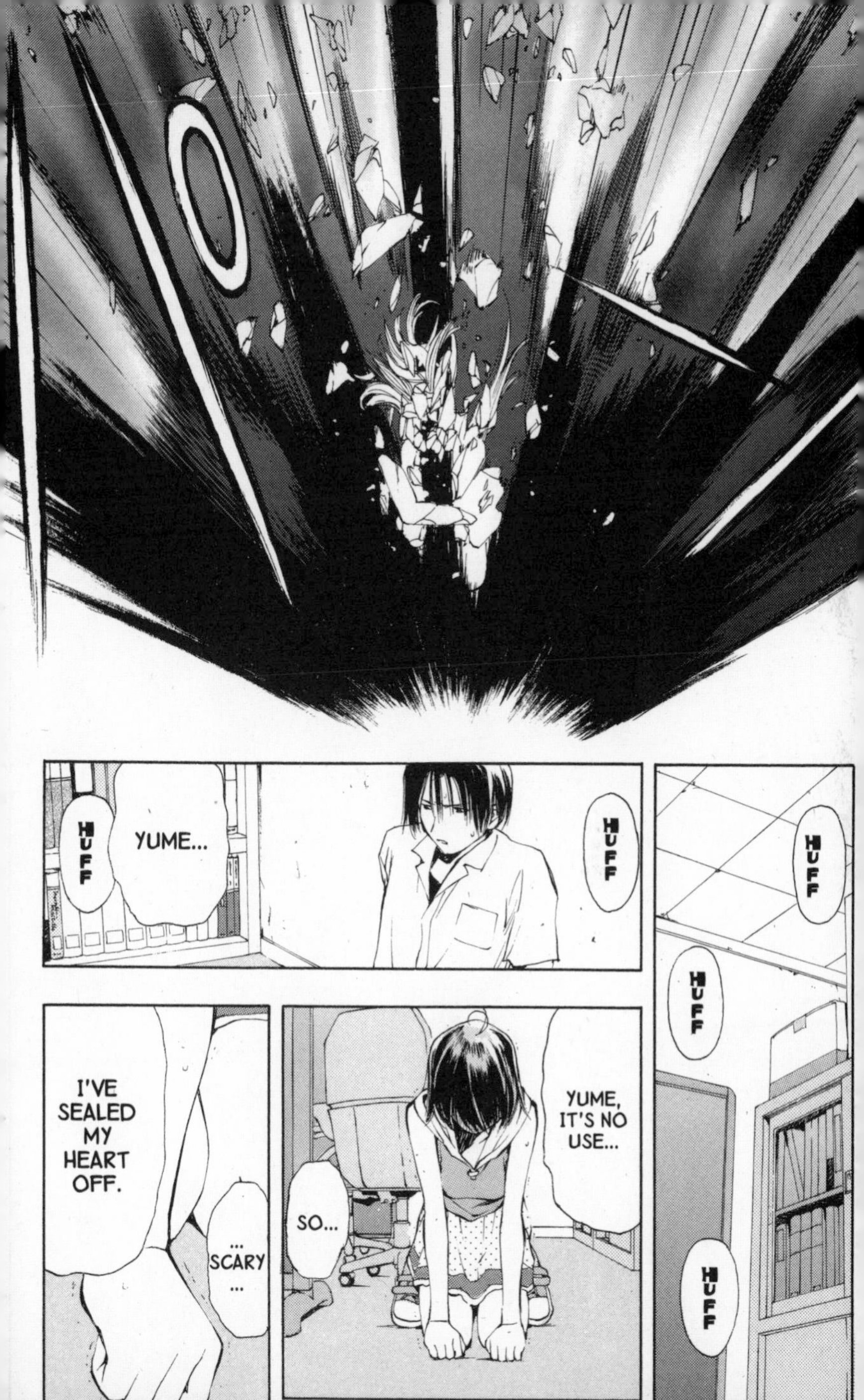
HUFF
HUFF
HUFF
HUFF
YUME...
HUFF
YUME, IT'S NO USE...
SO...
I'VE SEALED MY HEART OFF.
...SCARY...

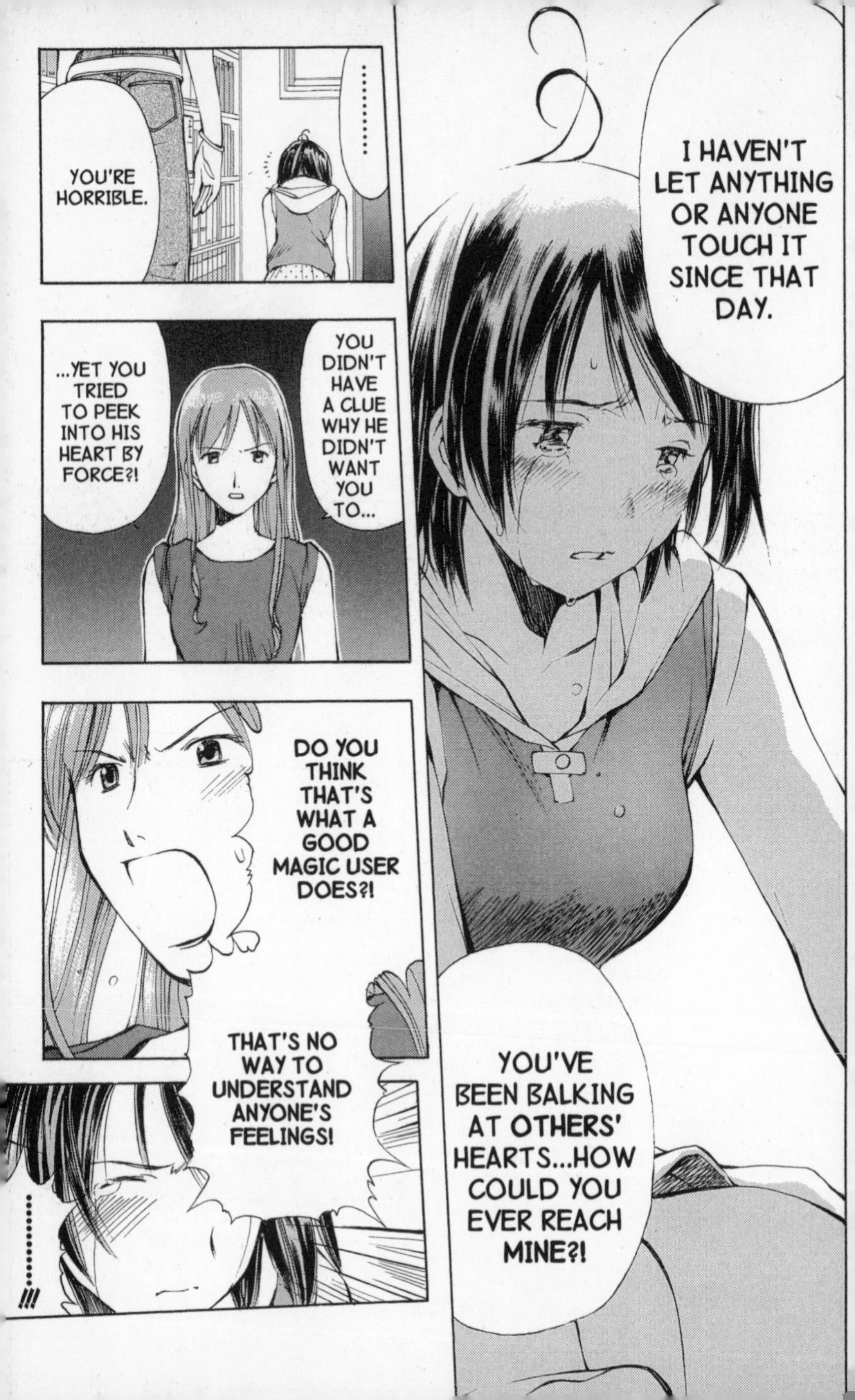

I HAVEN'T LET ANYTHING OR ANYONE TOUCH IT SINCE THAT DAY.
YOU'VE BEEN BALKING AT OTHERS' HEARTS...HOW COULD YOU EVER REACH MINE?!
......
YOU'RE HORRIBLE.
YOU DIDN'T HAVE A CLUE WHY HE DIDN'T WANT YOU TO...
...YET YOU TRIED TO PEEK INTO HIS HEART BY FORCE?!
DO YOU THINK THAT'S WHAT A GOOD MAGIC USER DOES?!
THAT'S NO WAY TO UNDERSTAND ANYONE'S FEELINGS!
.........!!!

I'M SORRY, MELINDA...

BUT RIGHT NOW...

MASAMI-CHAN!!

YUME-CHAN!!

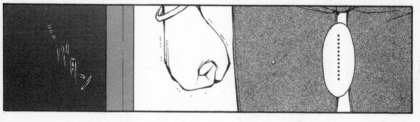

WHY AM I HERE...?

30

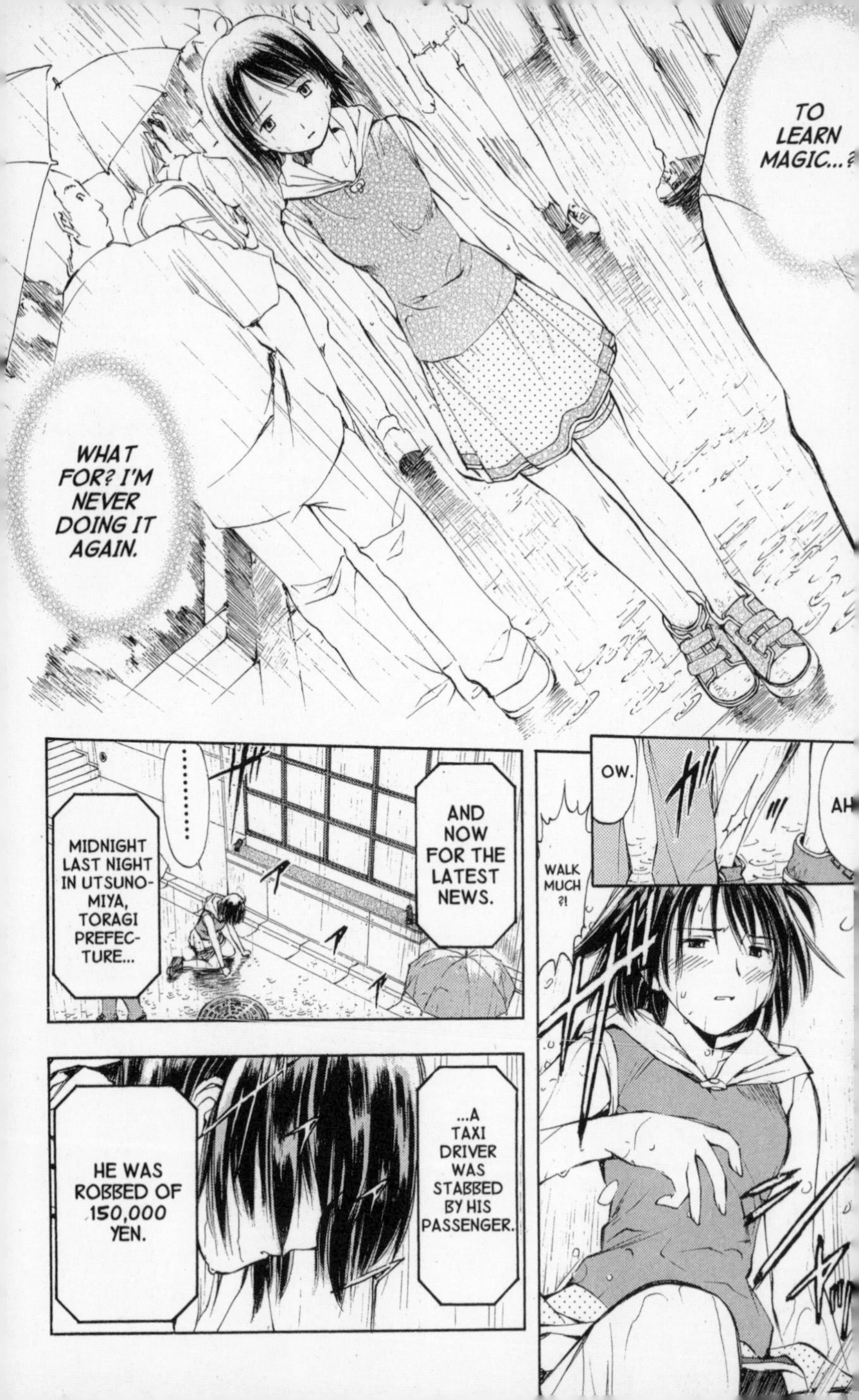

TO LEARN MAGIC...?
WHAT FOR? I'M NEVER DOING IT AGAIN.
AH
OW.
WALK MUCH ?!
AND NOW FOR THE LATEST NEWS.
MIDNIGHT LAST NIGHT IN UTSUNOMIYA, TORAGI PREFECTURE...
....
...A TAXI DRIVER WAS STABBED BY HIS PASSENGER.
HE WAS ROBBED OF 150,000 YEN.

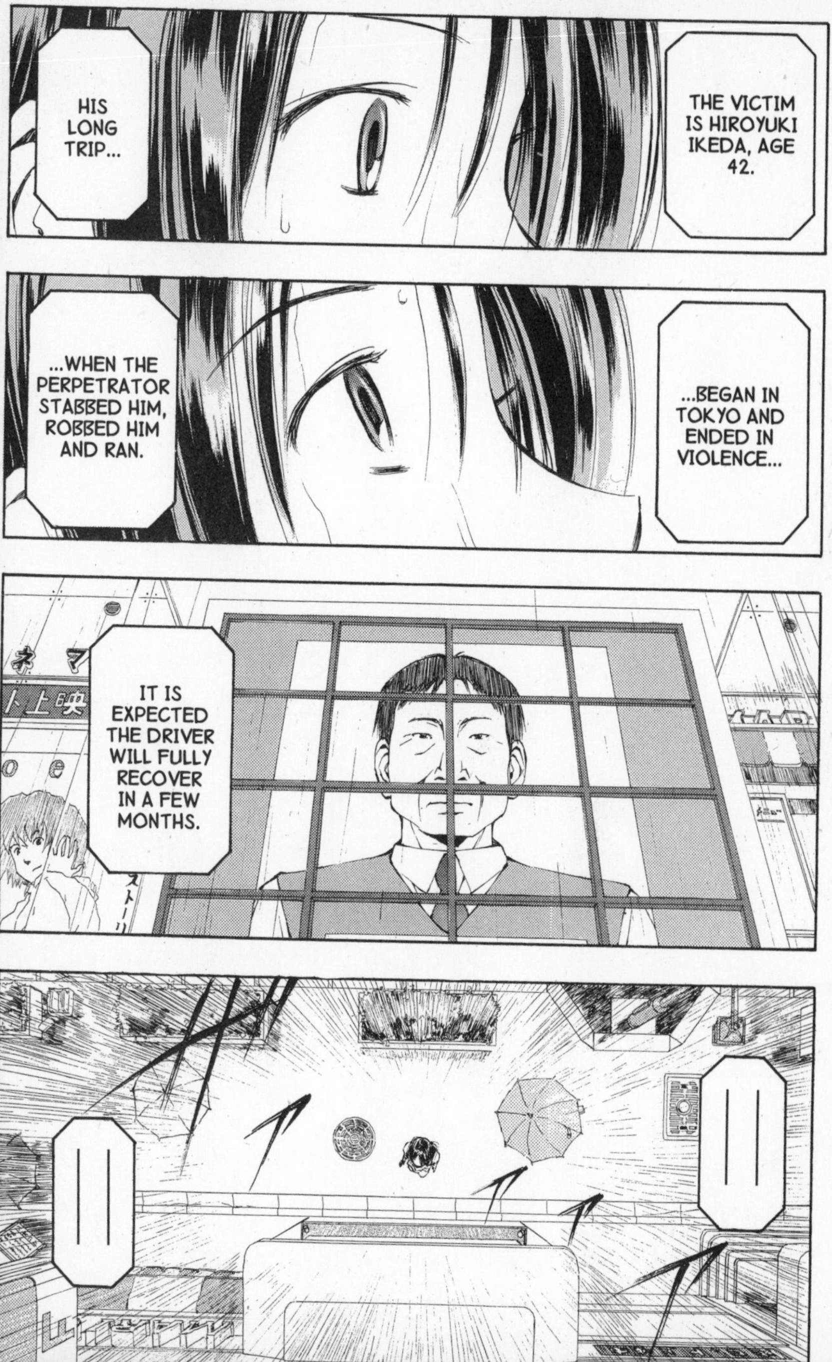
THE VICTIM IS HIROYUKI IKEDA, AGE 42.
HIS LONG TRIP...
...BEGAN IN TOKYO AND ENDED IN VIOLENCE...
...WHEN THE PERPETRATOR STABBED HIM, ROBBED HIM AND RAN.
IT IS EXPECTED THE DRIVER WILL FULLY RECOVER IN A FEW MONTHS.

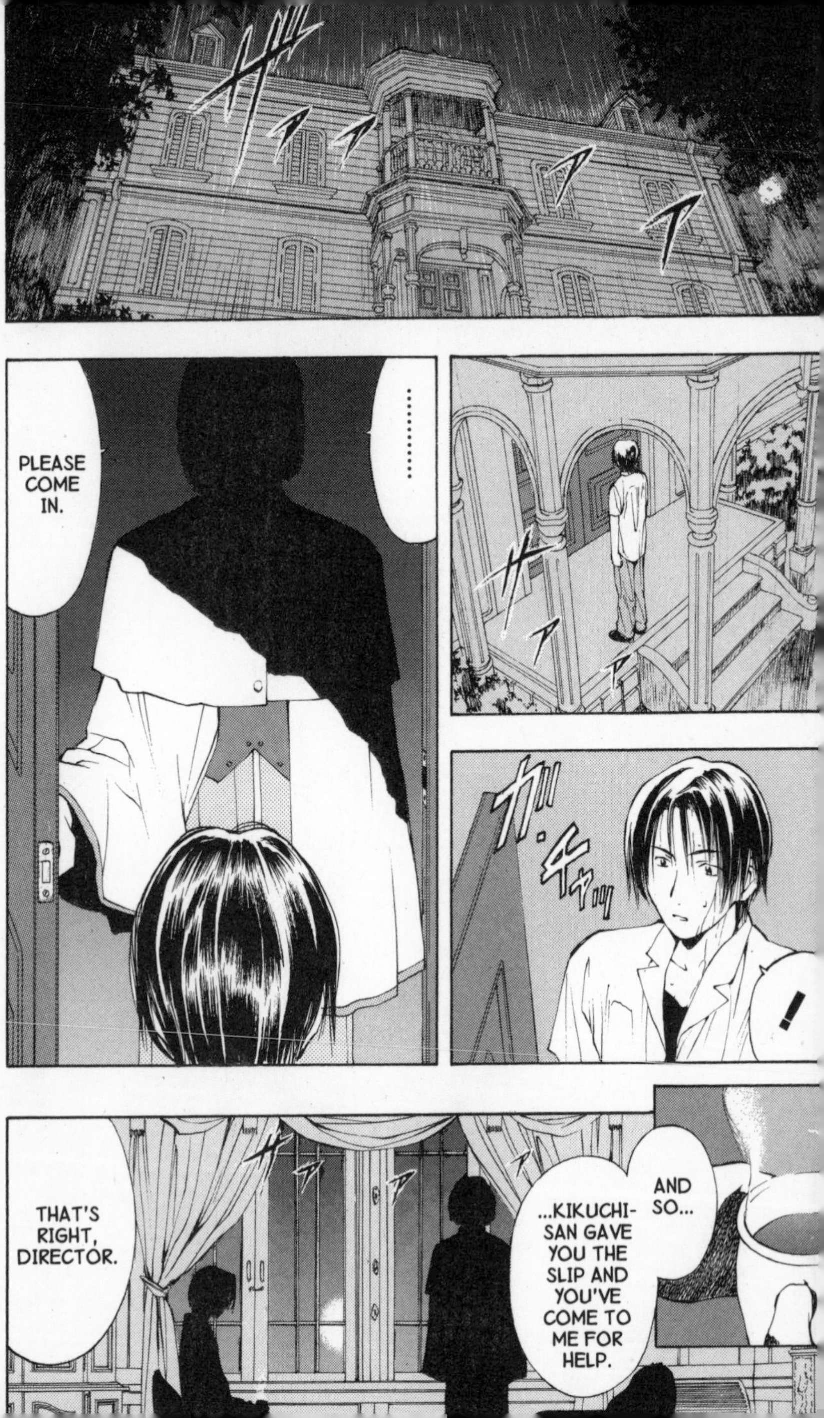
!
......
PLEASE COME IN.
AND SO...
...KIKUCHI-SAN GAVE YOU THE SLIP AND YOU'VE COME TO ME FOR HELP.
THAT'S RIGHT, DIRECTOR.

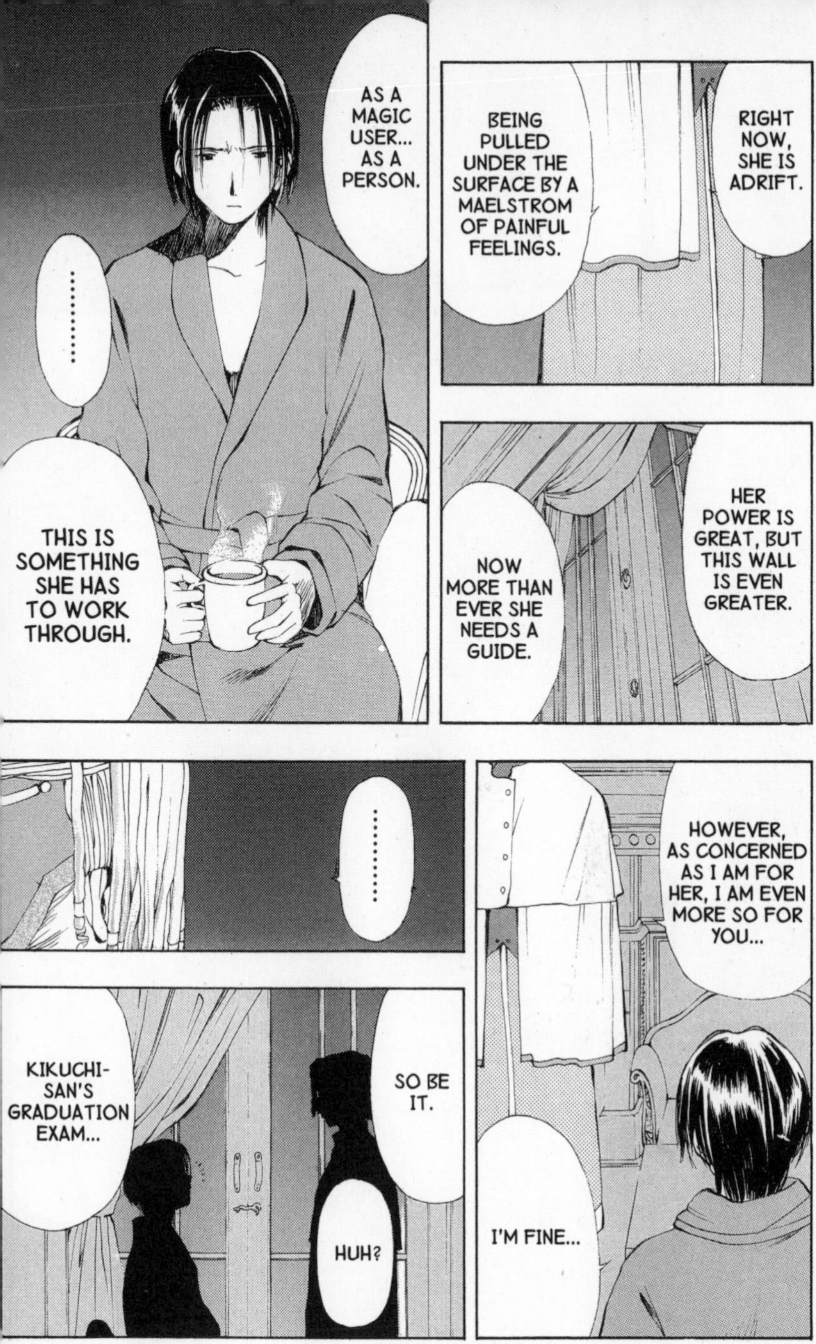
RIGHT NOW, SHE IS ADRIFT.
BEING PULLED UNDER THE SURFACE BY A MAELSTROM OF PAINFUL FEELINGS.
HER POWER IS GREAT, BUT THIS WALL IS EVEN GREATER.
NOW MORE THAN EVER SHE NEEDS A GUIDE.
AS A MAGIC USER... AS A PERSON.
....
THIS IS SOMETHING SHE HAS TO WORK THROUGH.
HOWEVER, AS CONCERNED AS I AM FOR HER, I AM EVEN MORE SO FOR YOU...
I'M FINE...
....
SO BE IT.
HUH?
KIKUCHI-SAN'S GRADUATION EXAM...

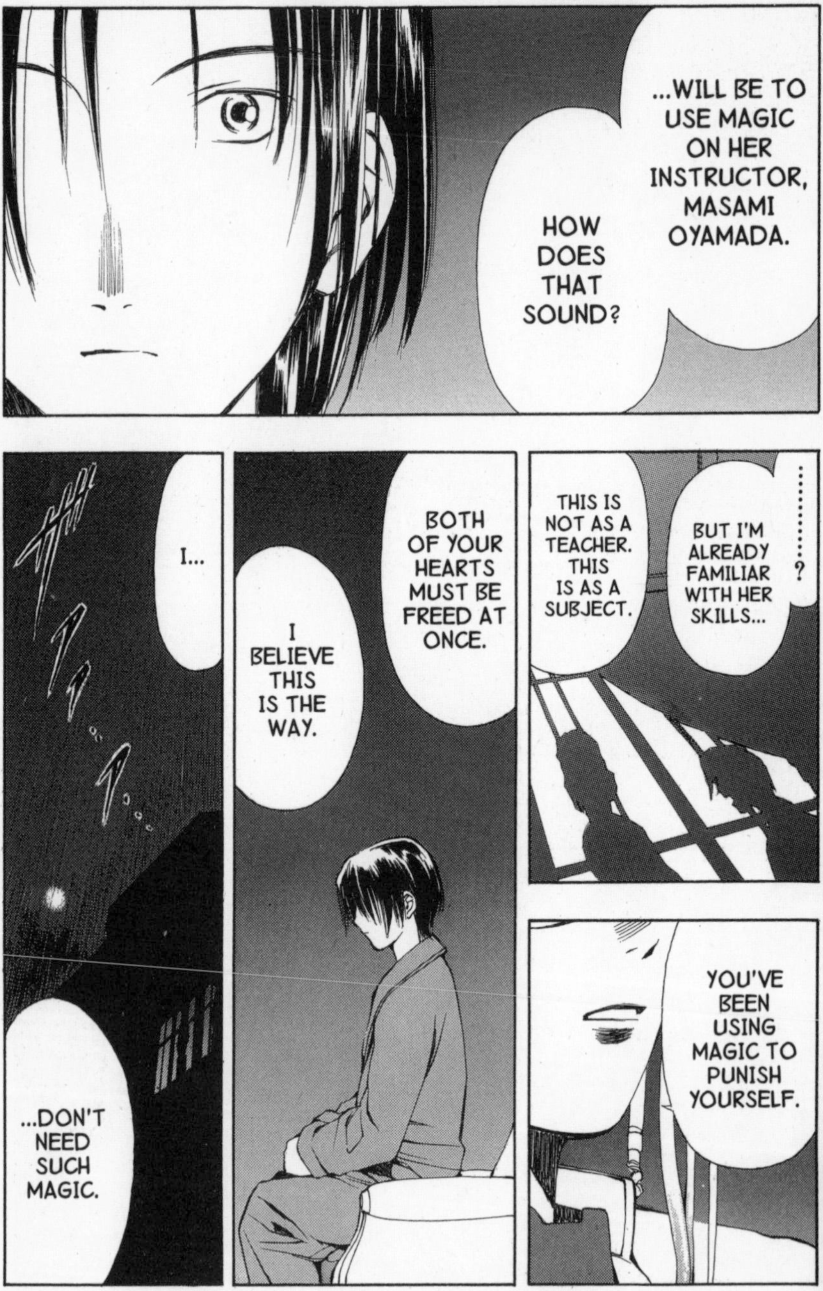
...WILL BE TO USE MAGIC ON HER INSTRUCTOR, MASAMI OYAMADA.
HOW DOES THAT SOUND?
........?
BUT I'M ALREADY FAMILIAR WITH HER SKILLS...
THIS IS NOT AS A TEACHER. THIS IS AS A SUBJECT.
YOU'VE BEEN USING MAGIC TO PUNISH YOURSELF.
BOTH OF YOUR HEARTS MUST BE FREED AT ONCE.
I BELIEVE THIS IS THE WAY.
I...
...DON'T NEED SUCH MAGIC.

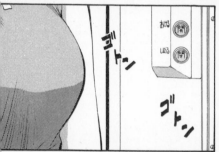プォ……オォン

ゴトッ

ゴトン

ゴトッ

ゴトン

ゴトン

ゴトン

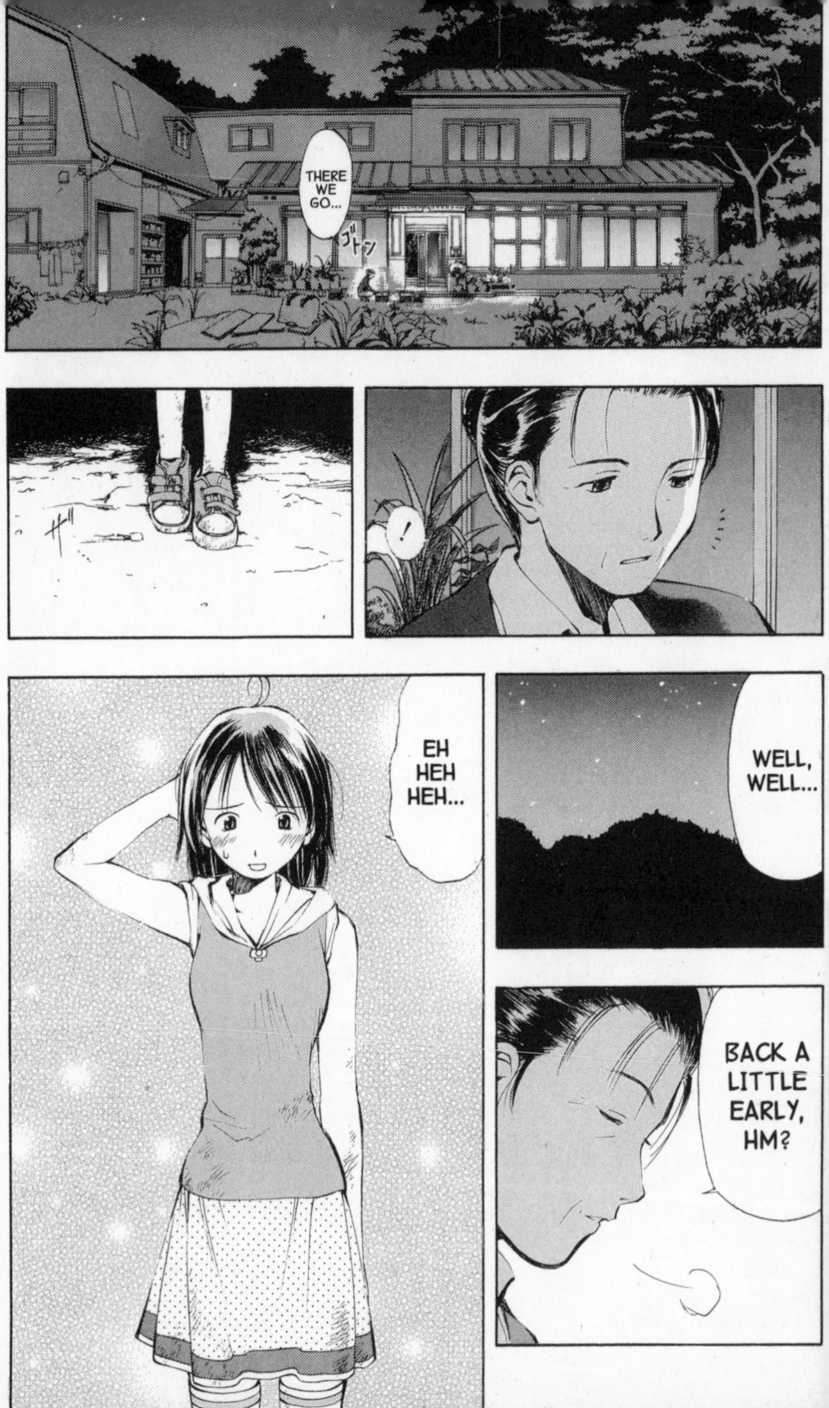
THERE WE GO...
ゴトン
!
WELL, WELL...
BACK A LITTLE EARLY, HM?
EH HEH HEH...

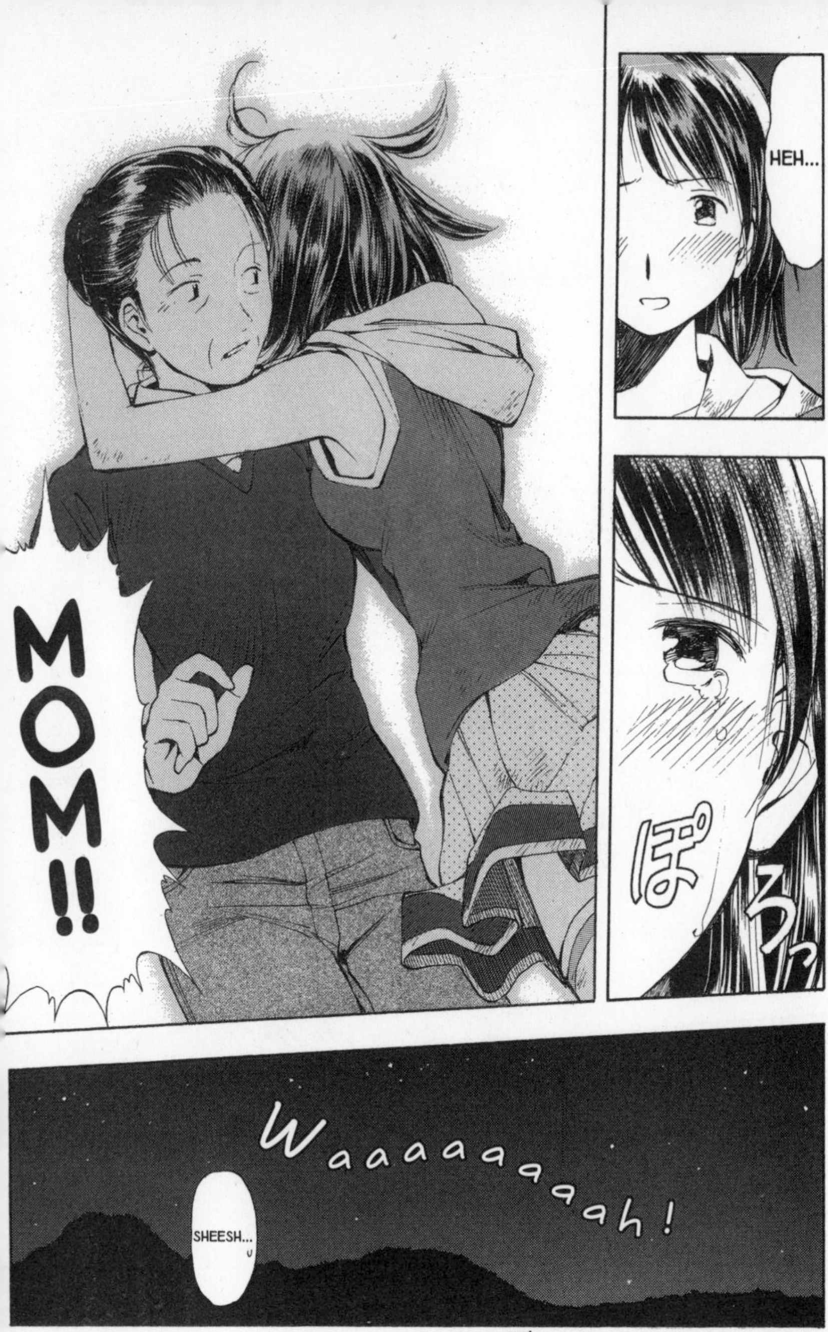
HEH...
ぽろっ
MOM!!
Waaaaaaaaaah!
SHEESH...

5th Dream ※ End

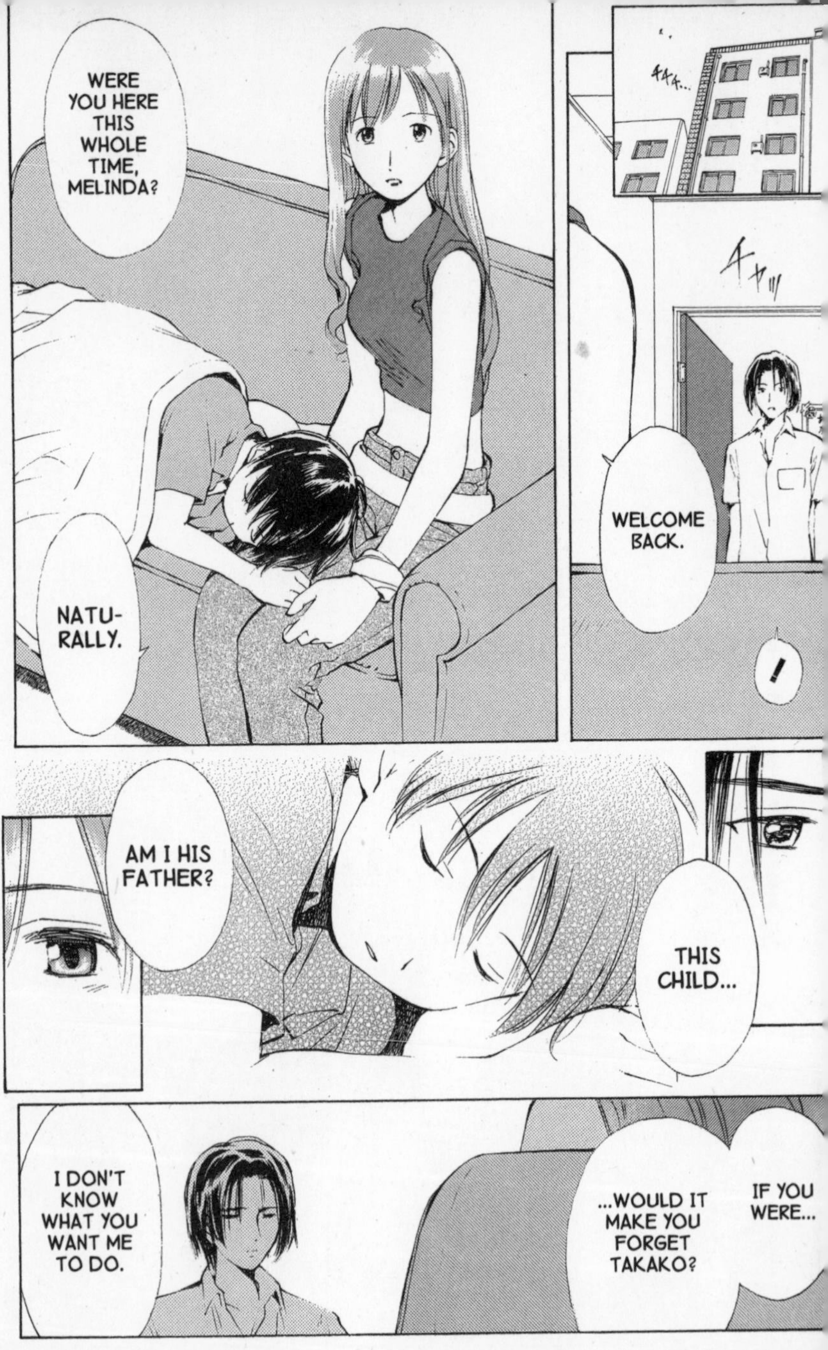
WELCOME BACK.
!
WERE YOU HERE THIS WHOLE TIME, MELINDA?
NATU-RALLY.
THIS CHILD...
AM I HIS FATHER?
IF YOU WERE...
...WOULD IT MAKE YOU FORGET TAKAKO?
I DON'T KNOW WHAT YOU WANT ME TO DO.

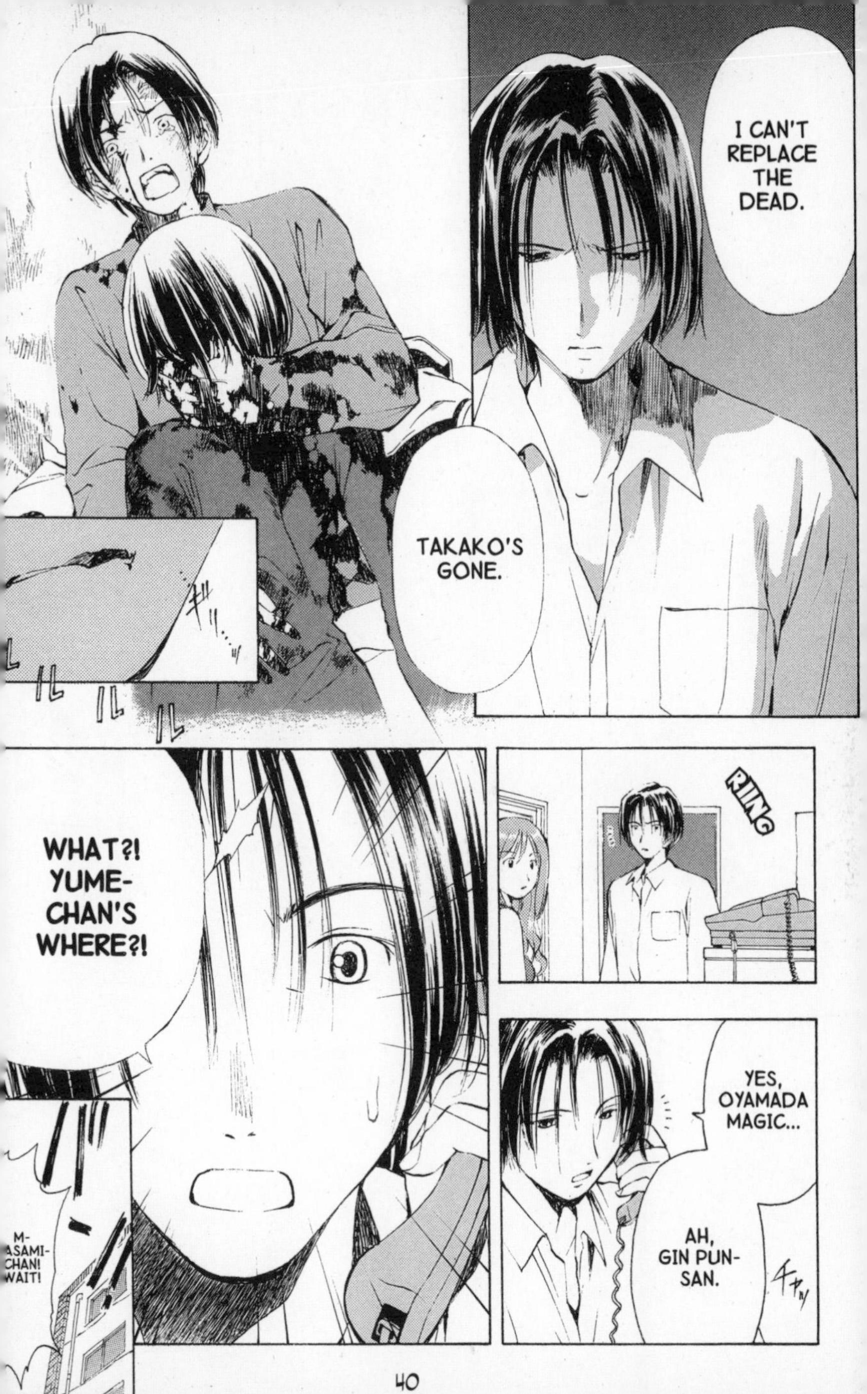
I CAN'T REPLACE THE DEAD.
TAKAKO'S GONE.
RIING
YES, OYAMADA MAGIC...
AH, GIN PUN-SAN.
WHAT?! YUME-CHAN'S WHERE?!
M-ASAMI-CHAN! WAIT!

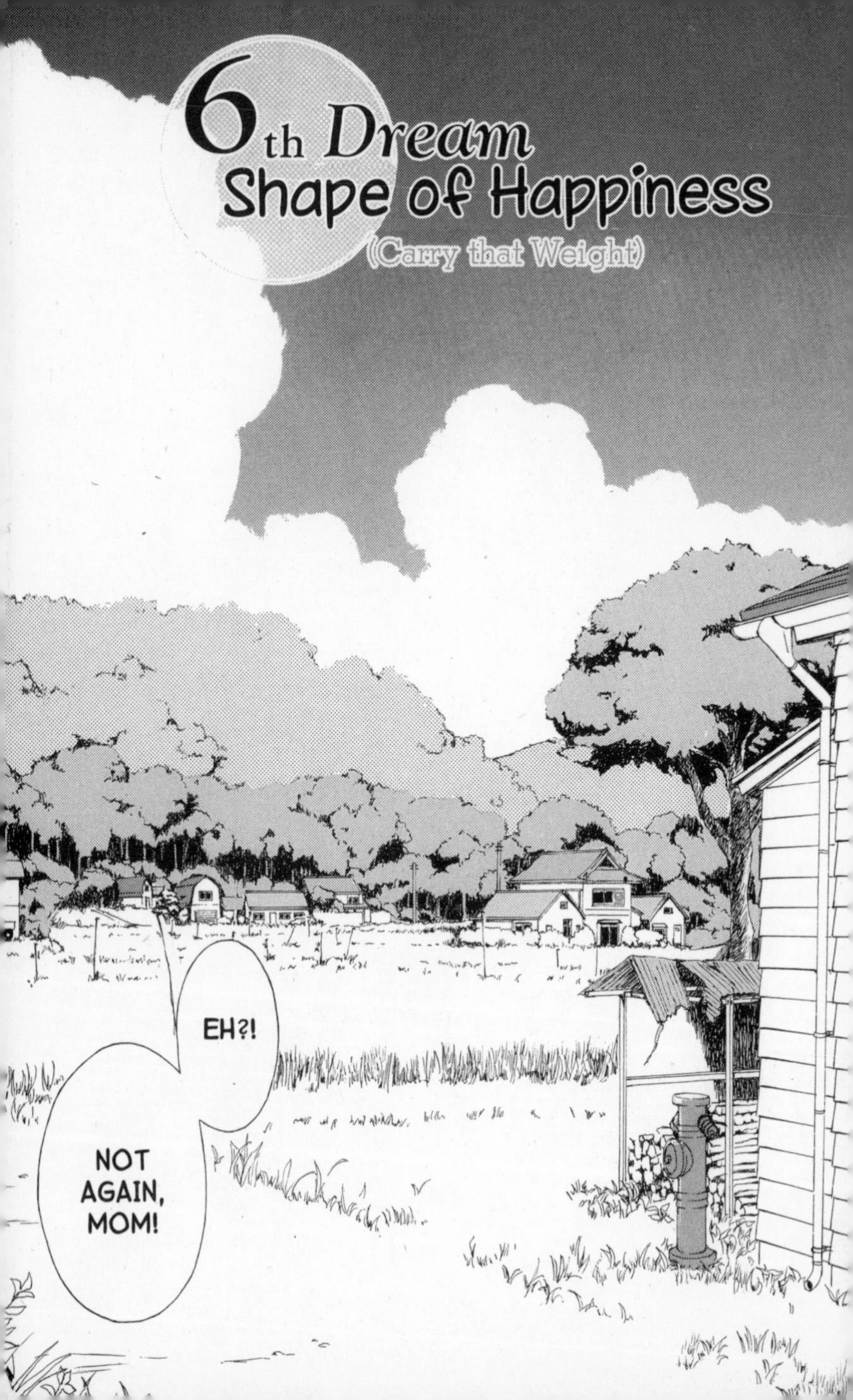
6th Dream
Shape of Happiness
(Carry that Weight)
EH?!
NOT AGAIN, MOM!

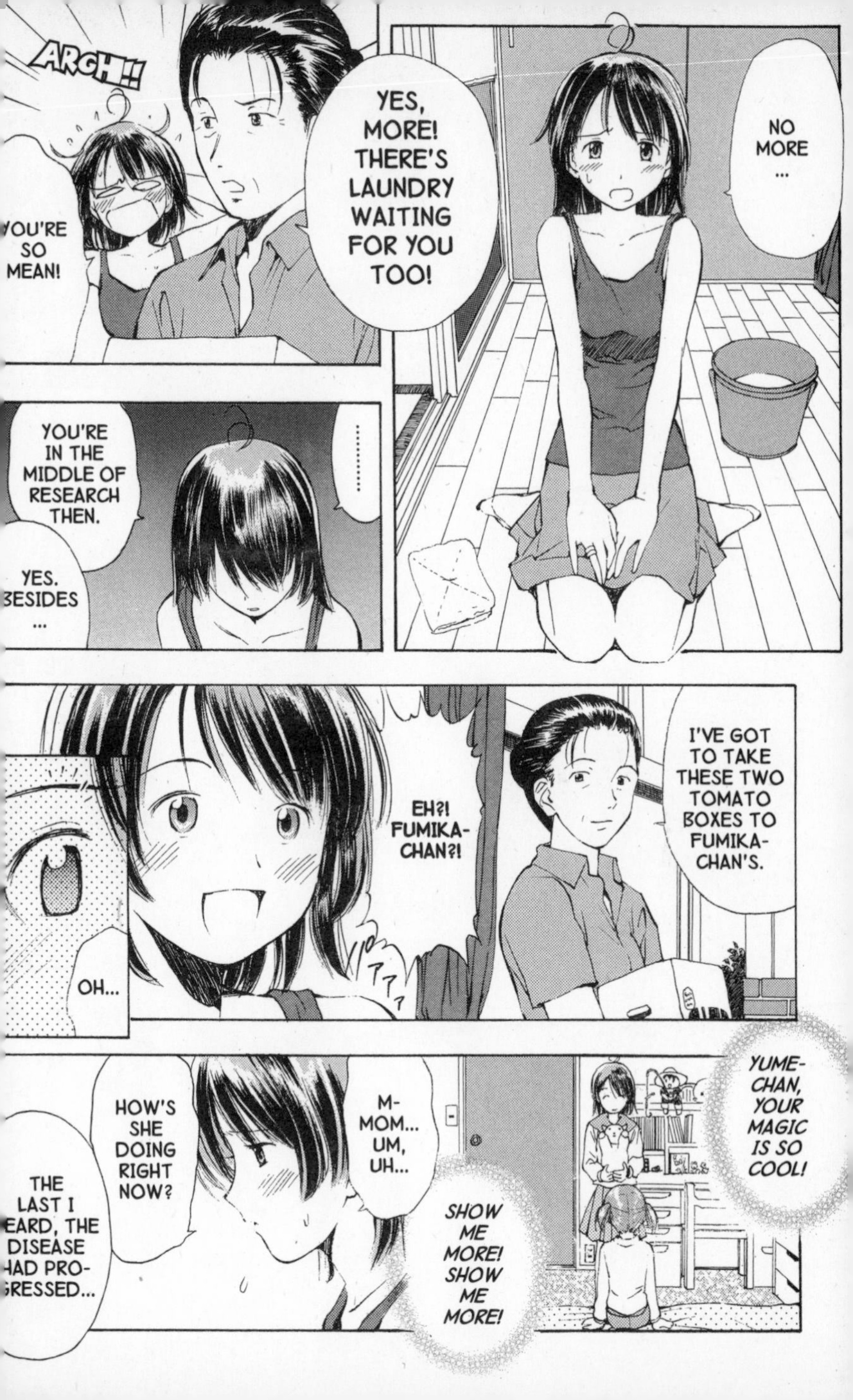
NO MORE ...
YES, MORE! THERE'S LAUNDRY WAITING FOR YOU TOO!
ARGH!!
YOU'RE SO MEAN!
......
YOU'RE IN THE MIDDLE OF RESEARCH THEN.
YES. BESIDES ...
I'VE GOT TO TAKE THESE TWO TOMATO BOXES TO FUMIKA-CHAN'S.
EH?! FUMIKA-CHAN?!
OH...
YUME-CHAN, YOUR MAGIC IS SO COOL!
SHOW ME MORE! SHOW ME MORE!
M-MOM... UM, UH...
HOW'S SHE DOING RIGHT NOW?
THE LAST I HEARD, THE DISEASE HAD PRO-GRESSED...

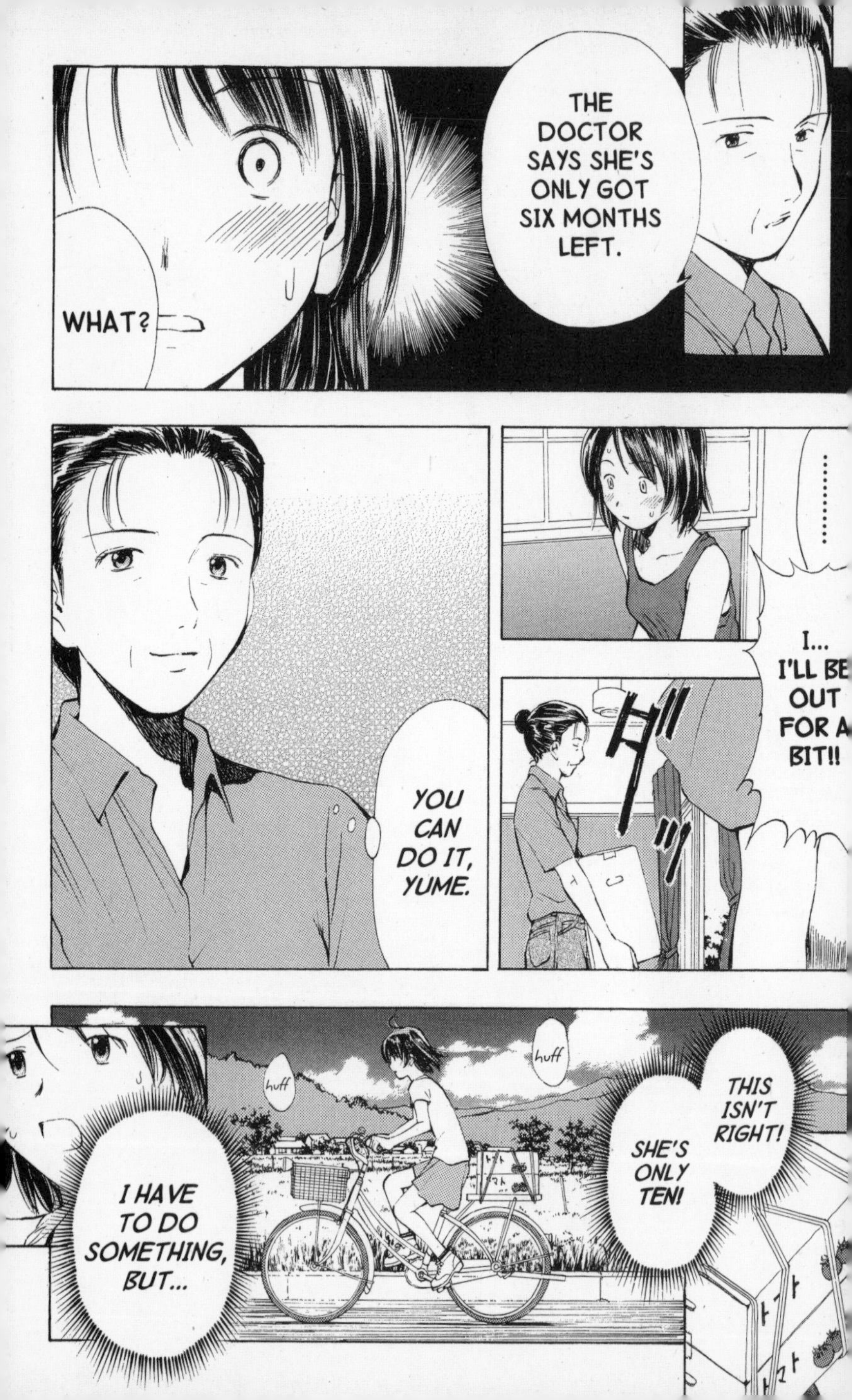
THE DOCTOR SAYS SHE'S ONLY GOT SIX MONTHS LEFT.
WHAT?
......
I... I'LL BE OUT FOR A BIT!!
YOU CAN DO IT, YUME.
huff
THIS ISN'T RIGHT!
SHE'S ONLY TEN!
huff
I HAVE TO DO SOMETHING, BUT...

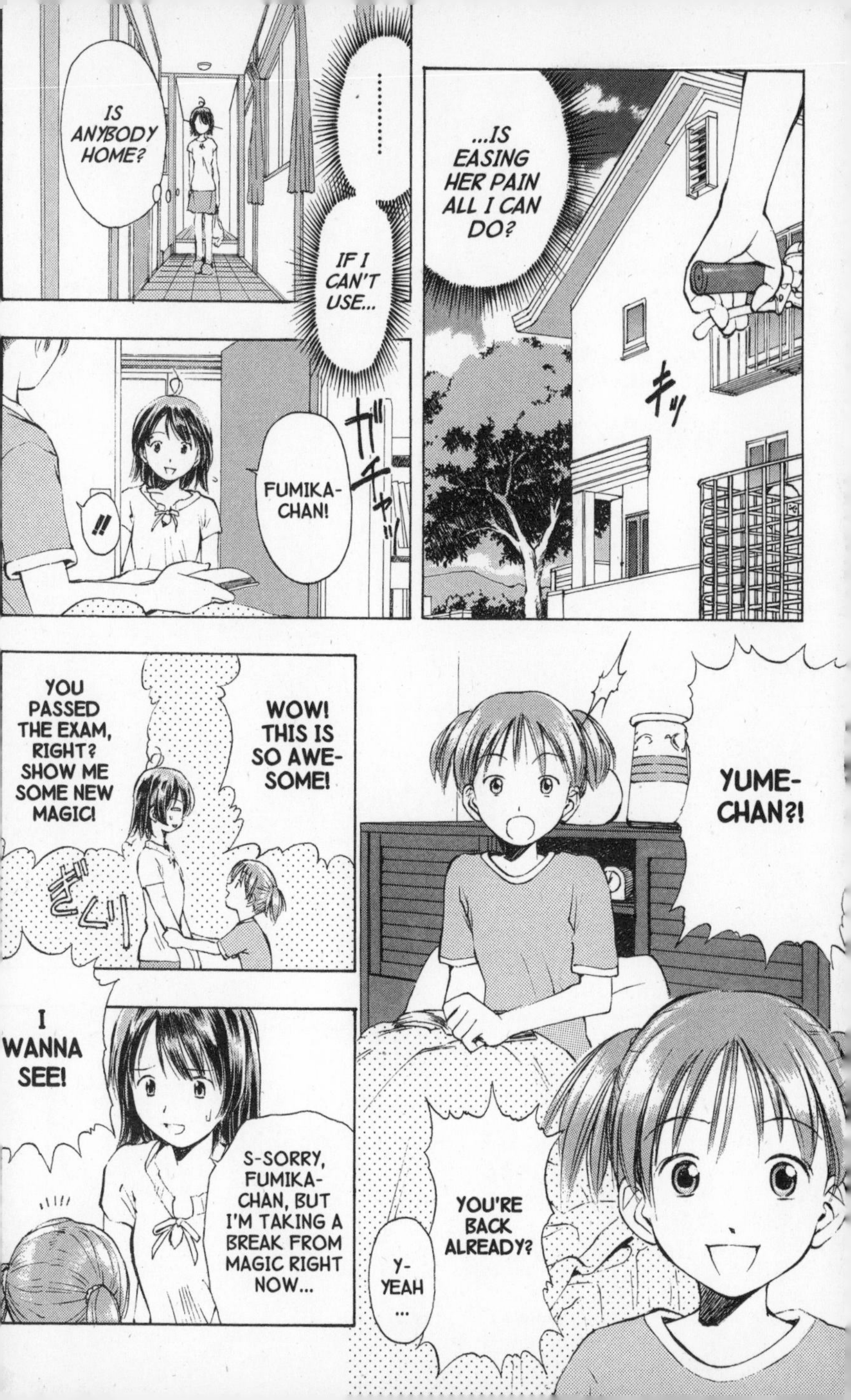

......
IF I CAN'T USE...
...IS EASING HER PAIN ALL I CAN DO?
キッ
IS ANYBODY HOME?
ガチャッ
FUMIKA-CHAN!
!!
YUME-CHAN?!
YOU'RE BACK ALREADY?
Y-YEAH ...
WOW! THIS IS SO AWE-SOME!
YOU PASSED THE EXAM, RIGHT? SHOW ME SOME NEW MAGIC!
ぎくり
I WANNA SEE!
S-SORRY, FUMIKA-CHAN, BUT I'M TAKING A BREAK FROM MAGIC RIGHT NOW...

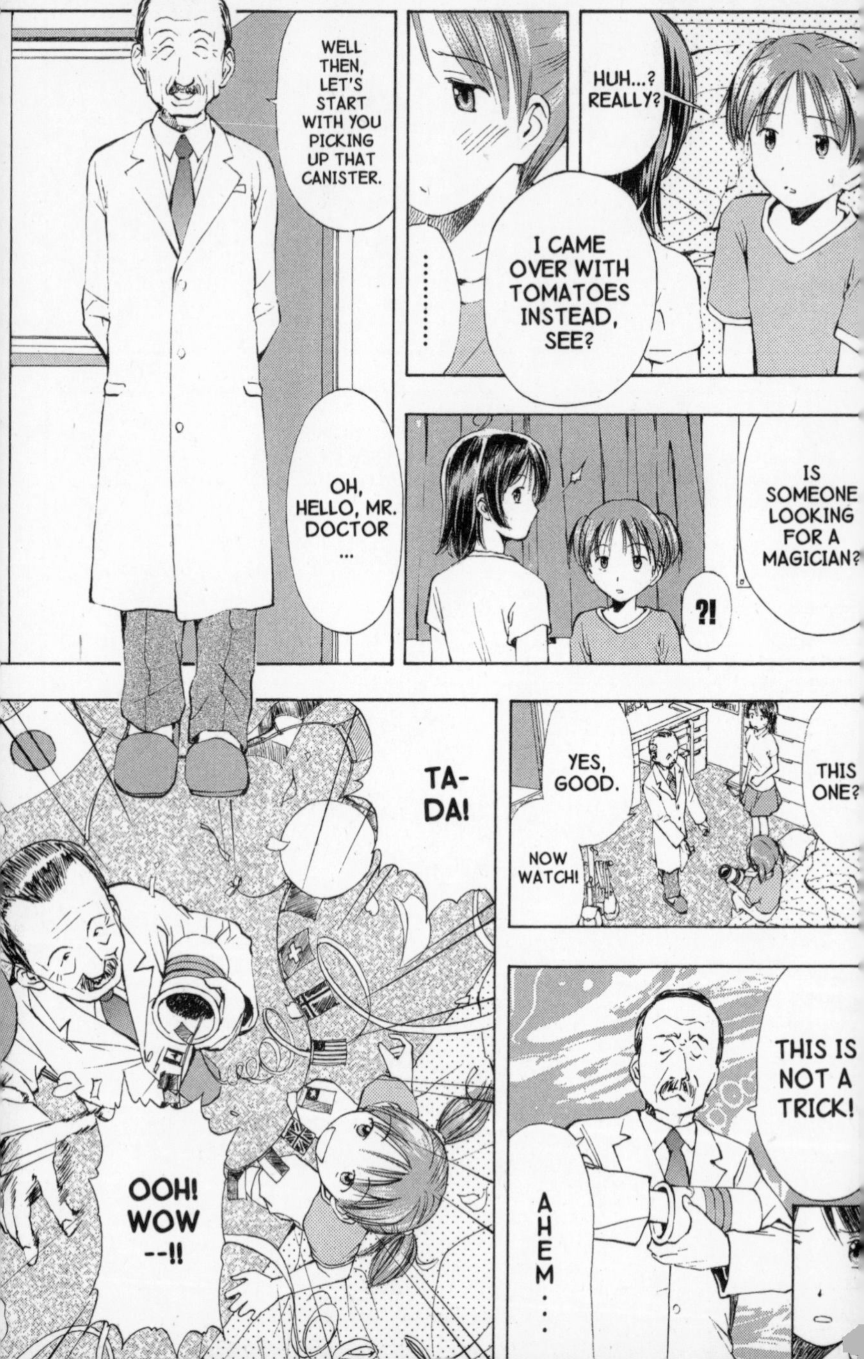
HUH...? REALLY?
I CAME OVER WITH TOMATOES INSTEAD, SEE?
....
IS SOMEONE LOOKING FOR A MAGICIAN?
?!
OH, HELLO, MR. DOCTOR ...
WELL THEN, LET'S START WITH YOU PICKING UP THAT CANISTER.
THIS ONE?
YES, GOOD.
NOW WATCH!
THIS IS NOT A TRICK!
AHEM...
TA-DA!
OOH! WOW --!!

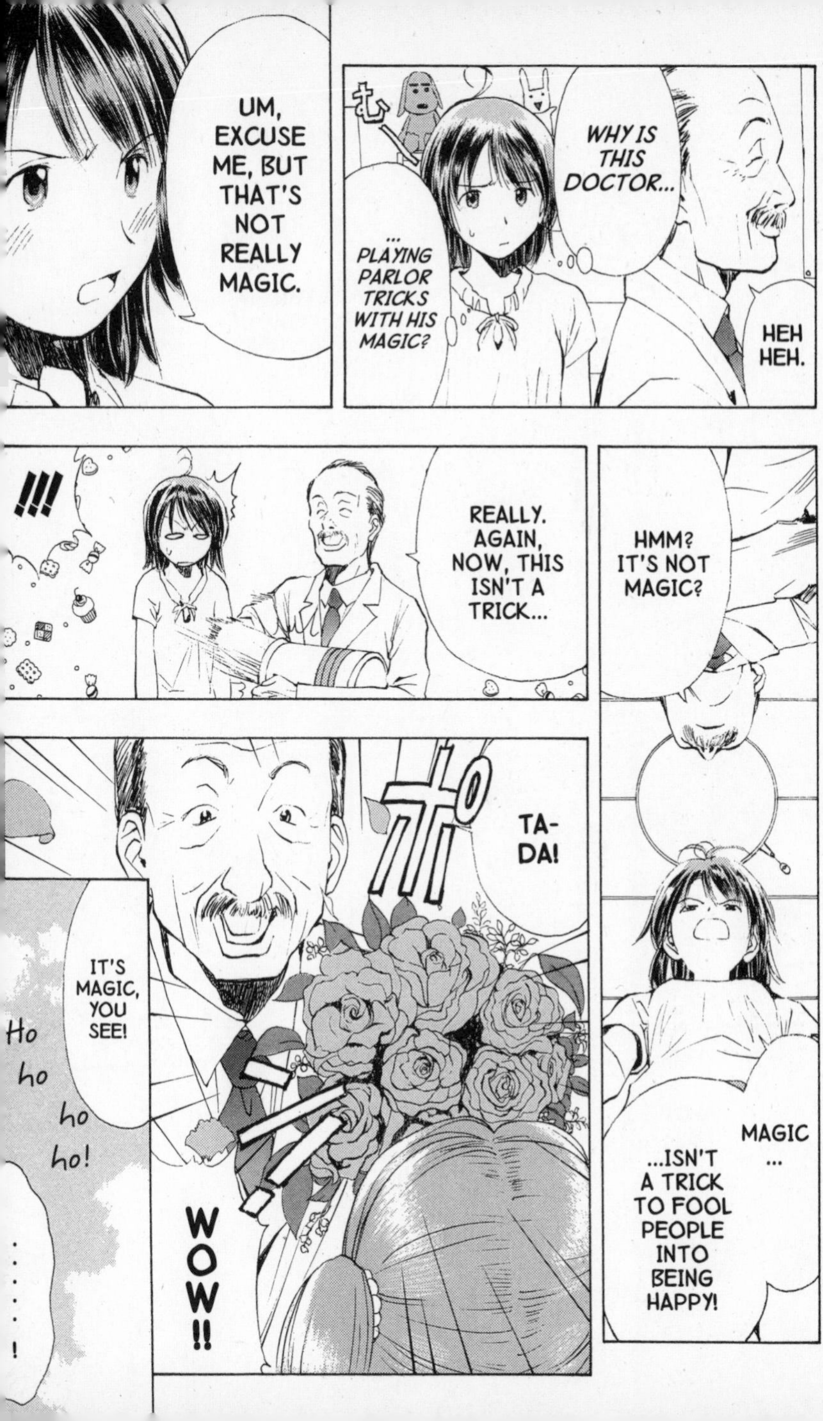
WHY IS THIS DOCTOR...
...PLAYING PARLOR TRICKS WITH HIS MAGIC?
HEH HEH.
UM, EXCUSE ME, BUT THAT'S NOT REALLY MAGIC.
HMM? IT'S NOT MAGIC?
MAGIC... ...ISN'T A TRICK TO FOOL PEOPLE INTO BEING HAPPY!
REALLY. AGAIN, NOW, THIS ISN'T A TRICK...
!!!
ポ
TA-DA!
IT'S MAGIC, YOU SEE!
Ho ho ho ho!
WOW!!
......!

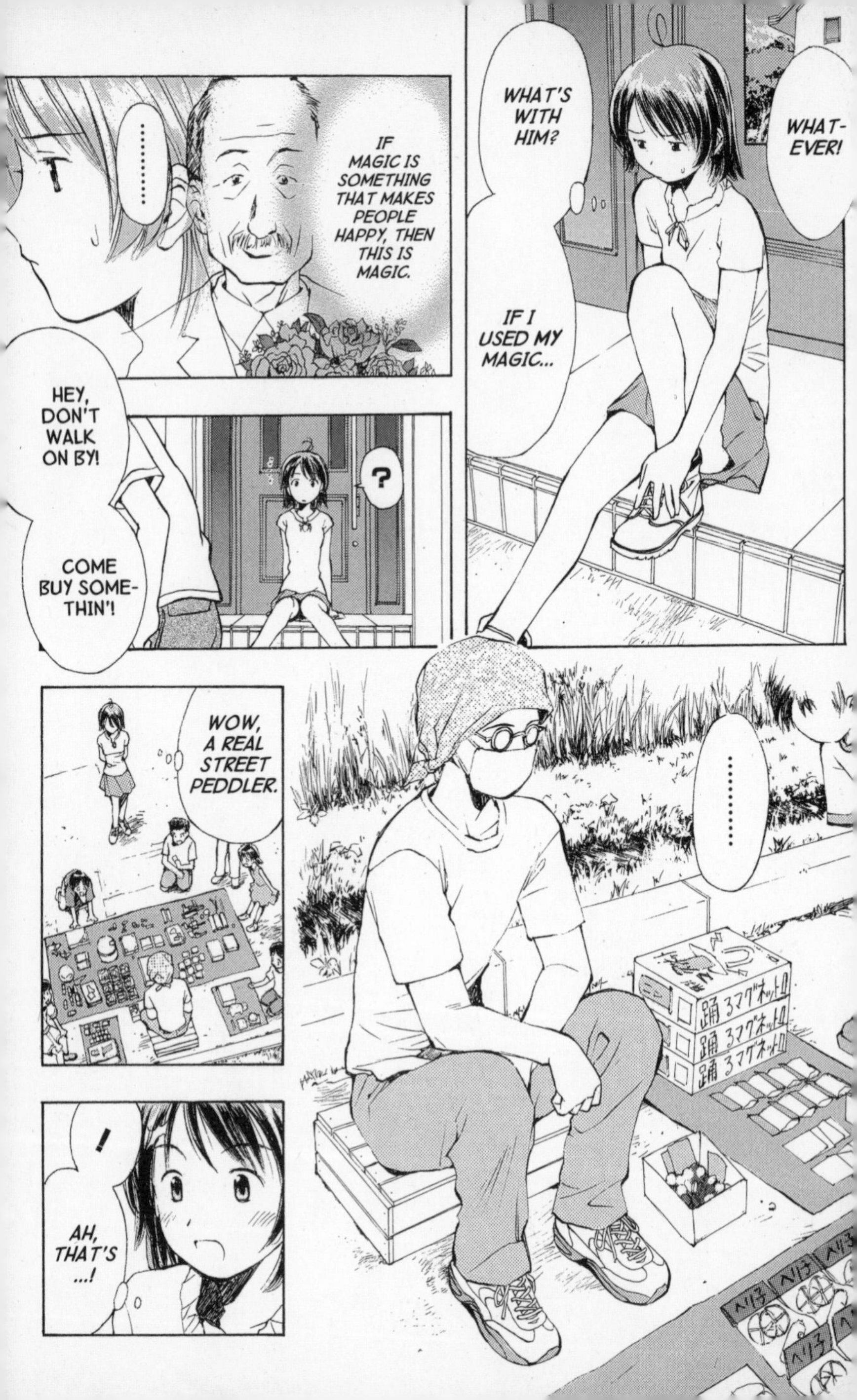
WHAT-EVER!
WHAT'S WITH HIM?
IF I USED MY MAGIC...
......
IF MAGIC IS SOMETHING THAT MAKES PEOPLE HAPPY, THEN THIS IS MAGIC.
?
HEY, DON'T WALK ON BY!
COME BUY SOME-THIN'!
......
踊るマグネット
踊るマグネット
踊るマグネット
WOW, A REAL STREET PEDDLER.
!
AH, THAT'S ...!

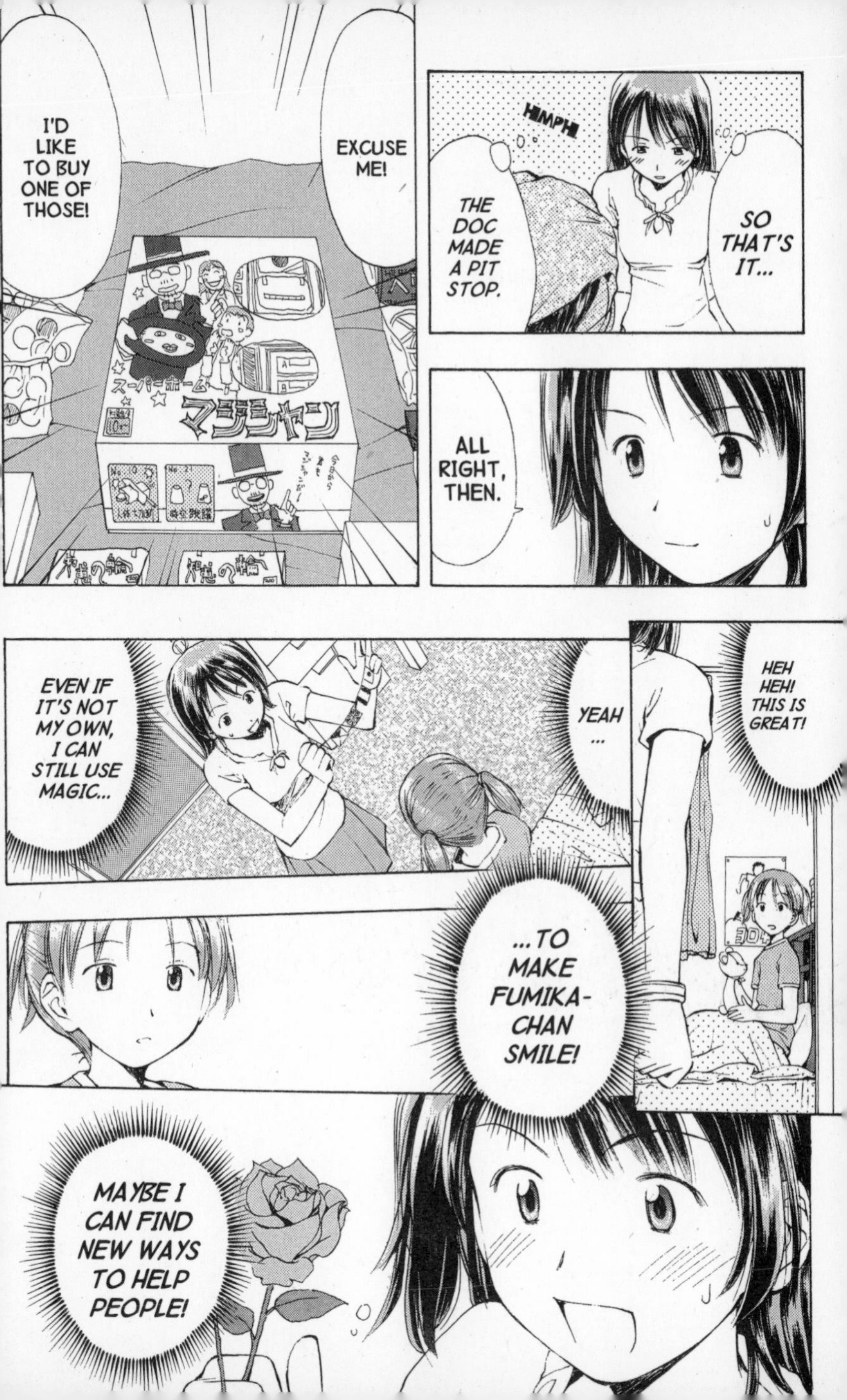
HMPH!
SO THAT'S IT...
THE DOC MADE A PIT STOP.
ALL RIGHT, THEN.
EXCUSE ME!
I'D LIKE TO BUY ONE OF THOSE!
スーパーホーム
マジシャン
HEH HEH! THIS IS GREAT!
YEAH ...
EVEN IF IT'S NOT MY OWN, I CAN STILL USE MAGIC...
...TO MAKE FUMIKA-CHAN SMILE!
MAYBE I CAN FIND NEW WAYS TO HELP PEOPLE!

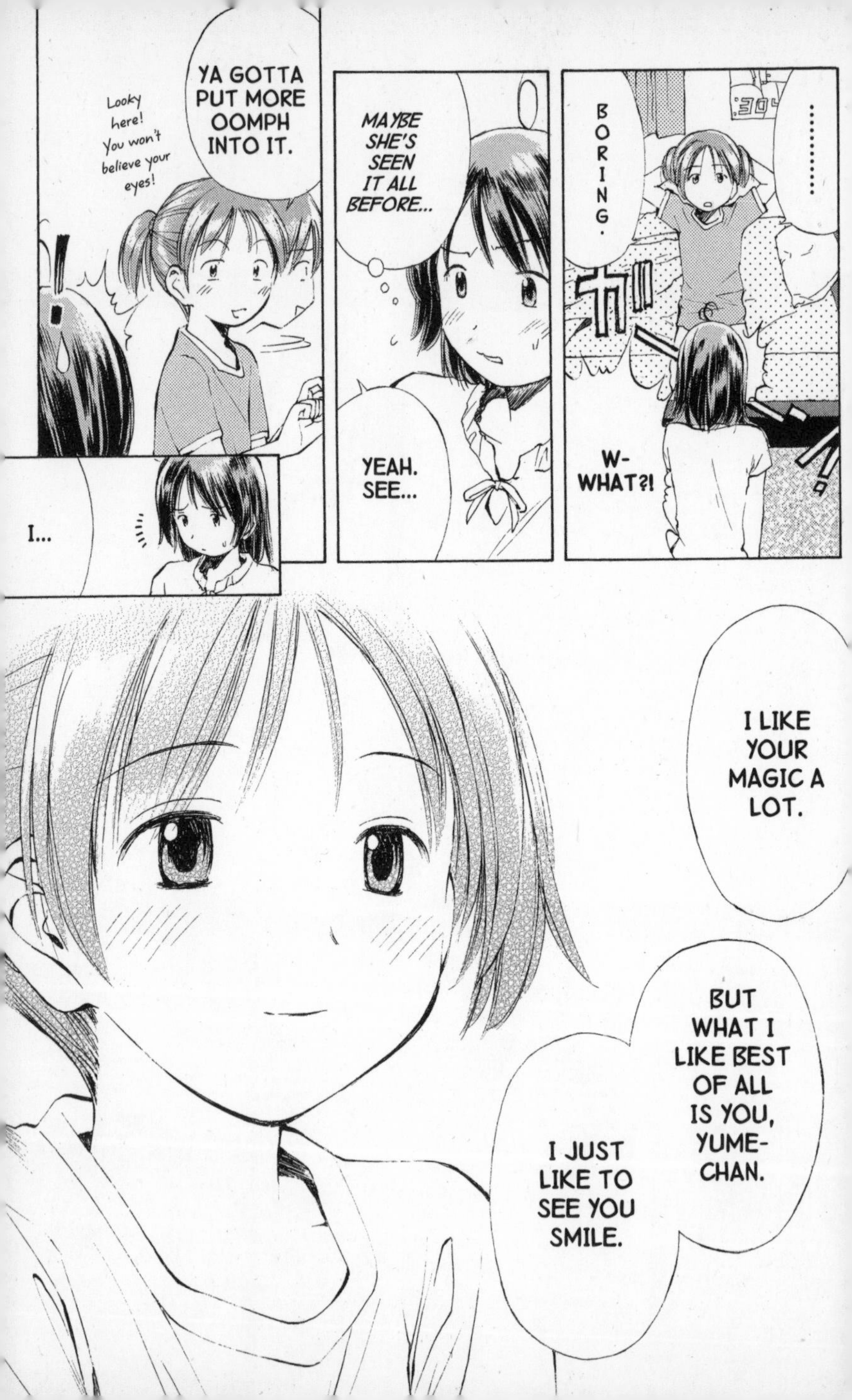
......
BORING.
W-WHAT?!
MAYBE SHE'S SEEN IT ALL BEFORE...
YEAH. SEE...
YA GOTTA PUT MORE OOMPH INTO IT.
Looky here! You won't believe your eyes!
I...
I LIKE YOUR MAGIC A LOT.
BUT WHAT I LIKE BEST OF ALL IS YOU, YUME-CHAN.
I JUST LIKE TO SEE YOU SMILE.

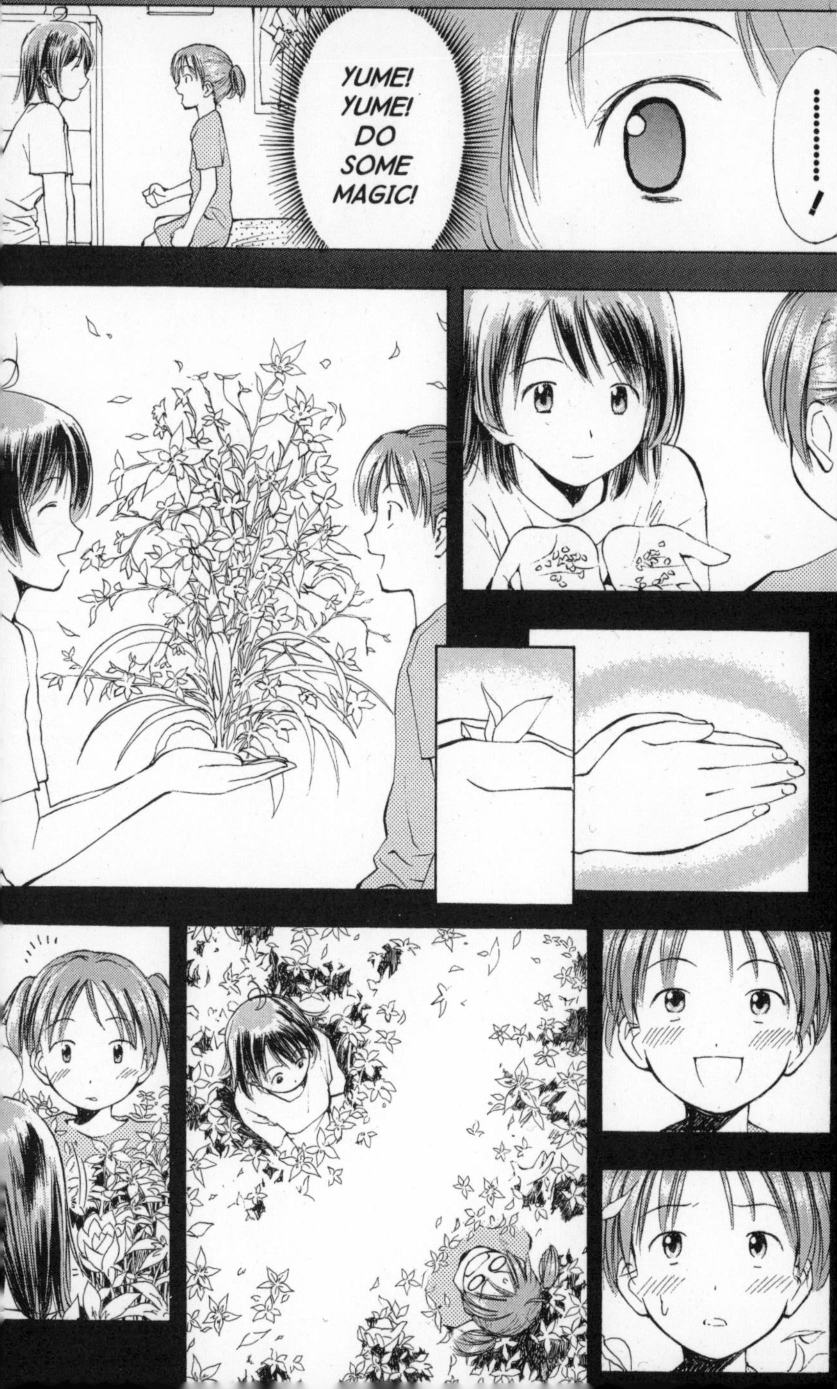
......!
YUME! YUME! DO SOME MAGIC!

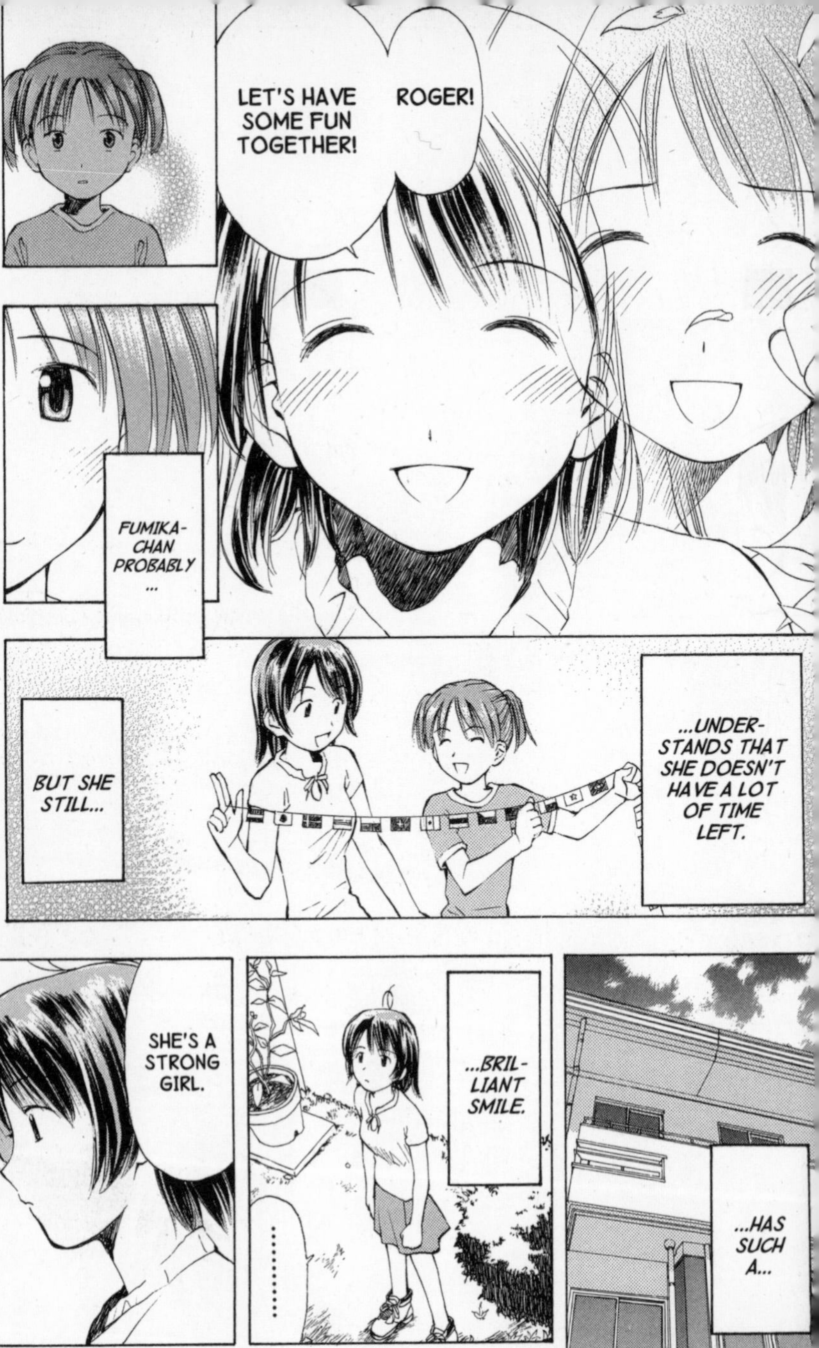
ROGER!
LET'S HAVE SOME FUN TOGETHER!
FUMIKA-CHAN PROBABLY ...
...UNDER-STANDS THAT SHE DOESN'T HAVE A LOT OF TIME LEFT.
BUT SHE STILL...
...HAS SUCH A...
...BRIL-LIANT SMILE.
....
SHE'S A STRONG GIRL.
.....

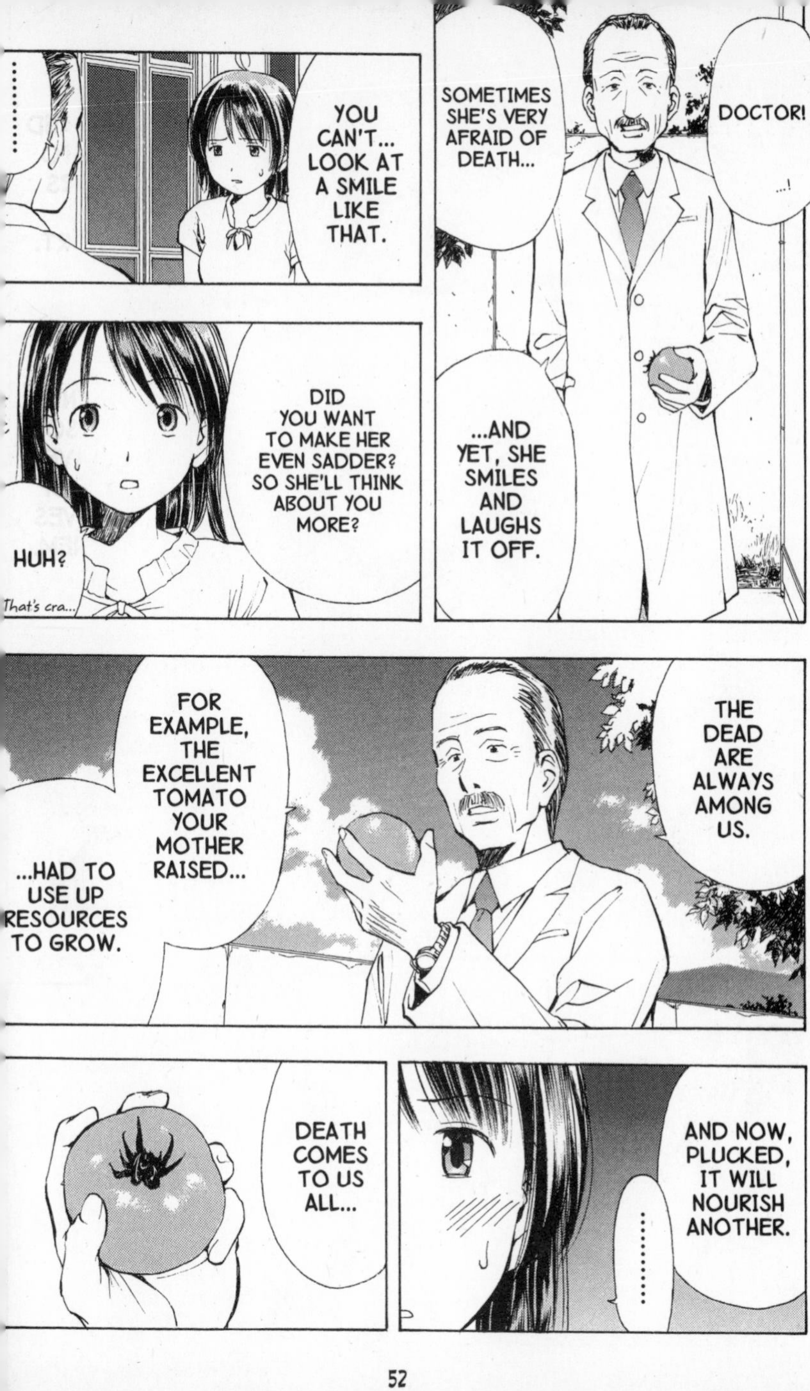
DOCTOR!
...!
SOMETIMES SHE'S VERY AFRAID OF DEATH...
...AND YET, SHE SMILES AND LAUGHS IT OFF.
YOU CAN'T... LOOK AT A SMILE LIKE THAT.
......
DID YOU WANT TO MAKE HER EVEN SADDER? SO SHE'LL THINK ABOUT YOU MORE?
HUH?
That's cra...
THE DEAD ARE ALWAYS AMONG US.
FOR EXAMPLE, THE EXCELLENT TOMATO YOUR MOTHER RAISED...
...HAD TO USE UP RESOURCES TO GROW.
AND NOW, PLUCKED, IT WILL NOURISH ANOTHER.
......
DEATH COMES TO US ALL...

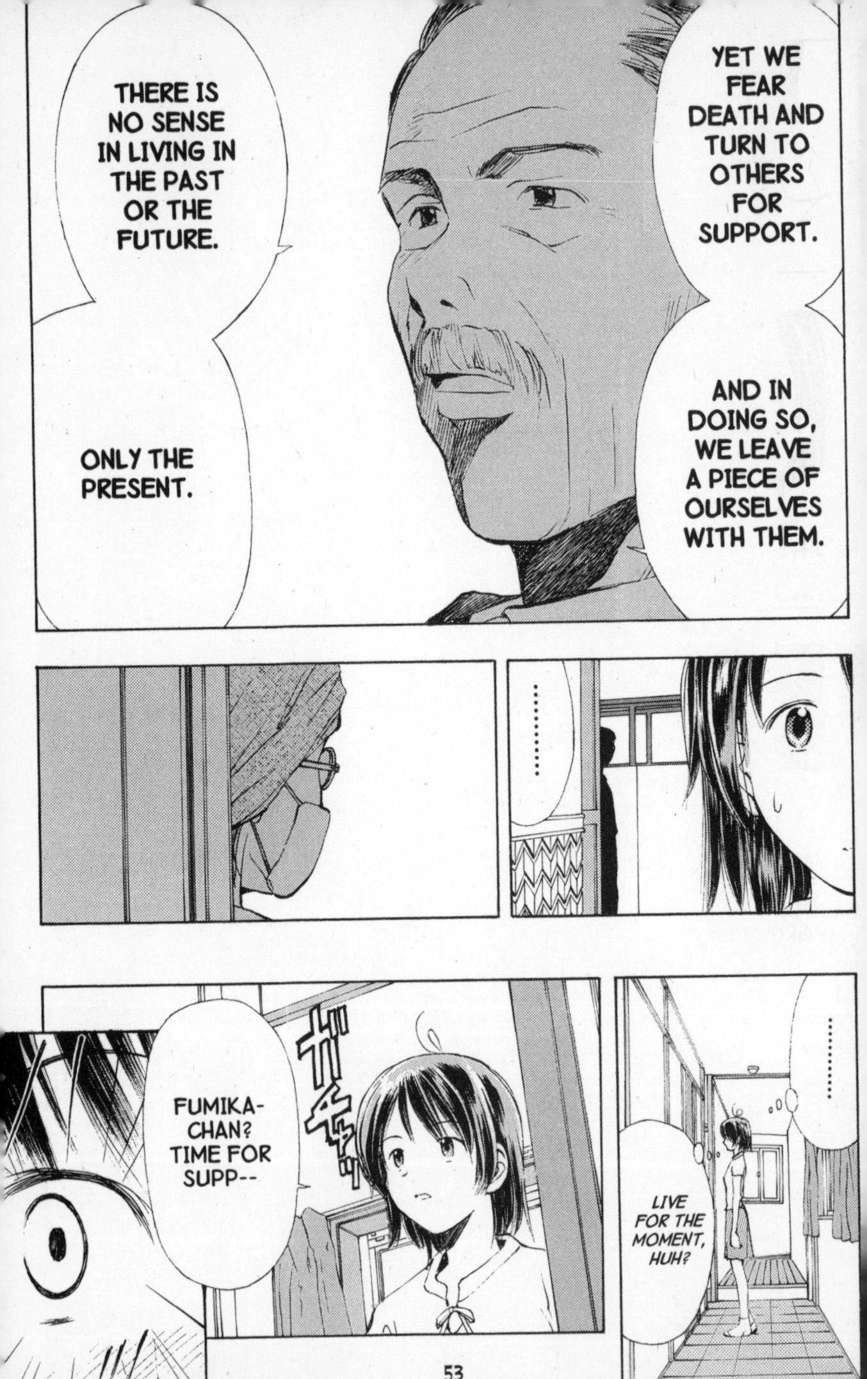
YET WE FEAR DEATH AND TURN TO OTHERS FOR SUPPORT.
THERE IS NO SENSE IN LIVING IN THE PAST OR THE FUTURE.
AND IN DOING SO, WE LEAVE A PIECE OF OURSELVES WITH THEM.
ONLY THE PRESENT.
....
....
LIVE FOR THE MOMENT, HUH?
ガチャッ
FUMIKA-CHAN? TIME FOR SUPP--

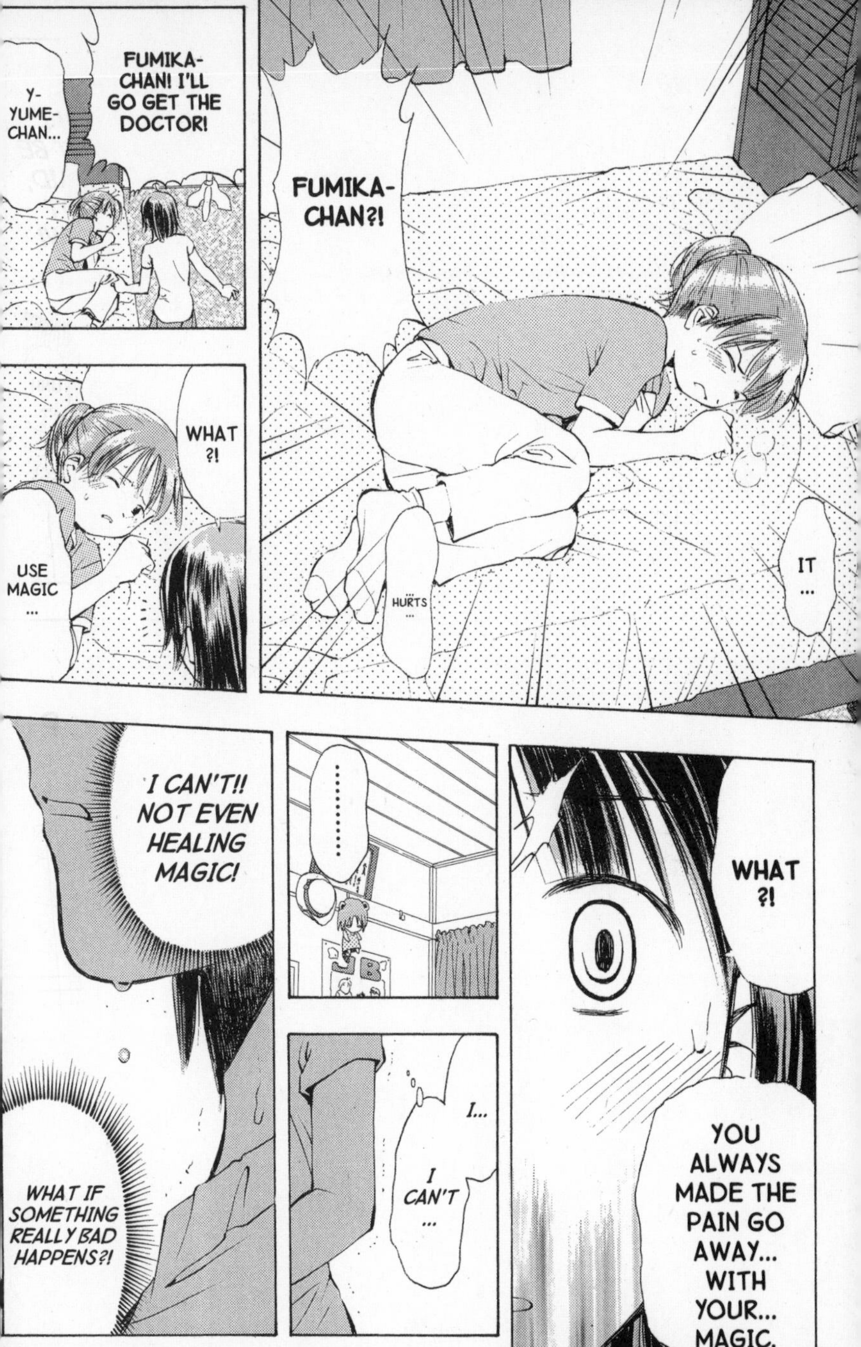
FUMIKA-CHAN?!
IT...
...HURTS...
FUMIKA-CHAN! I'LL GO GET THE DOCTOR!
Y-YUME-CHAN...
WHAT?!
USE MAGIC...
WHAT?!
YOU ALWAYS MADE THE PAIN GO AWAY... WITH YOUR... MAGIC.
....
I...
I CAN'T...
I CAN'T!! NOT EVEN HEALING MAGIC!
WHAT IF SOMETHING REALLY BAD HAPPENS?!

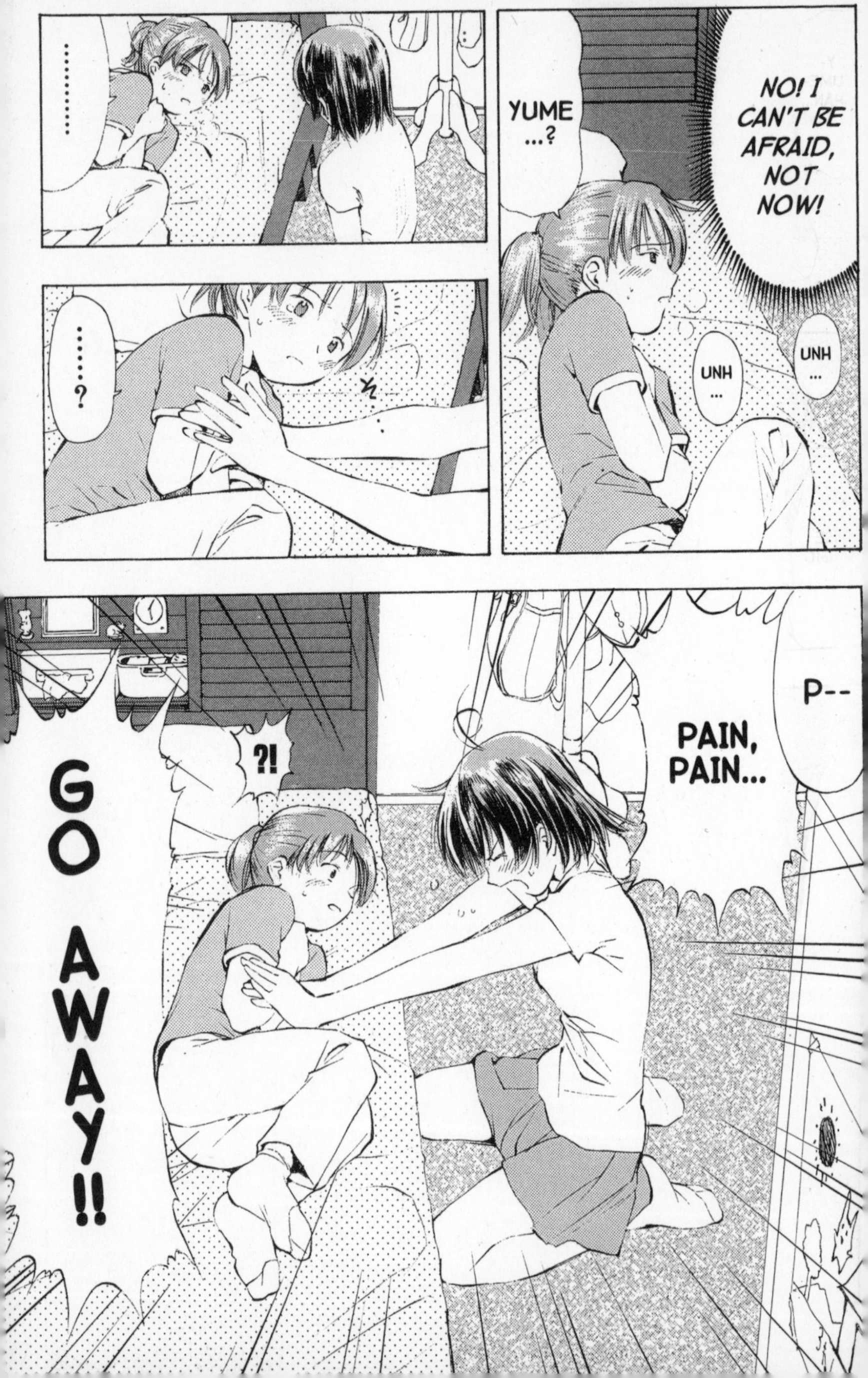
NO! I CAN'T BE AFRAID, NOT NOW!
YUME ...?
UNH ...
UNH ...
....
......?
P--
PAIN, PAIN...
?!
GO AWAY!!

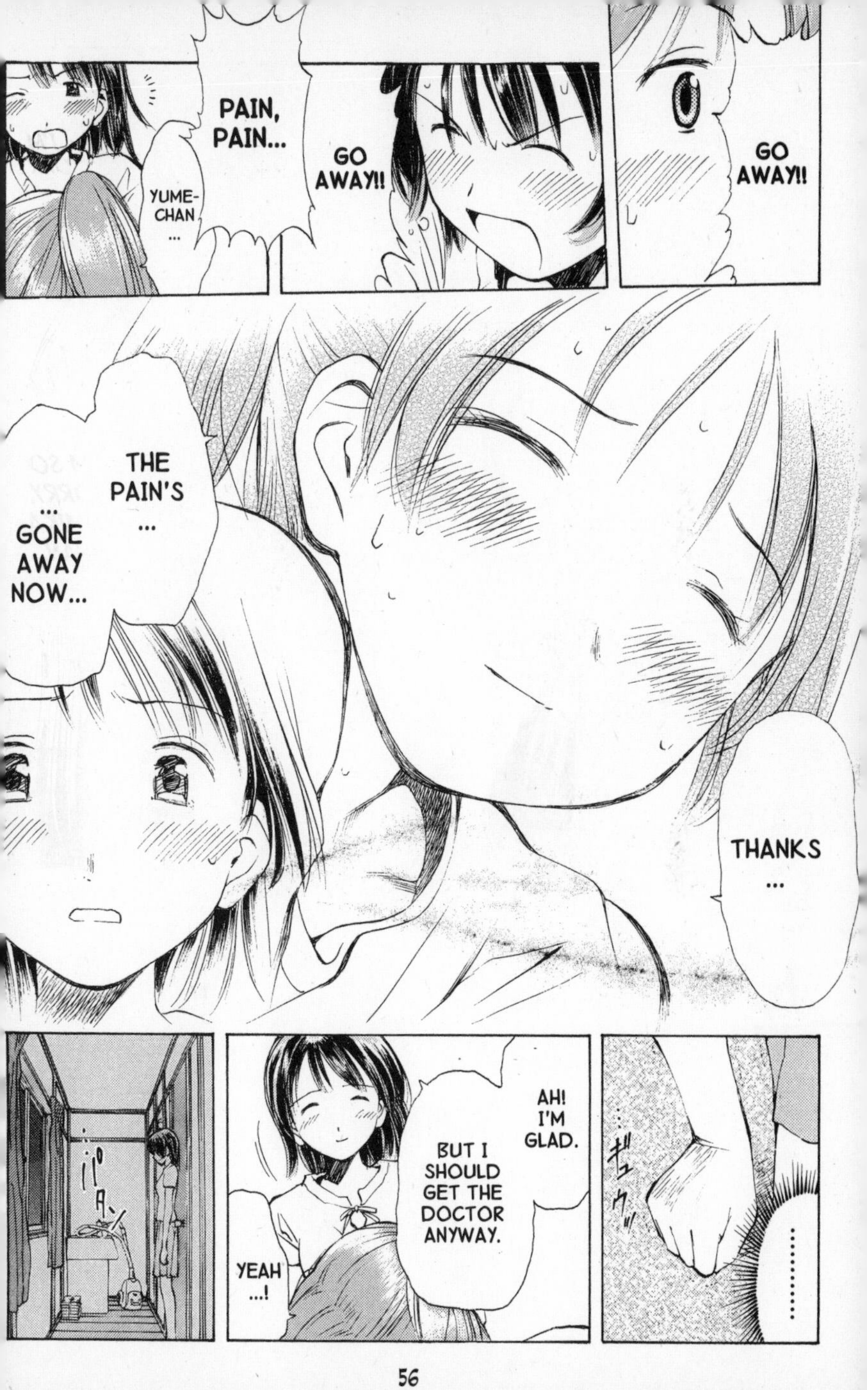
GO AWAY!!
GO AWAY!!
PAIN, PAIN...
YUME-CHAN ...
THE PAIN'S ... ... GONE AWAY NOW...
THANKS ...
....
ギュウ
AH! I'M GLAD.
BUT I SHOULD GET THE DOCTOR ANYWAY.
YEAH ...!
パタン

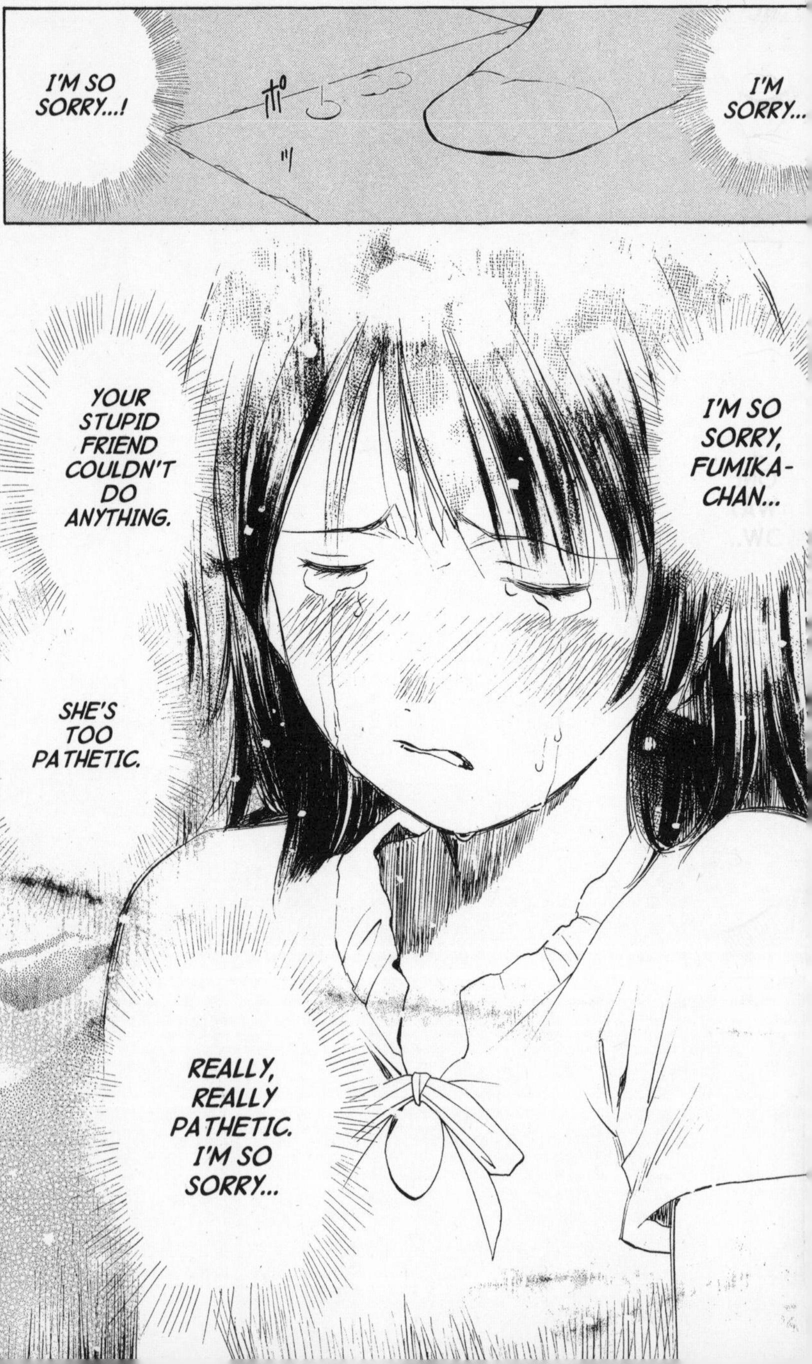
I'M SORRY...
ポツ
I'M SO SORRY...!
I'M SO SORRY, FUMIKA-CHAN...
YOUR STUPID FRIEND COULDN'T DO ANYTHING.
SHE'S TOO PATHETIC.
REALLY, REALLY PATHETIC. I'M SO SORRY...

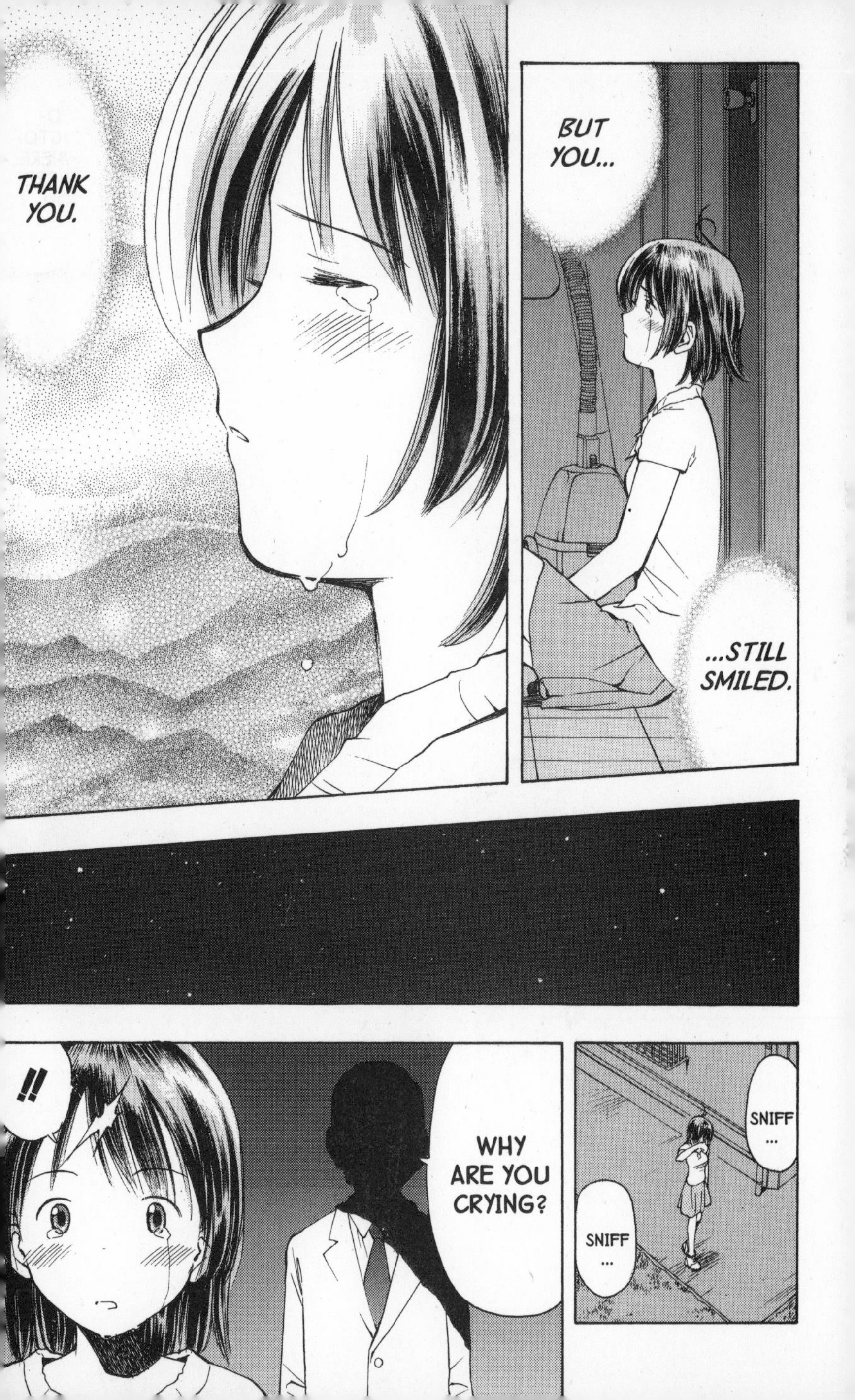
BUT YOU...
...STILL SMILED.
THANK YOU.
SNIFF ...
SNIFF ...
WHY ARE YOU CRYING?
!!

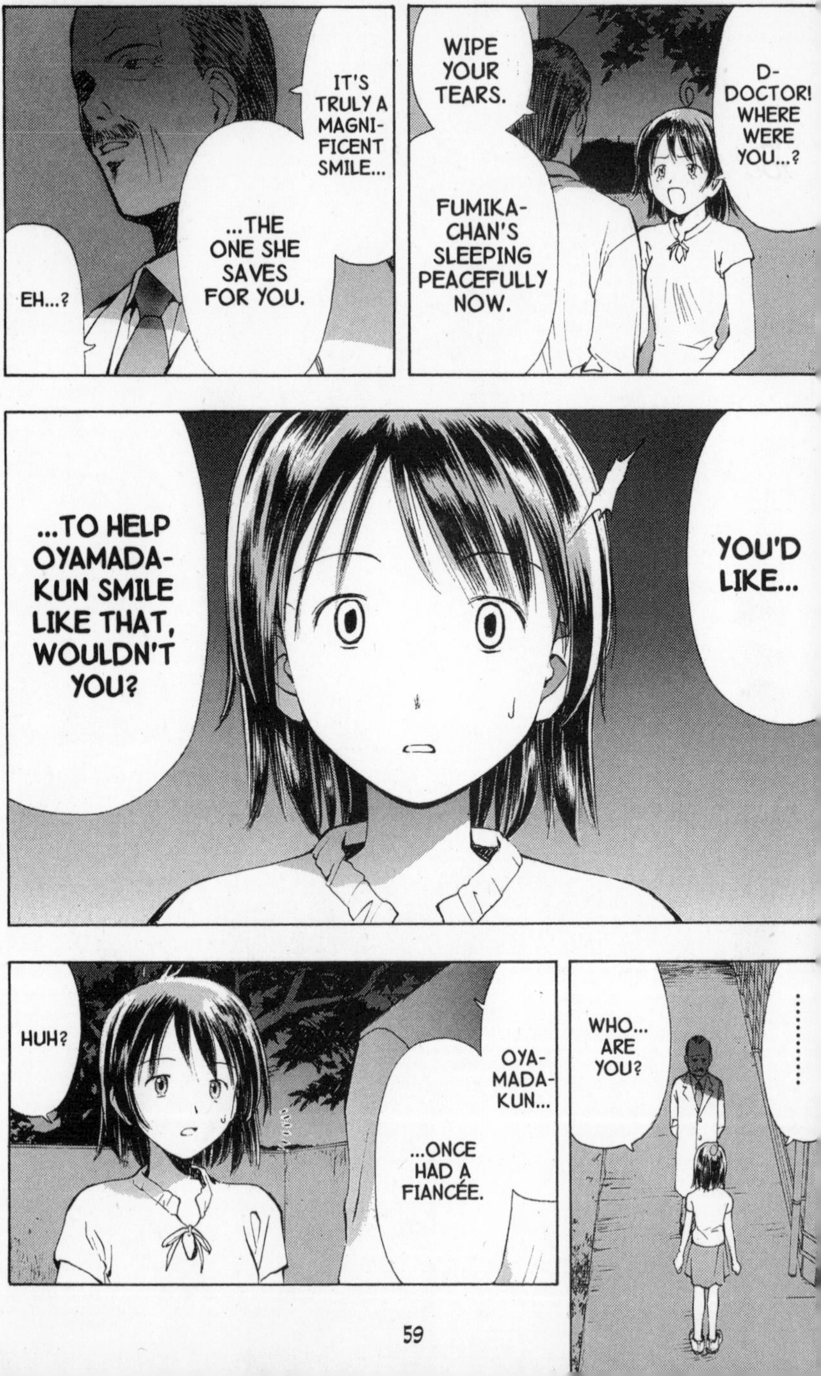
D-DOCTOR! WHERE WERE YOU...?
WIPE YOUR TEARS.
FUMIKA-CHAN'S SLEEPING PEACEFULLY NOW.
IT'S TRULY A MAGNIFICENT SMILE...
...THE ONE SHE SAVES FOR YOU.
EH...?
YOU'D LIKE...
...TO HELP OYAMADA-KUN SMILE LIKE THAT, WOULDN'T YOU?
....
WHO... ARE YOU?
OYA-MADA-KUN...
...ONCE HAD A FIANCÉE.
HUH?

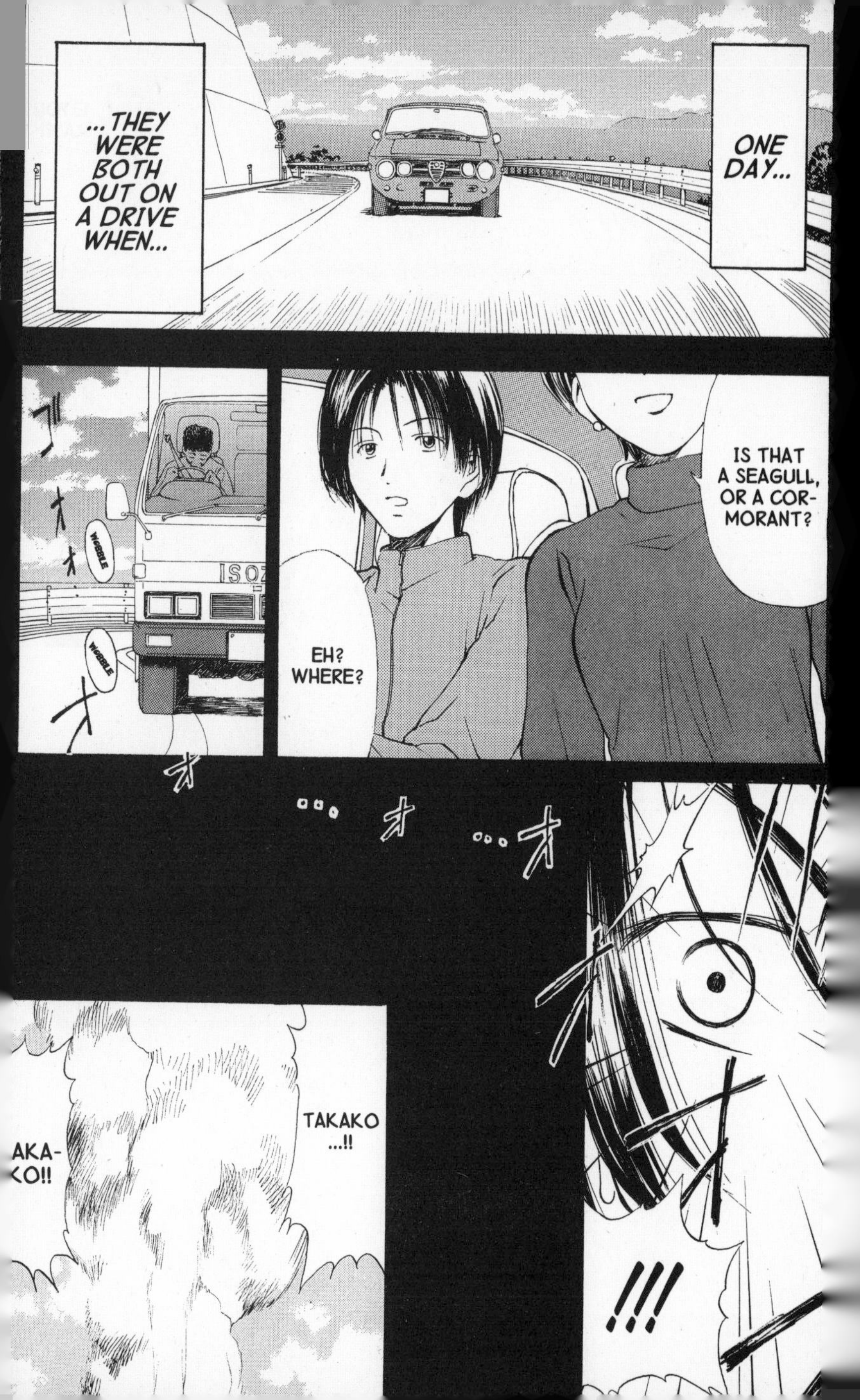
ONE DAY...
...THEY WERE BOTH OUT ON A DRIVE WHEN...
IS THAT A SEAGULL, OR A COR-MORANT?
EH? WHERE?
WOBBLE
WOBBLE
!!!
TAKAKO ...!!
AKA-KO!!

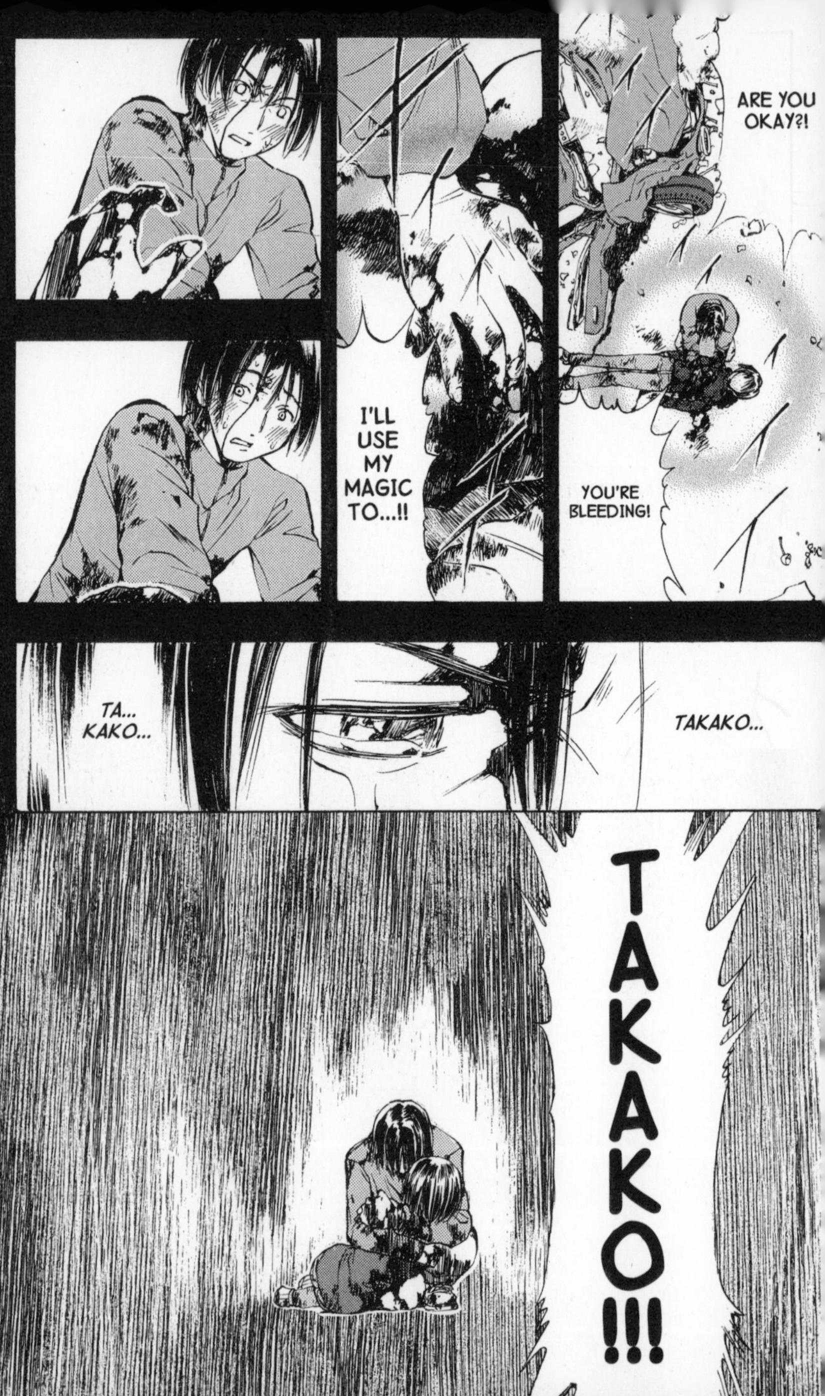
ARE YOU OKAY?!
YOU'RE BLEEDING!
I'LL USE MY MAGIC TO...!!
TAKAKO...
TA... KAKO...
TAKAKO!!!

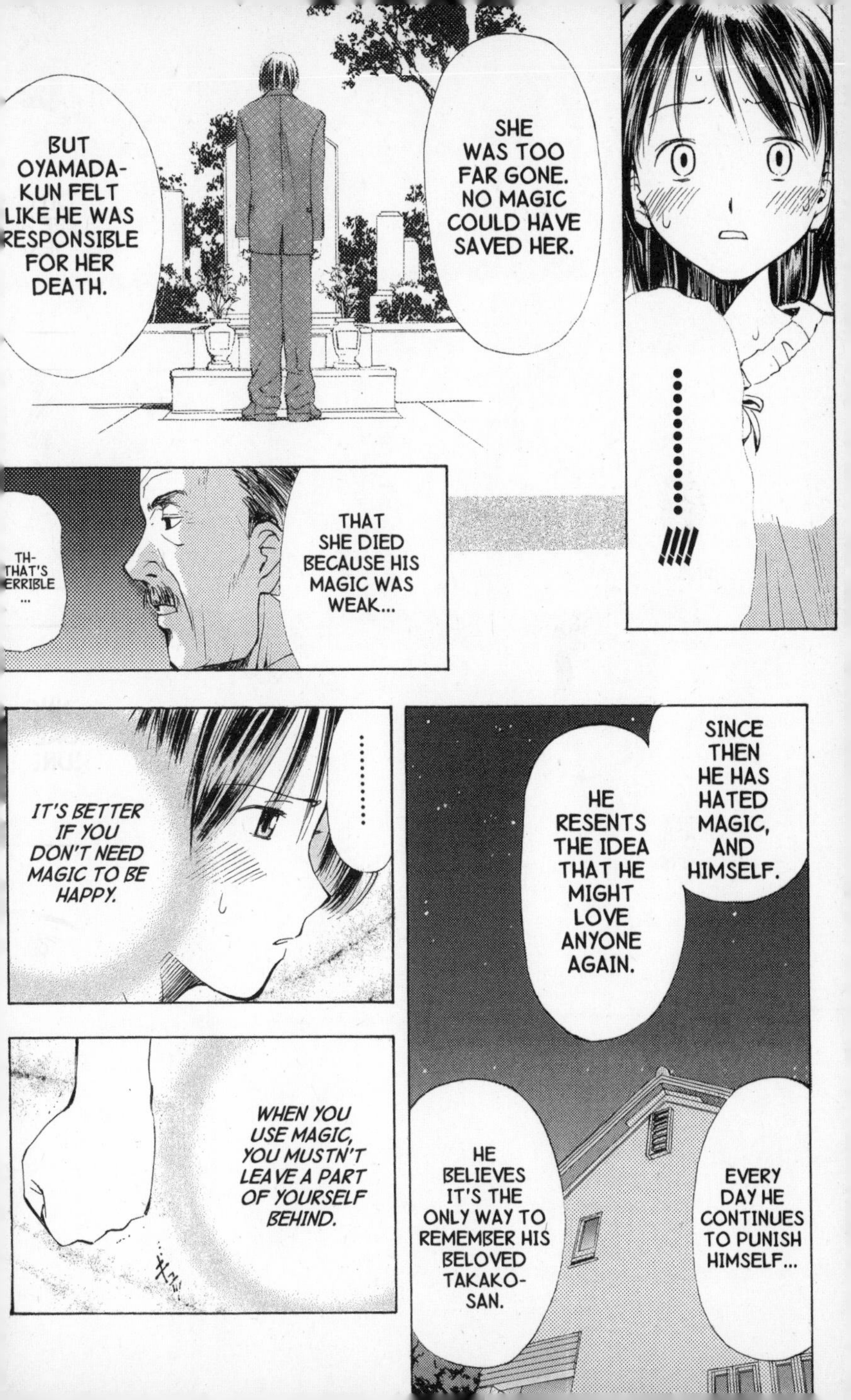
SHE WAS TOO FAR GONE. NO MAGIC COULD HAVE SAVED HER.
BUT OYAMADA-KUN FELT LIKE HE WAS RESPONSIBLE FOR HER DEATH.
......!!!!!
THAT SHE DIED BECAUSE HIS MAGIC WAS WEAK...
TH- THAT'S ERRIBLE ...
SINCE THEN HE HAS HATED MAGIC, AND HIMSELF.
HE RESENTS THE IDEA THAT HE MIGHT LOVE ANYONE AGAIN.
EVERY DAY HE CONTINUES TO PUNISH HIMSELF...
HE BELIEVES IT'S THE ONLY WAY TO REMEMBER HIS BELOVED TAKAKO-SAN.
......
IT'S BETTER IF YOU DON'T NEED MAGIC TO BE HAPPY.
WHEN YOU USE MAGIC, YOU MUSTN'T LEAVE A PART OF YOURSELF BEHIND.

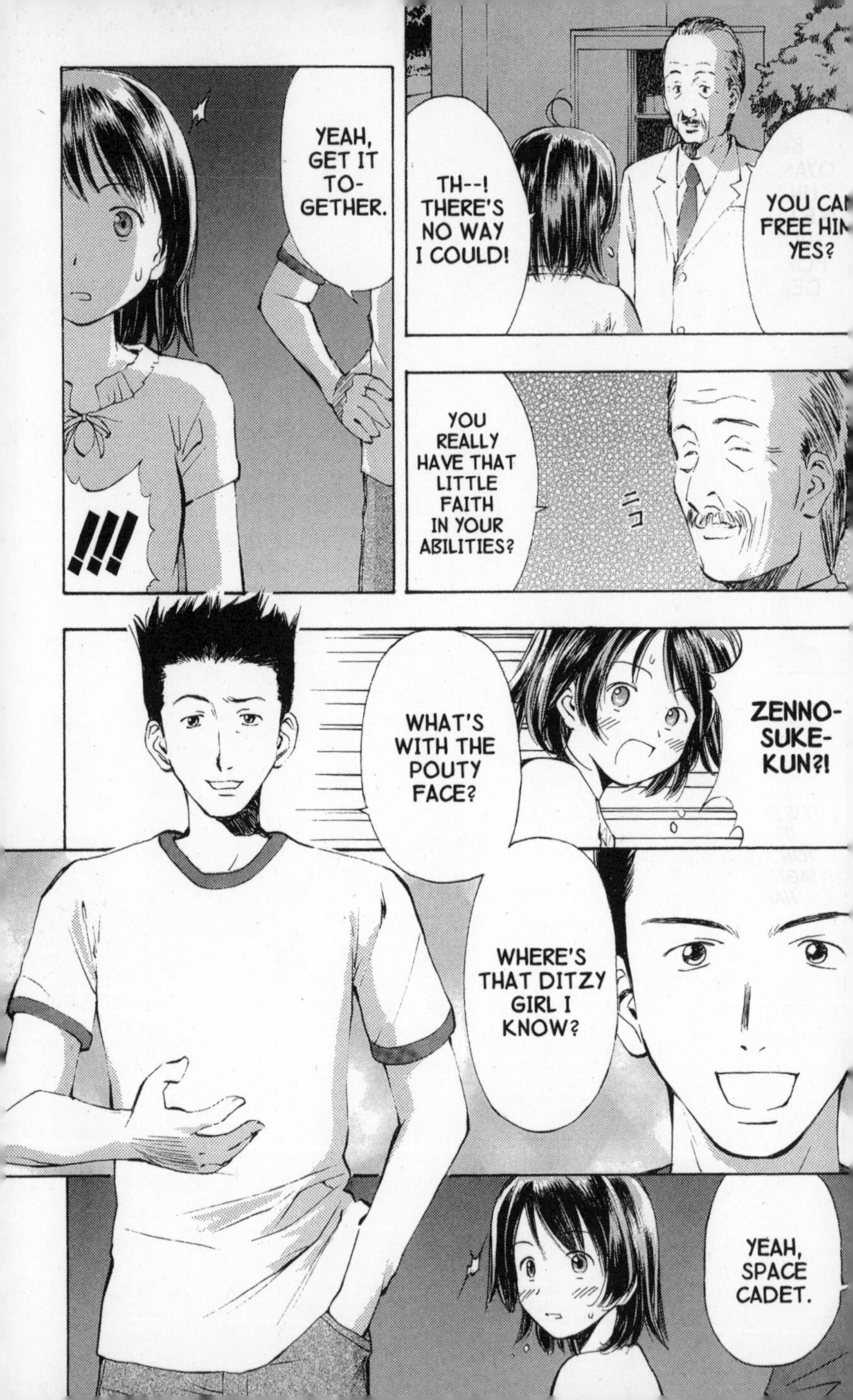
YOU CA FREE HI YES?
TH--! THERE'S NO WAY I COULD!
YOU REALLY HAVE THAT LITTLE FAITH IN YOUR ABILITIES?
ニコ
YEAH, GET IT TO-GETHER.
!!!
ZENNO-SUKE-KUN?!
WHAT'S WITH THE POUTY FACE?
WHERE'S THAT DITZY GIRL I KNOW?
YEAH, SPACE CADET.

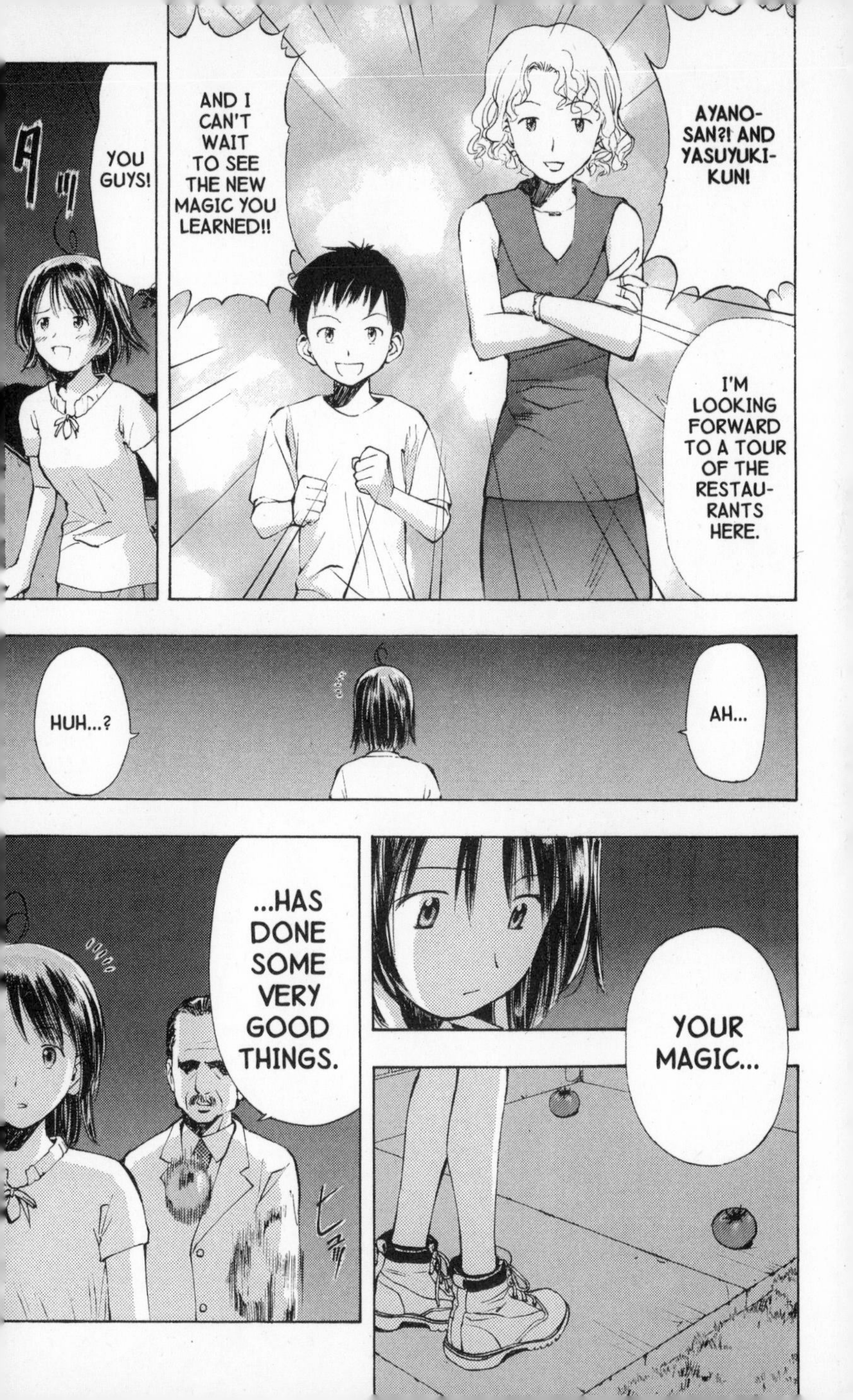
AYANO-SAN?! AND YASUYUKI-KUN!
I'M LOOKING FORWARD TO A TOUR OF THE RESTAURANTS HERE.
AND I CAN'T WAIT TO SEE THE NEW MAGIC YOU LEARNED!!
YOU GUYS!
AH...
HUH...?
YOUR MAGIC...
...HAS DONE SOME VERY GOOD THINGS.

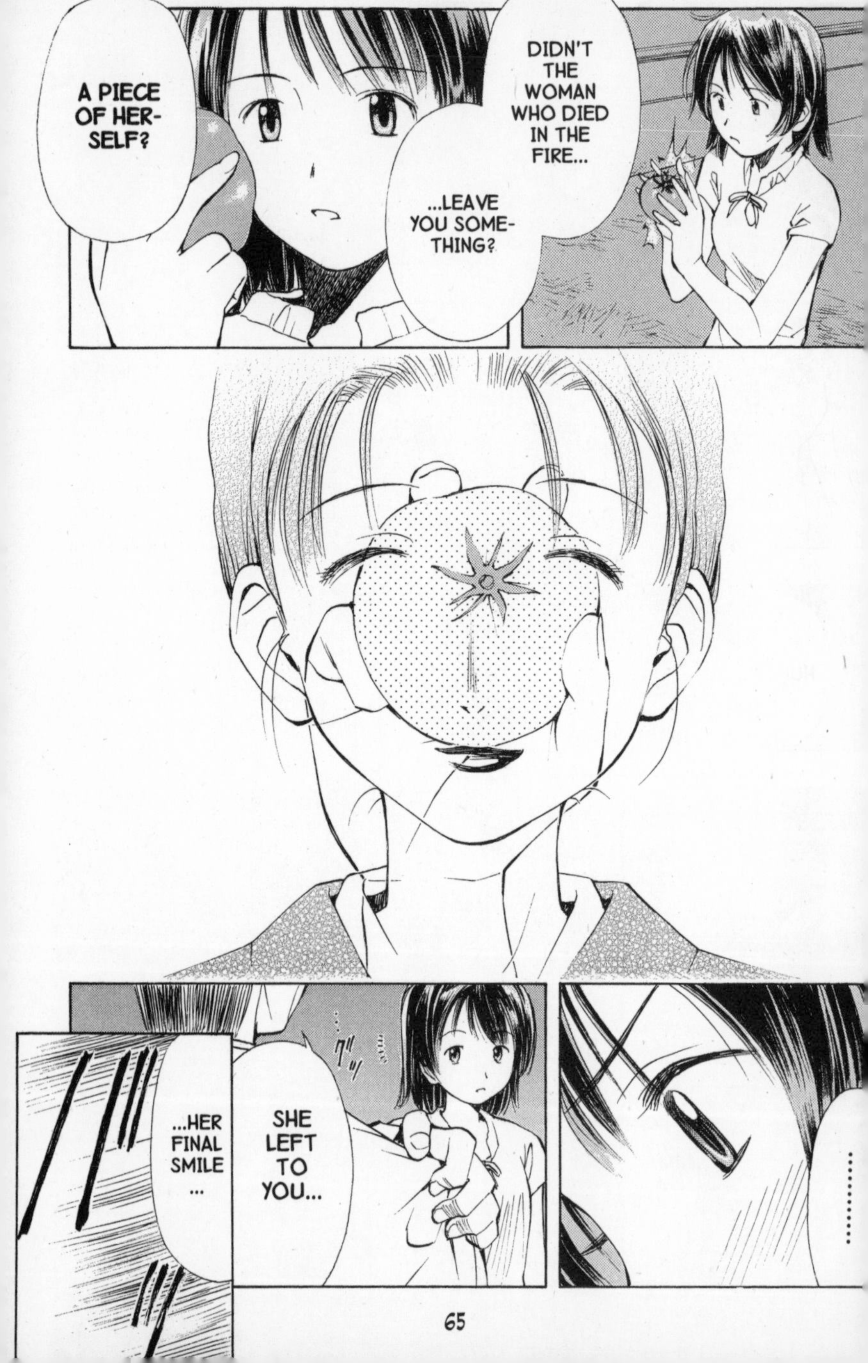
DIDN'T THE WOMAN WHO DIED IN THE FIRE...
...LEAVE YOU SOMETHING?
A PIECE OF HER-SELF?
......
グッ
SHE LEFT TO YOU...
...HER FINAL SMILE ...

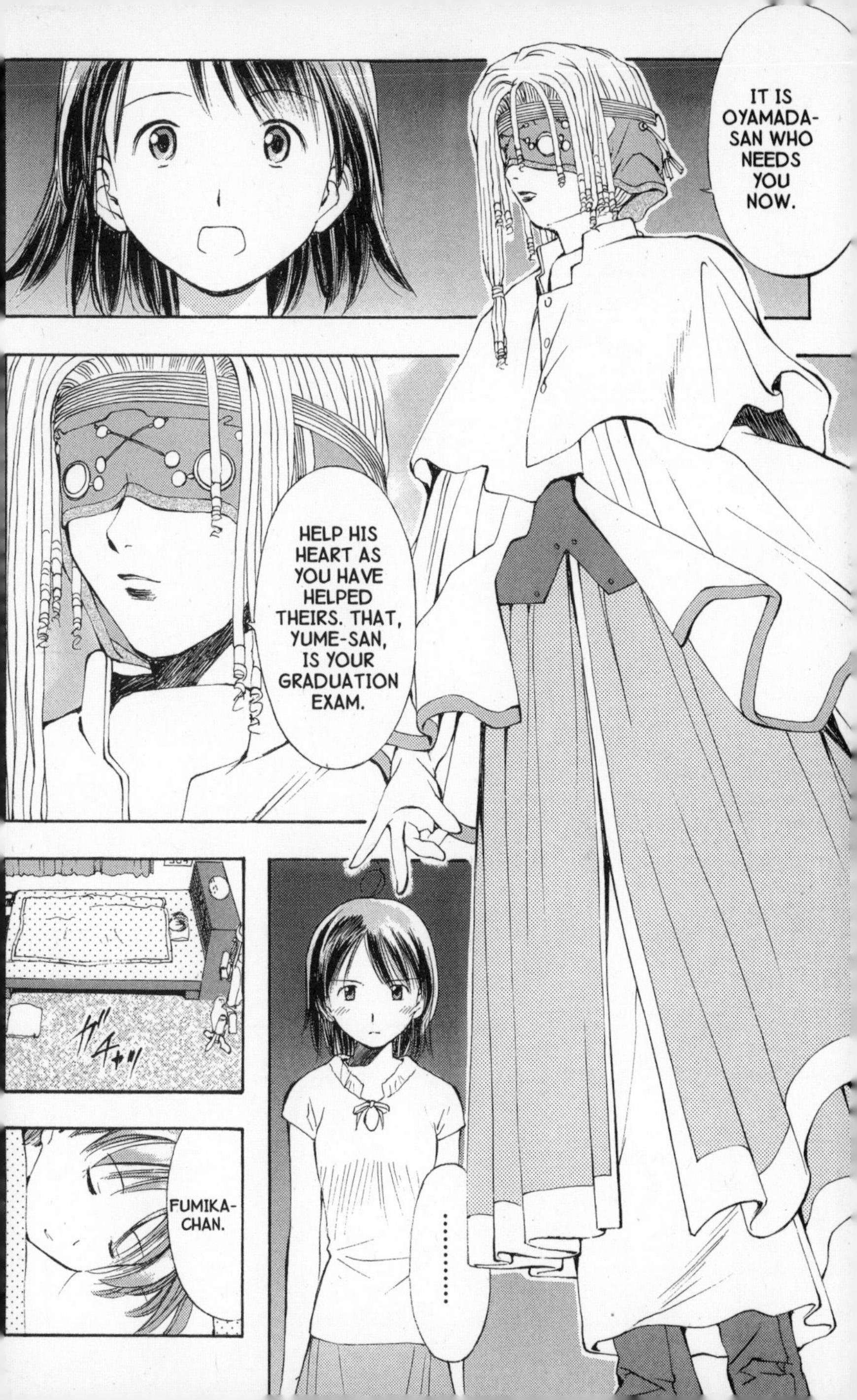
IT IS OYAMADA-SAN WHO NEEDS YOU NOW.
HELP HIS HEART AS YOU HAVE HELPED THEIRS. THAT, YUME-SAN, IS YOUR GRADUATION EXAM.
......
FUMIKA-CHAN.

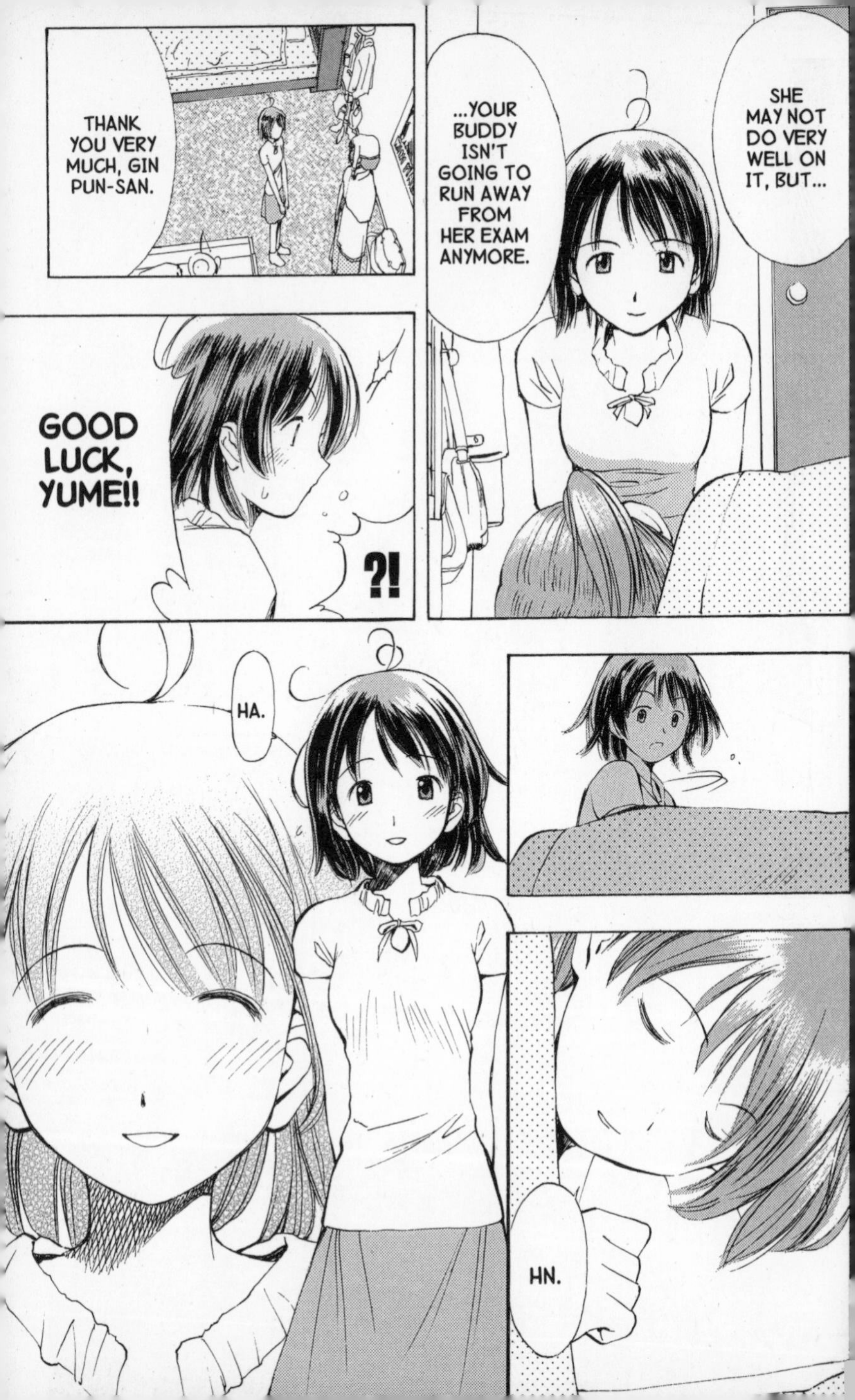
SHE MAY NOT DO VERY WELL ON IT, BUT...
...YOUR BUDDY ISN'T GOING TO RUN AWAY FROM HER EXAM ANYMORE.
THANK YOU VERY MUCH, GIN PUN-SAN.
GOOD LUCK, YUME!!
?!
HN.
HA.

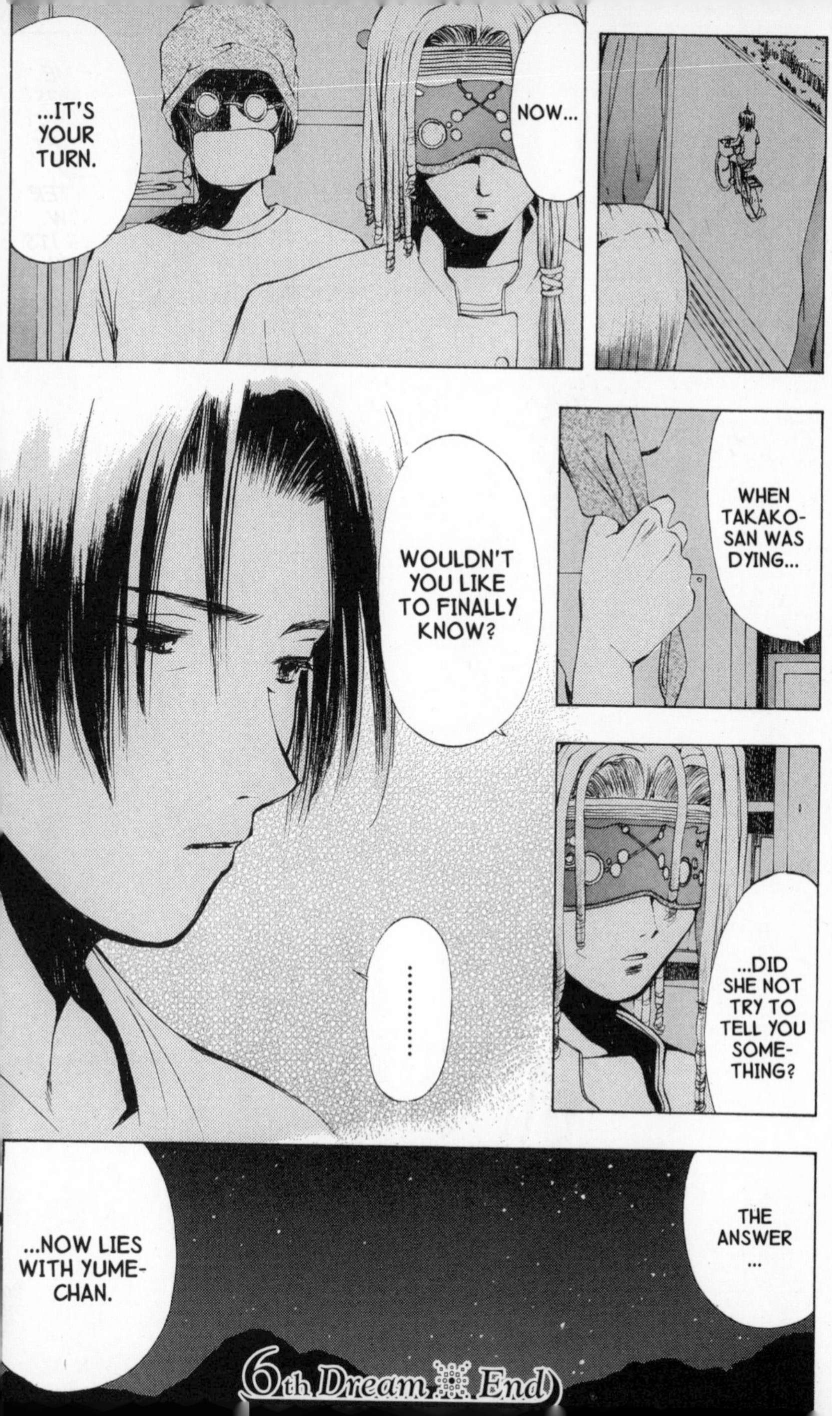
NOW...
...IT'S YOUR TURN.
WHEN TAKAKO-SAN WAS DYING...
...DID SHE NOT TRY TO TELL YOU SOMETHING?
WOULDN'T YOU LIKE TO FINALLY KNOW?
....
THE ANSWER ...
...NOW LIES WITH YUME-CHAN.
6th Dream End

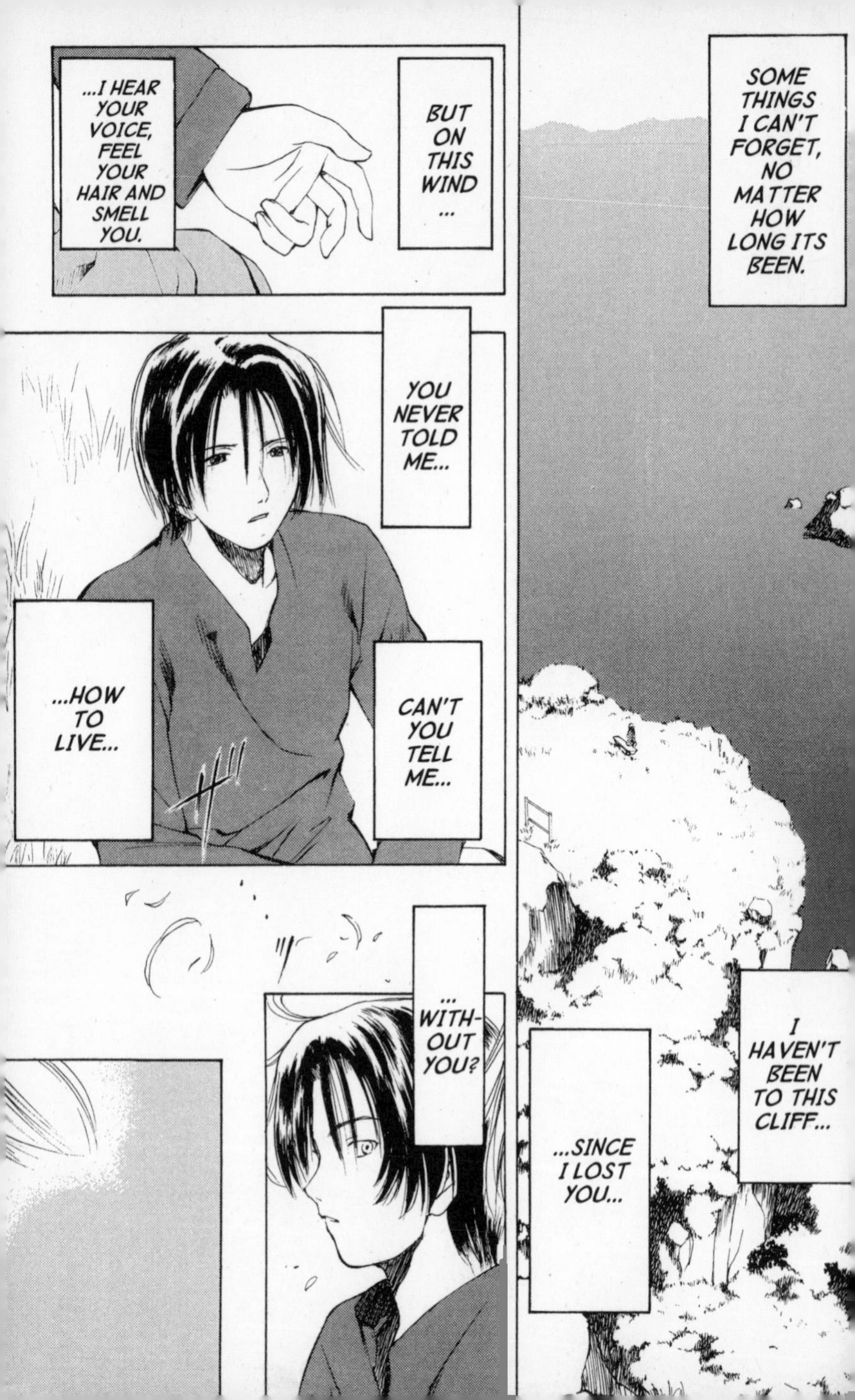
SOME THINGS I CAN'T FORGET, NO MATTER HOW LONG ITS BEEN.
I HAVEN'T BEEN TO THIS CLIFF...
...SINCE I LOST YOU...
BUT ON THIS WIND...
...I HEAR YOUR VOICE, FEEL YOUR HAIR AND SMELL YOU.
YOU NEVER TOLD ME...
CAN'T YOU TELL ME...
...HOW TO LIVE...
...WITH-OUT YOU?

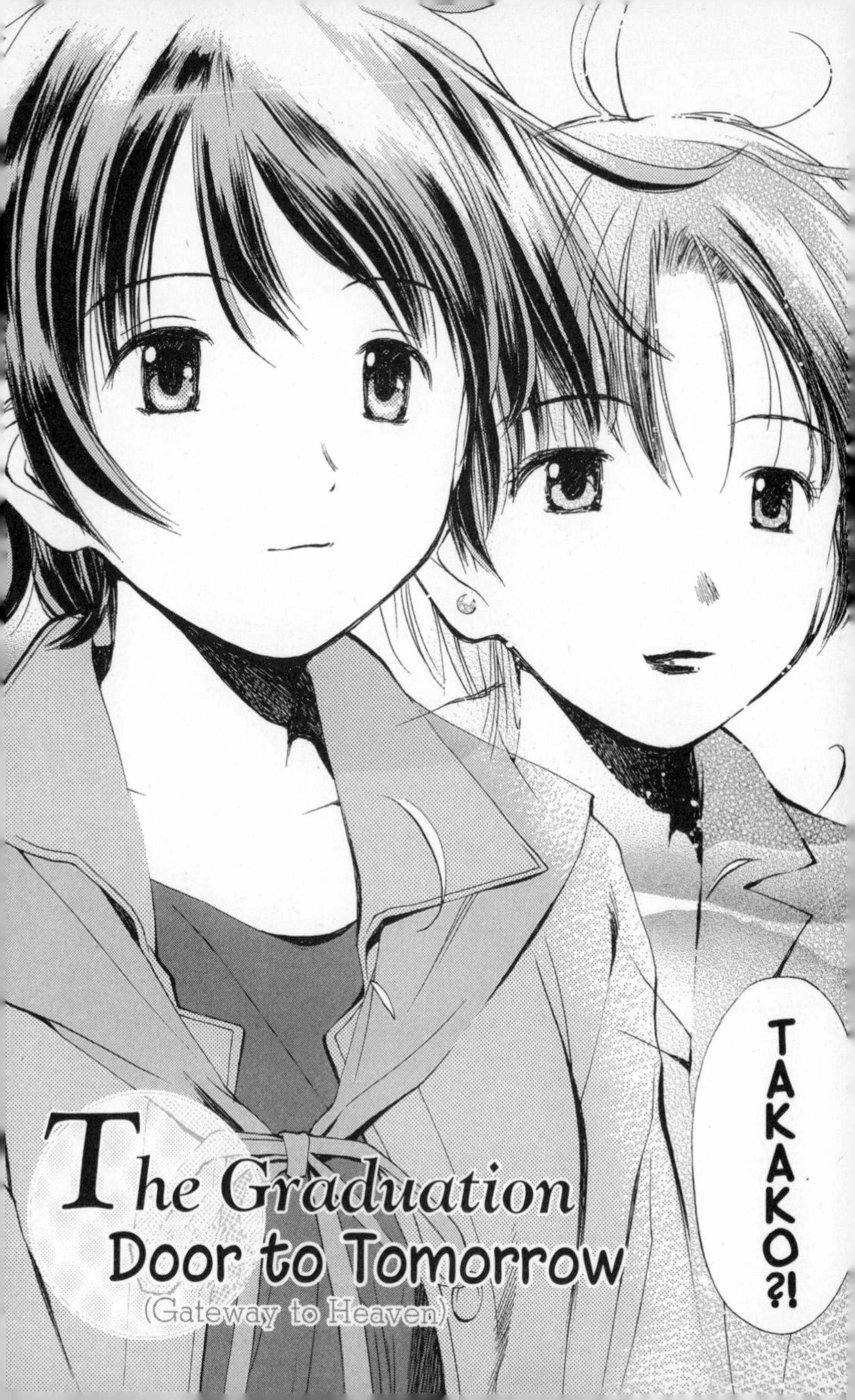
TAKAKO?!
The Graduation
Door to Tomorrow
(Gateway to Heaven)

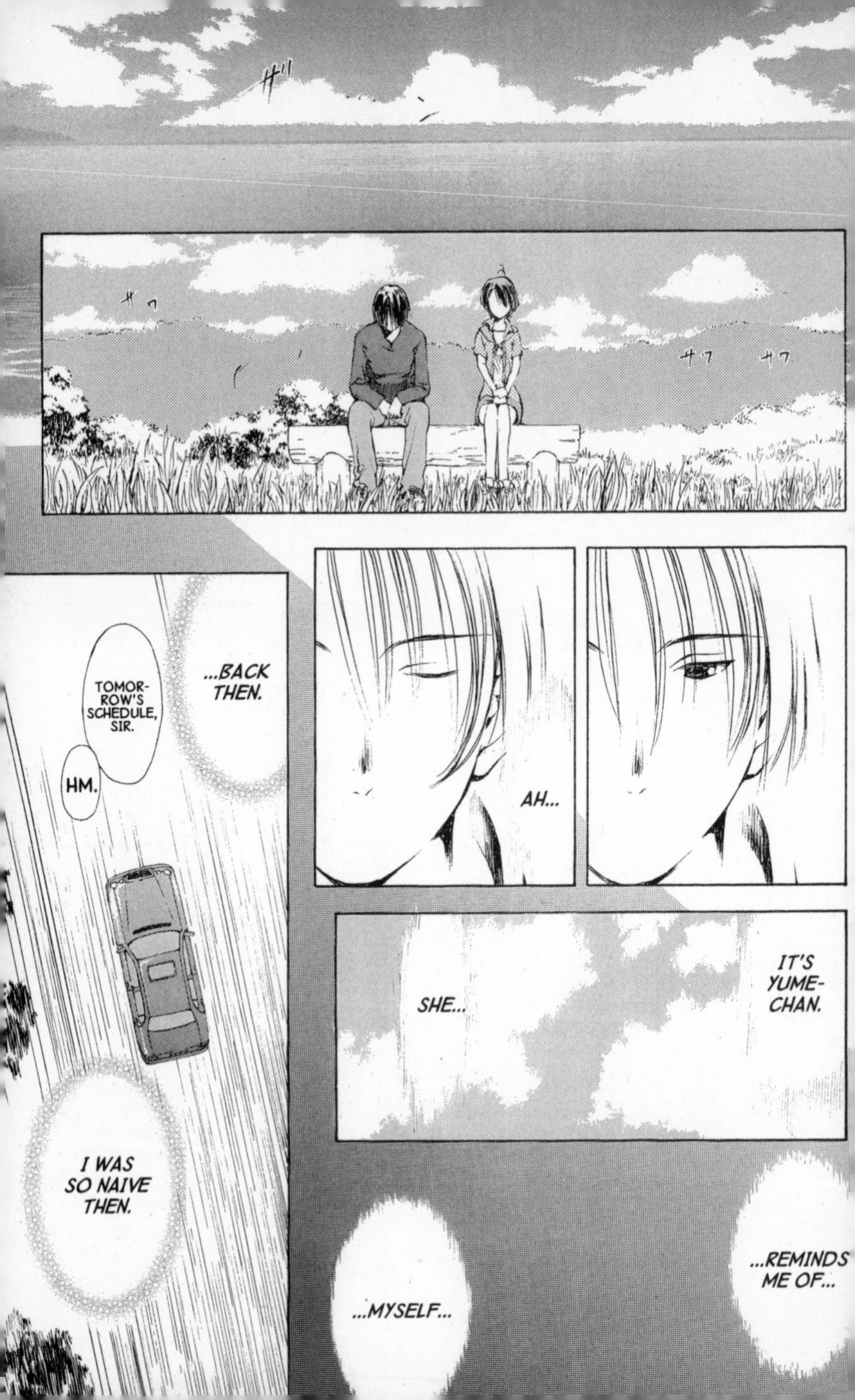
AH...
IT'S YUME-CHAN.
SHE...
...REMINDS ME OF...
...MYSELF...
...BACK THEN.
TOMORROW'S SCHEDULE, SIR.
HM.
I WAS SO NAIVE THEN.

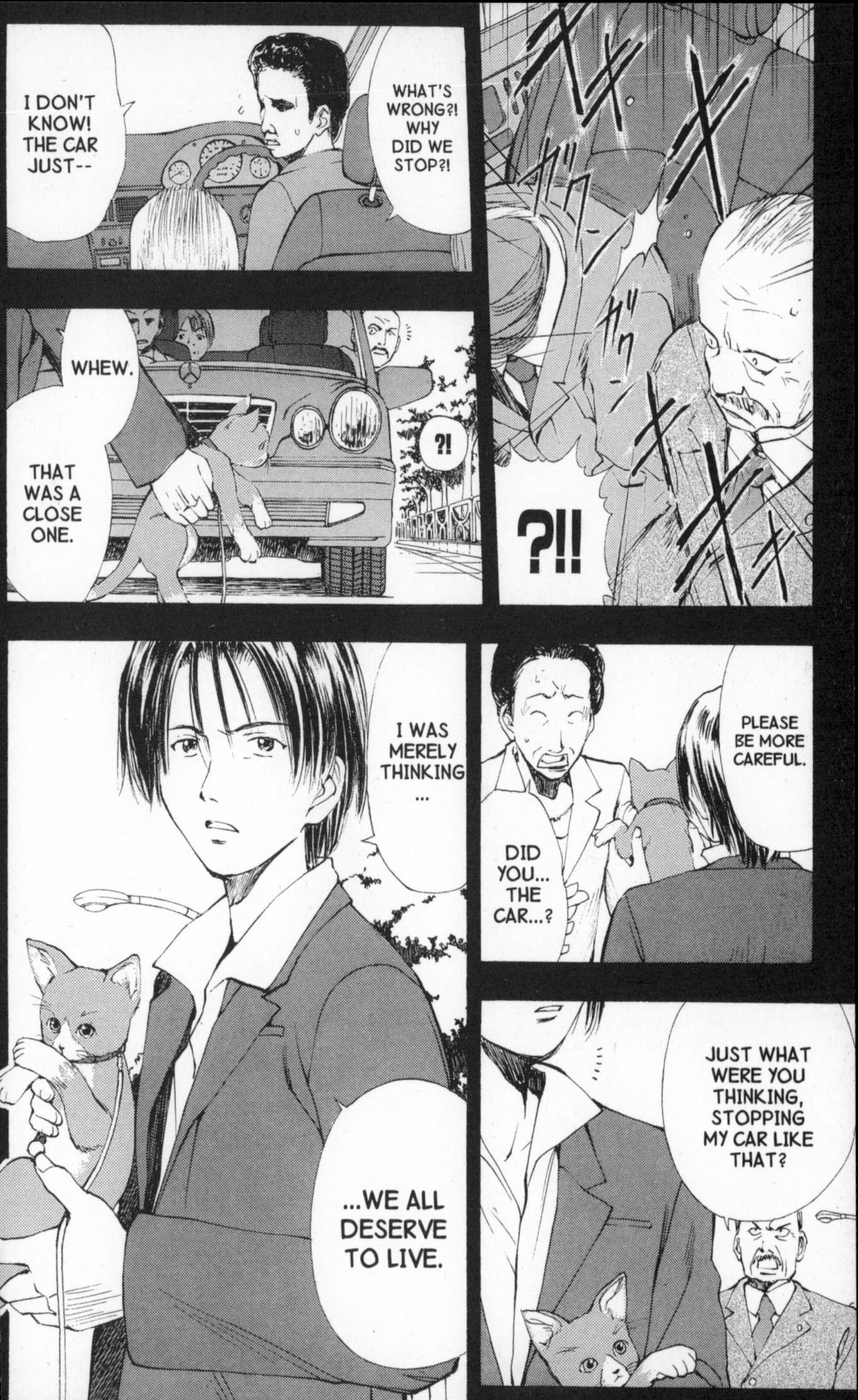
?!!
WHAT'S WRONG?! WHY DID WE STOP?!
I DON'T KNOW! THE CAR JUST--
WHEW.
?!
THAT WAS A CLOSE ONE.
PLEASE BE MORE CAREFUL.
DID YOU... THE CAR...?
JUST WHAT WERE YOU THINKING, STOPPING MY CAR LIKE THAT?
I WAS MERELY THINKING...
...WE ALL DESERVE TO LIVE.

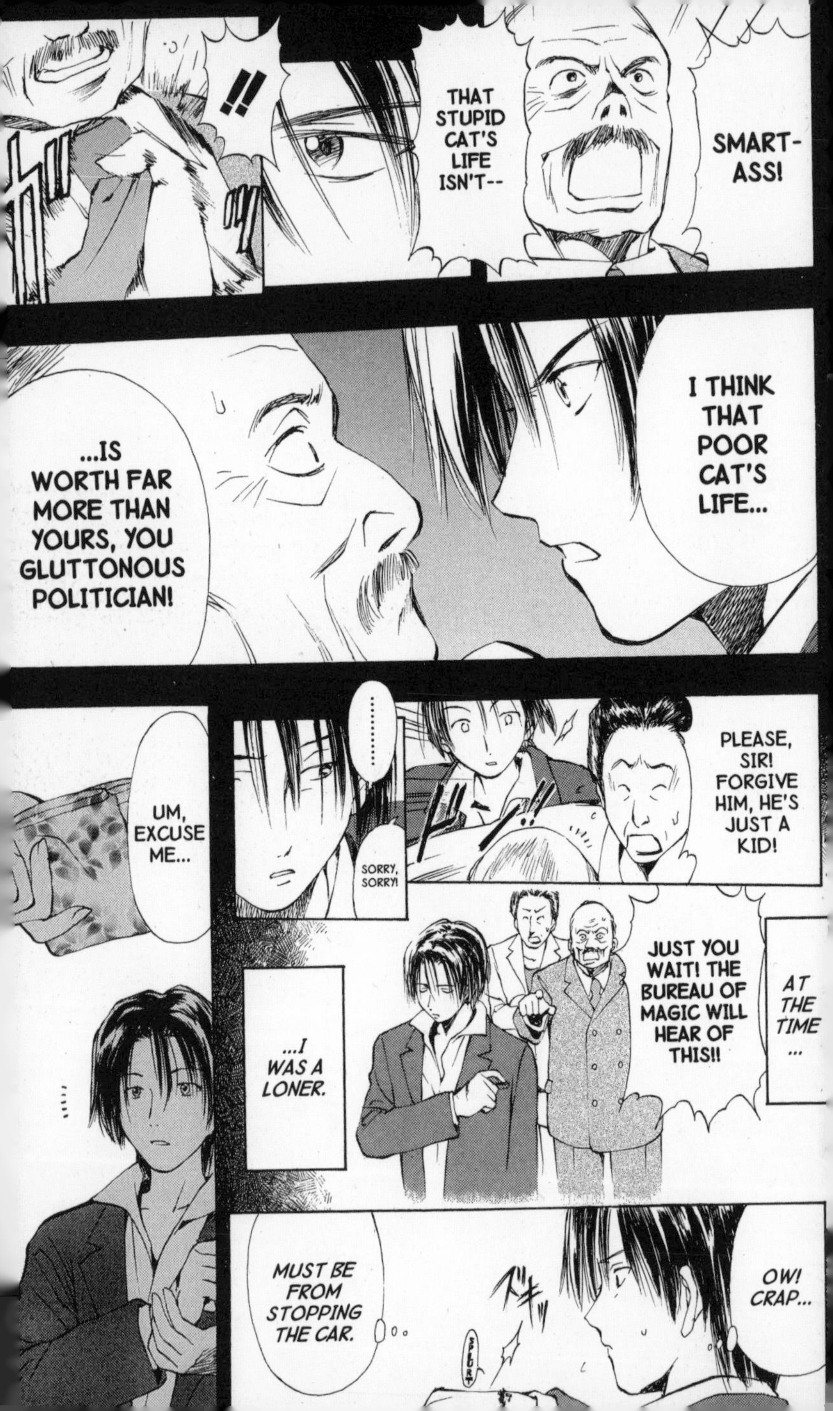
SMART-ASS!
THAT STUPID CAT'S LIFE ISN'T--
!!
I THINK THAT POOR CAT'S LIFE...
...IS WORTH FAR MORE THAN YOURS, YOU GLUTTONOUS POLITICIAN!
PLEASE, SIR! FORGIVE HIM, HE'S JUST A KID!
SORRY, SORRY!
....
AT THE TIME...
JUST YOU WAIT! THE BUREAU OF MAGIC WILL HEAR OF THIS!!
...I WAS A LONER.
OW! CRAP...
SPLURT
MUST BE FROM STOPPING THE CAR.
UM, EXCUSE ME...
...

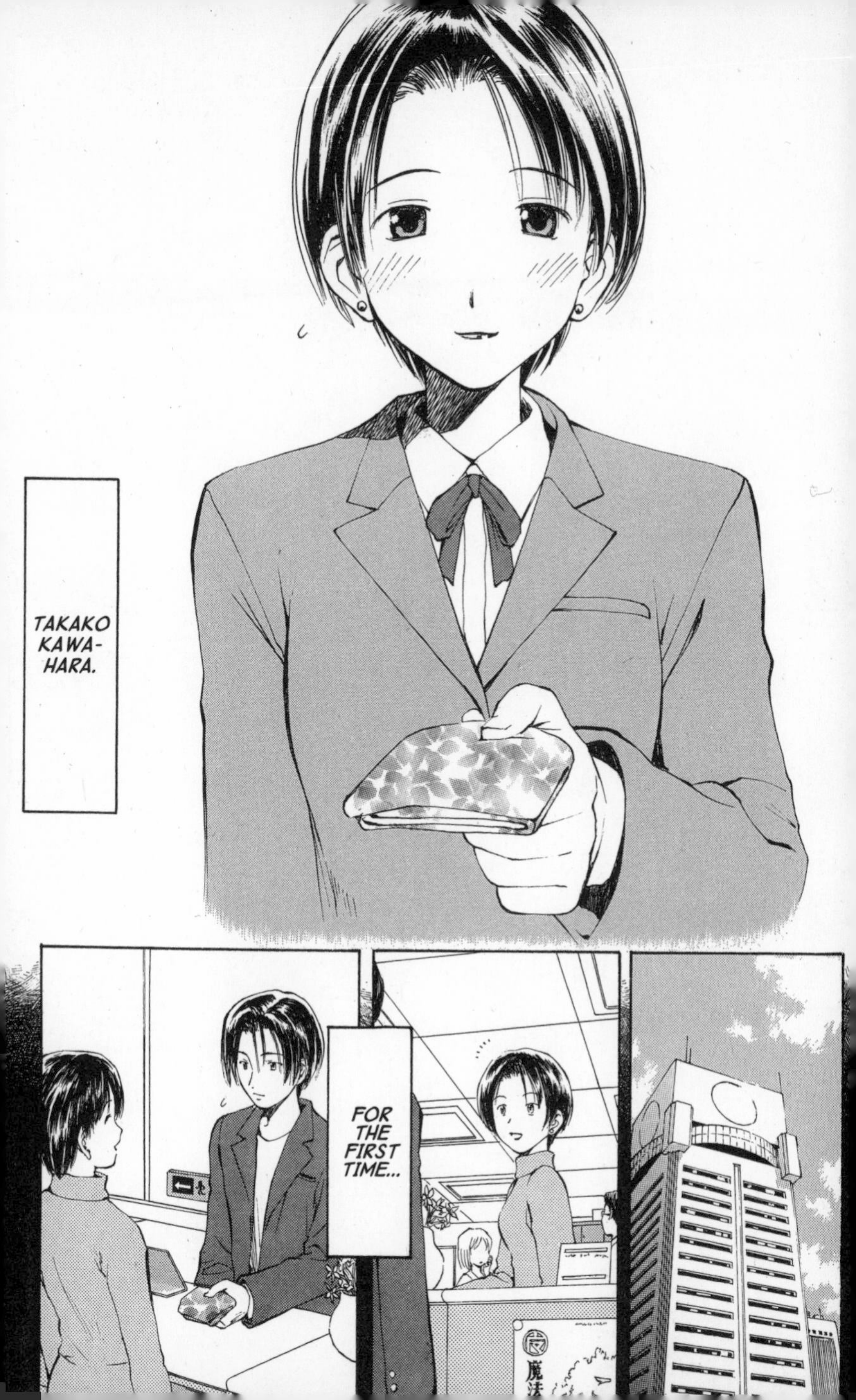
TAKAKO KAWA-HARA.
FOR THE FIRST TIME...

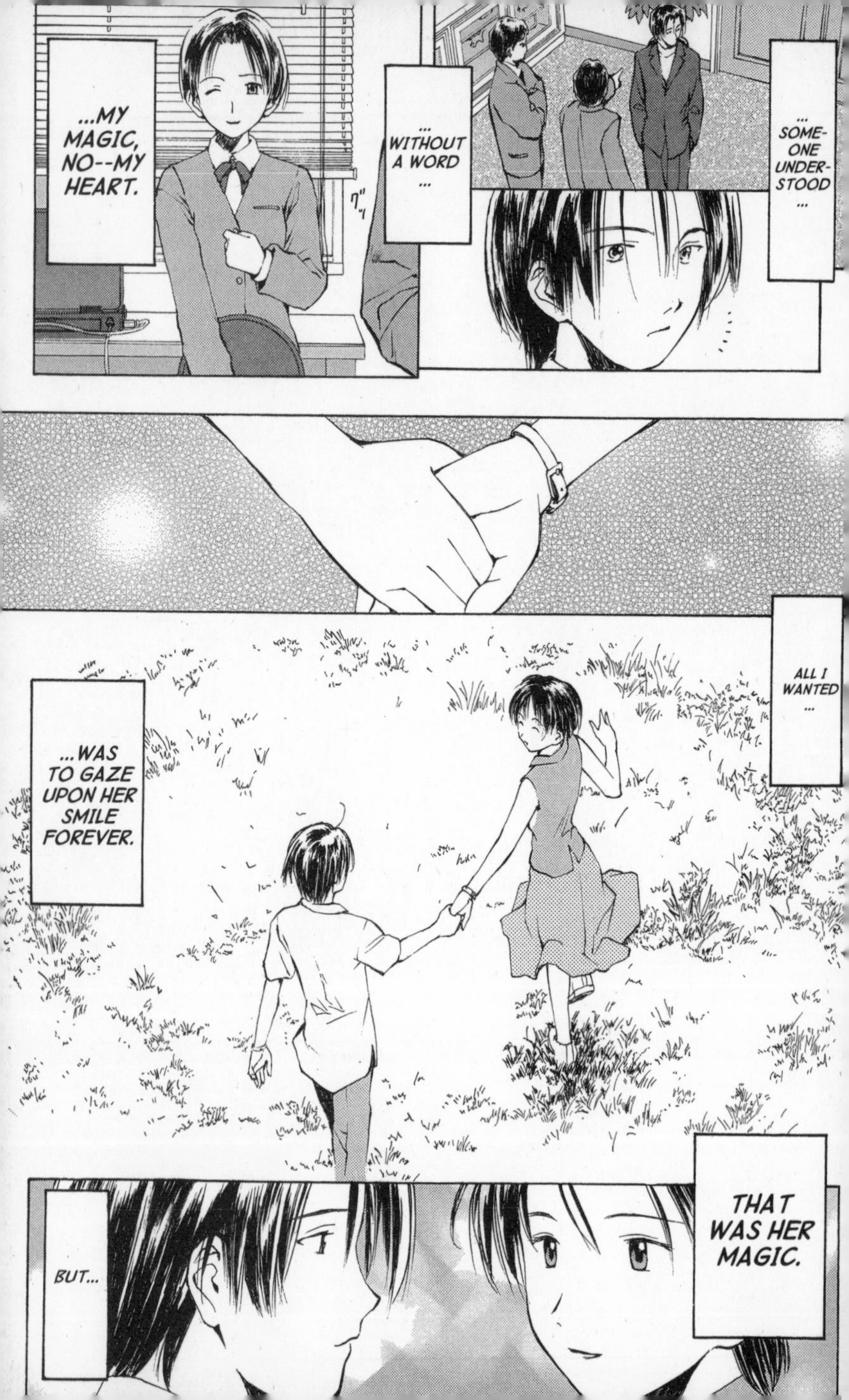
...SOME-ONE UNDER-STOOD...
...WITHOUT A WORD...
...MY MAGIC, NO--MY HEART.
グッ
ALL I WANTED...
...WAS TO GAZE UPON HER SMILE FOREVER.
THAT WAS HER MAGIC.
BUT...

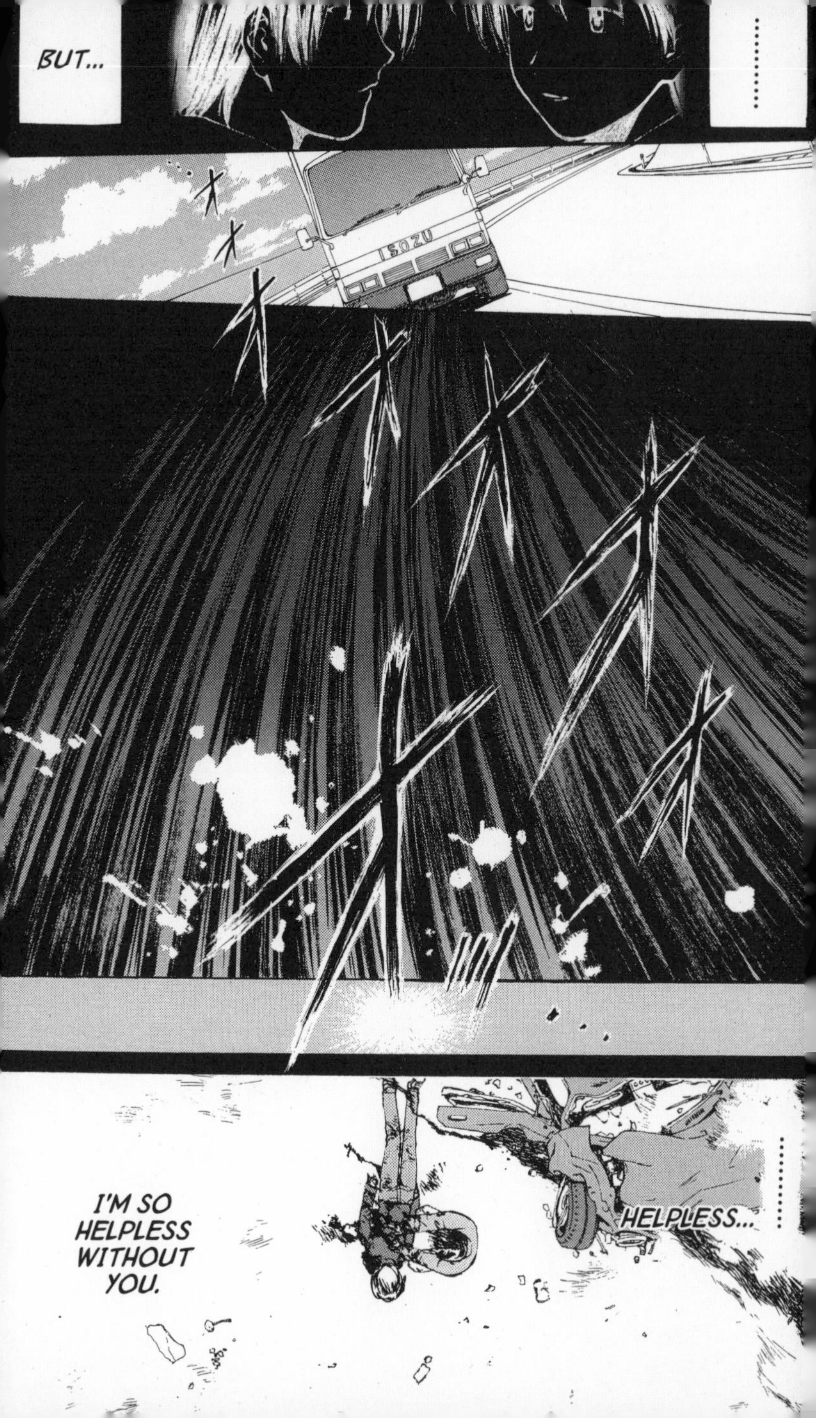
......
BUT...
......
HELPLESS...
I'M SO HELPLESS WITHOUT YOU.

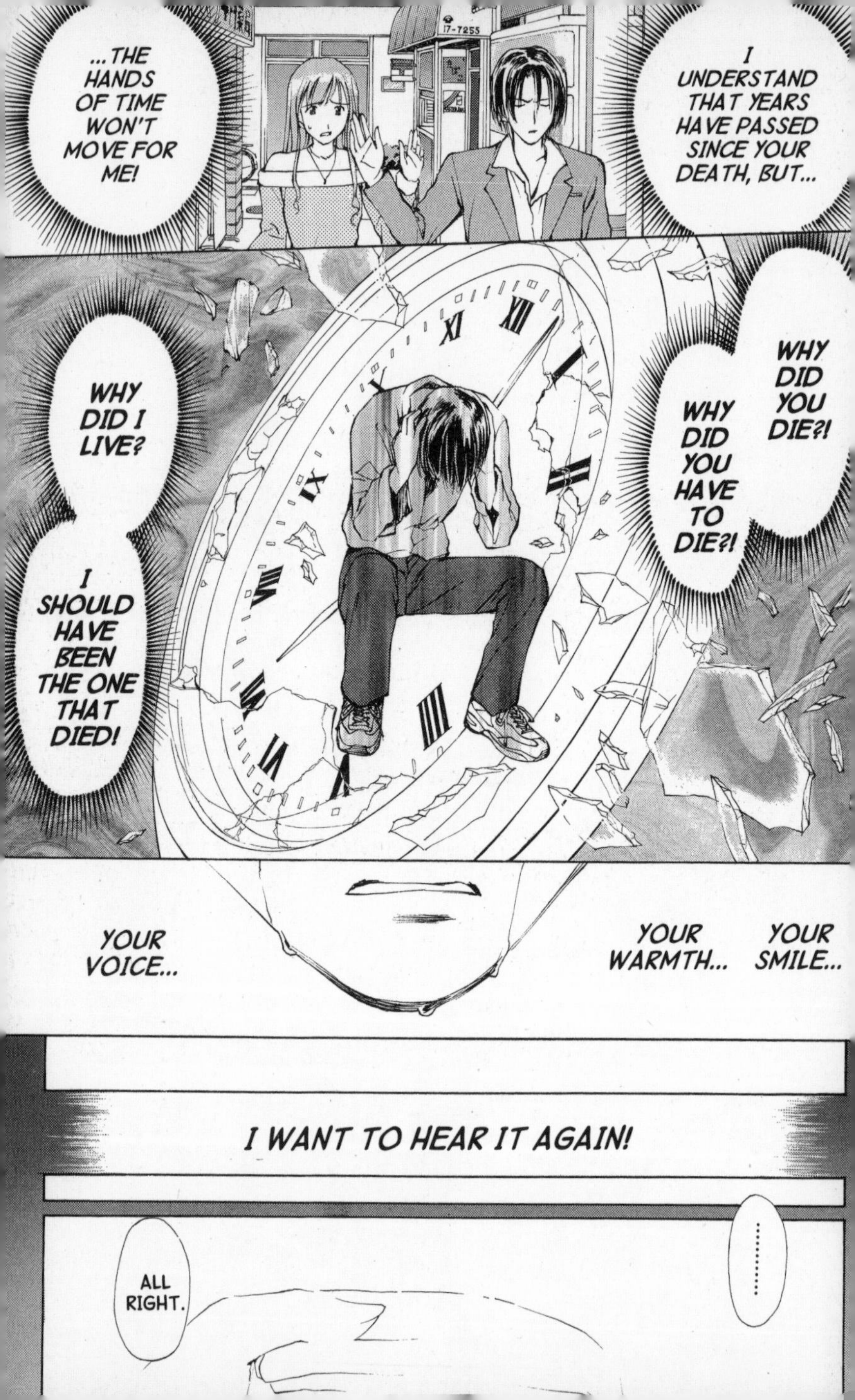
I UNDERSTAND THAT YEARS HAVE PASSED SINCE YOUR DEATH, BUT...
...THE HANDS OF TIME WON'T MOVE FOR ME!
WHY DID YOU DIE?!
WHY DID YOU HAVE TO DIE?!
WHY DID I LIVE?
I SHOULD HAVE BEEN THE ONE THAT DIED!
YOUR SMILE...
YOUR WARMTH...
YOUR VOICE...
I WANT TO HEAR IT AGAIN!
......
ALL RIGHT.

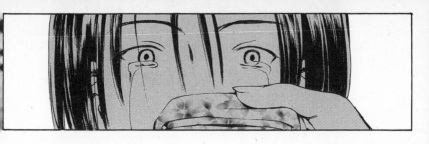

EVERY DAY.

I WATCH YOU.

EVERY MOMENT SINCE THAT DAY, I'VE BEEN WATCHING YOU.

EVERY SINGLE MOMENT YOU'VE SUFFERED ...

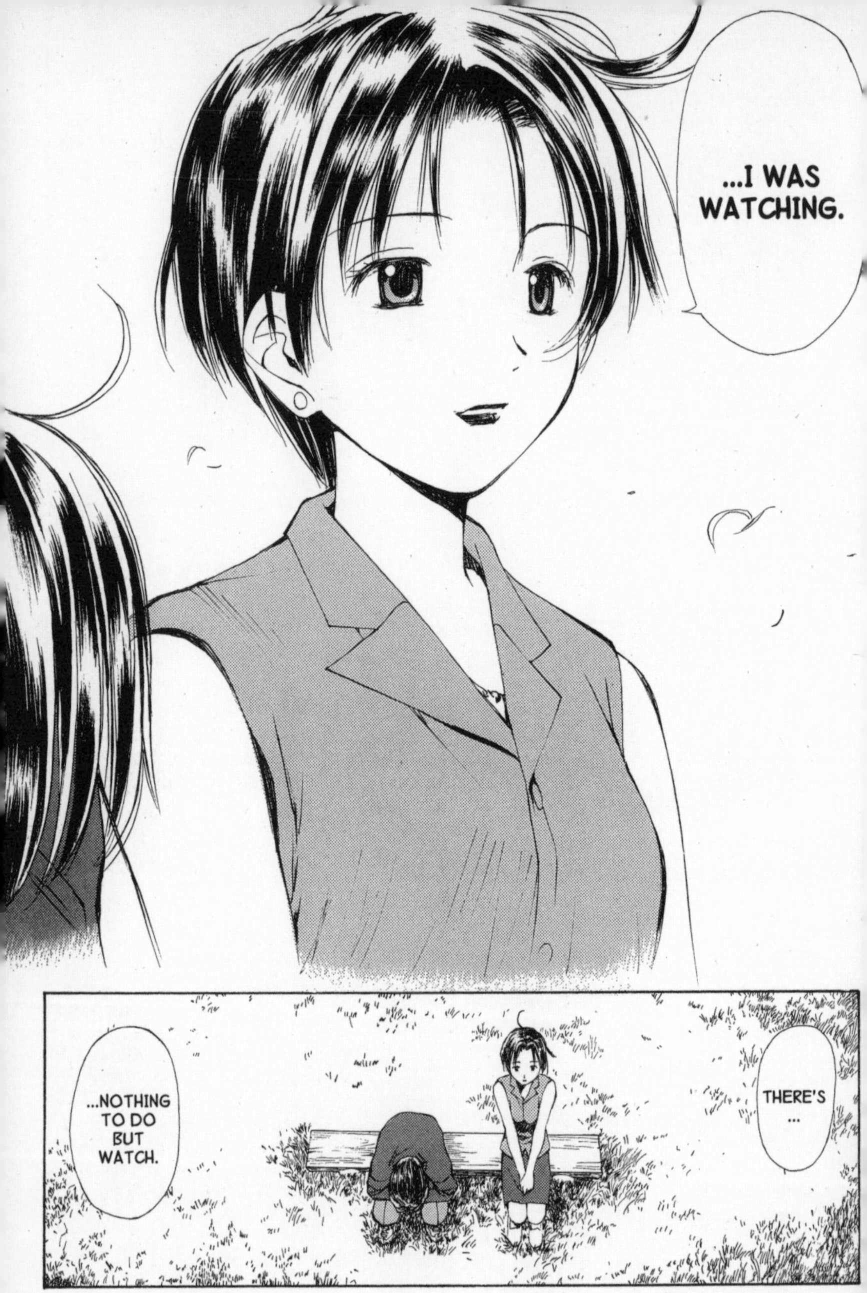

...I WAS WATCHING.
THERE'S ...
...NOTHING TO DO BUT WATCH.

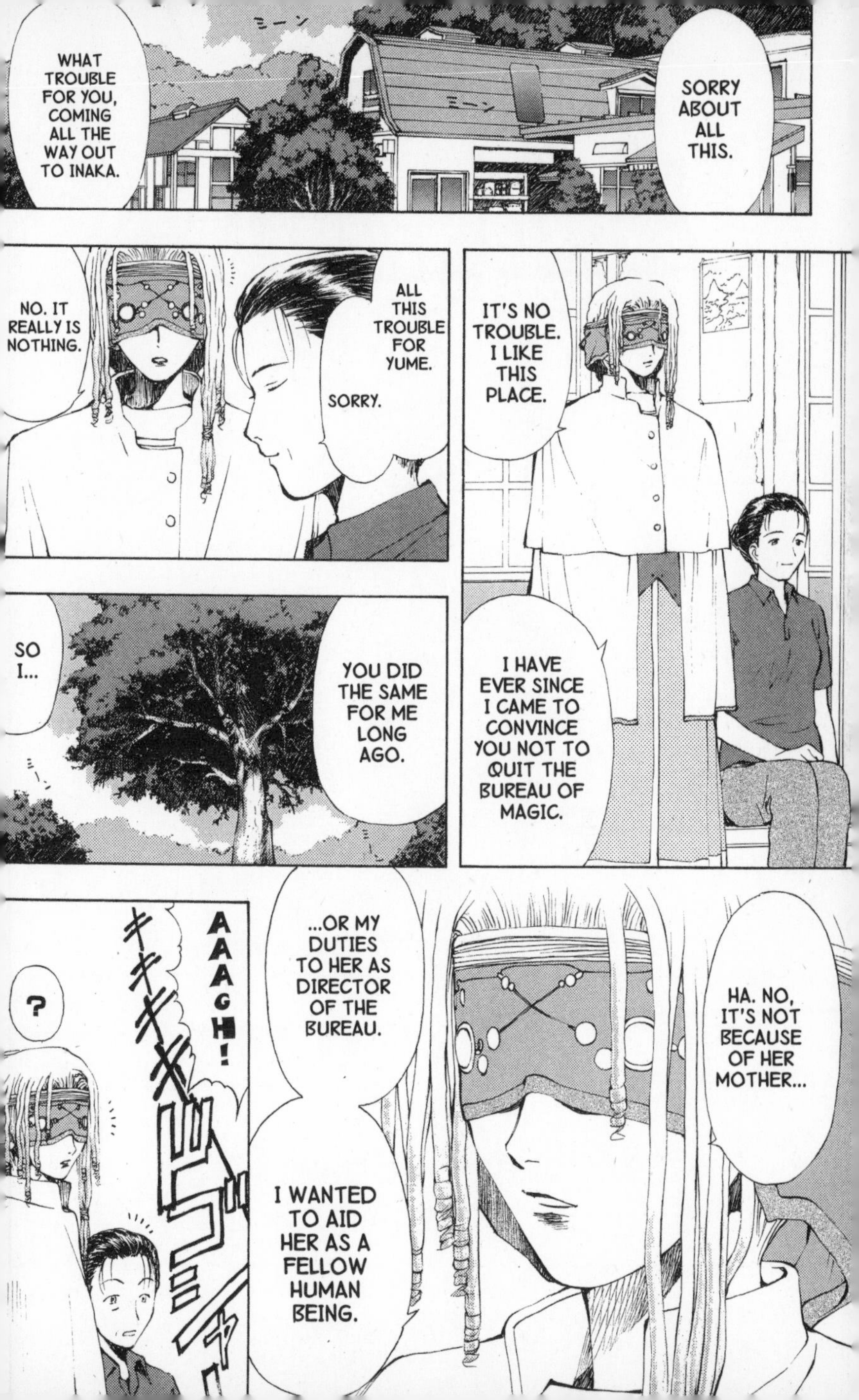
SORRY ABOUT ALL THIS.
WHAT TROUBLE FOR YOU, COMING ALL THE WAY OUT TO INAKA.
IT'S NO TROUBLE. I LIKE THIS PLACE.
I HAVE EVER SINCE I CAME TO CONVINCE YOU NOT TO QUIT THE BUREAU OF MAGIC.
ALL THIS TROUBLE FOR YUME.
SORRY.
NO. IT REALLY IS NOTHING.
YOU DID THE SAME FOR ME LONG AGO.
SO I...
HA. NO, IT'S NOT BECAUSE OF HER MOTHER...
...OR MY DUTIES TO HER AS DIRECTOR OF THE BUREAU.
I WANTED TO AID HER AS A FELLOW HUMAN BEING.
AAAAGH!
?

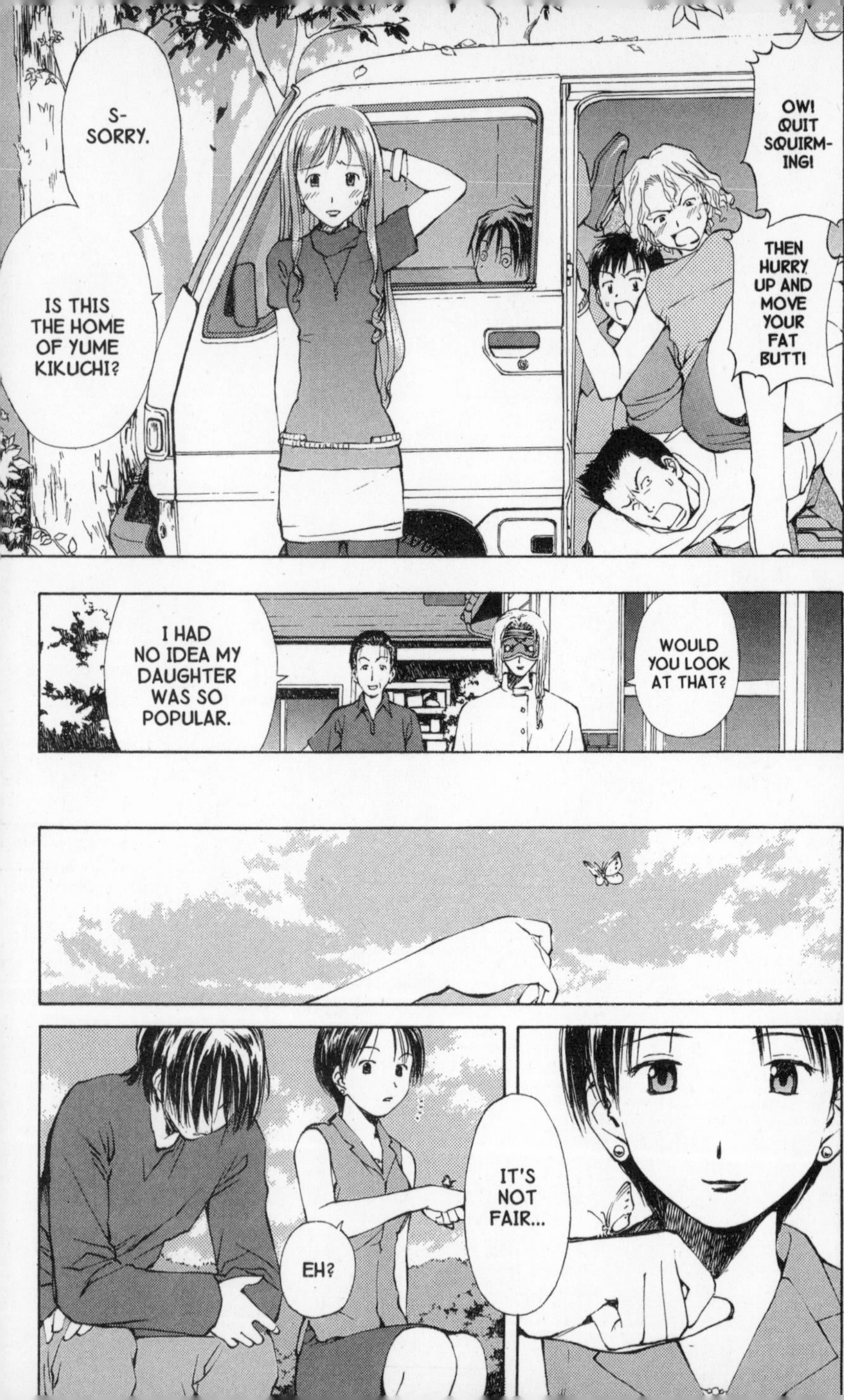
OW! QUIT SQUIRMING!
S- SORRY.
THEN HURRY UP AND MOVE YOUR FAT BUTT!
IS THIS THE HOME OF YUME KIKUCHI?
WOULD YOU LOOK AT THAT?
I HAD NO IDEA MY DAUGHTER WAS SO POPULAR.
IT'S NOT FAIR...
EH?

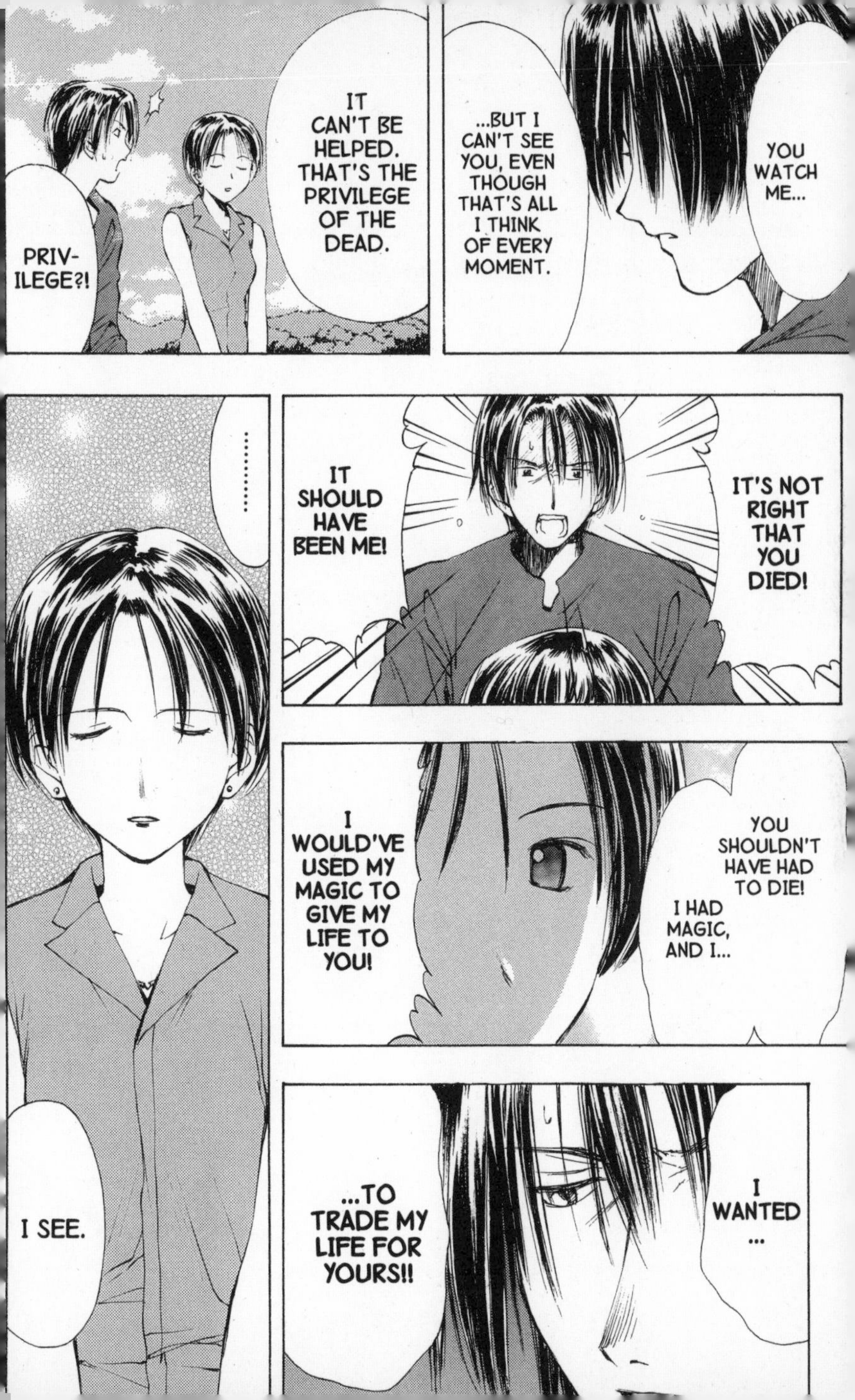
YOU WATCH ME...
...BUT I CAN'T SEE YOU, EVEN THOUGH THAT'S ALL I THINK OF EVERY MOMENT.
IT CAN'T BE HELPED. THAT'S THE PRIVILEGE OF THE DEAD.
PRIV-ILEGE?!
IT'S NOT RIGHT THAT YOU DIED!
IT SHOULD HAVE BEEN ME!
YOU SHOULDN'T HAVE HAD TO DIE!
I HAD MAGIC, AND I...
I WOULD'VE USED MY MAGIC TO GIVE MY LIFE TO YOU!
I WANTED...
...TO TRADE MY LIFE FOR YOURS!!
....
I SEE.

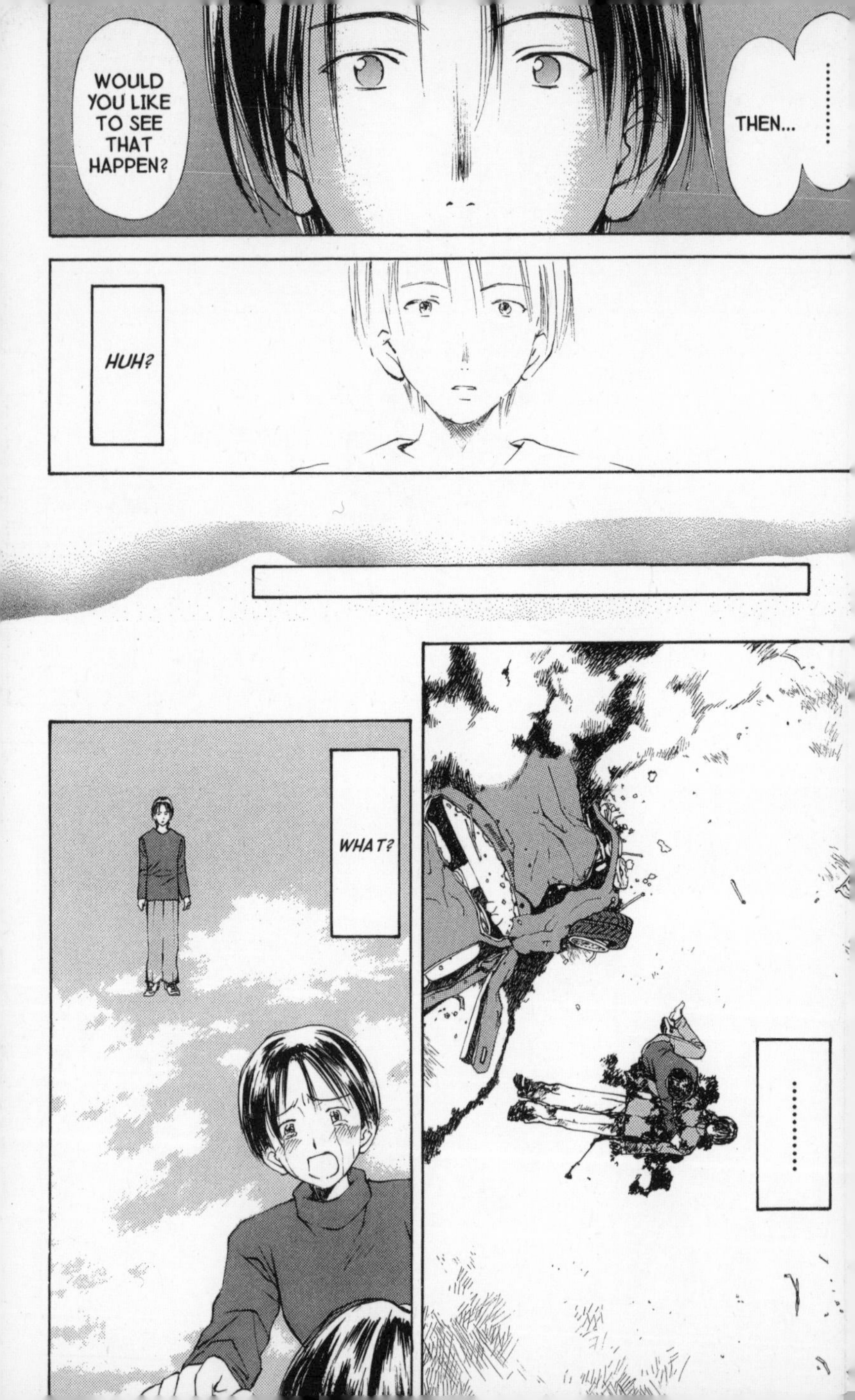

......
THEN...
WOULD YOU LIKE TO SEE THAT HAPPEN?
HUH?
....
WHAT?

I DIED INSTEAD!

THAT'S ME!!

TH- THAT'S...

OH, I SEE.

I SAVED TAKAKO.

THANK GOD...

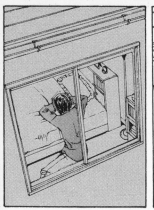

84

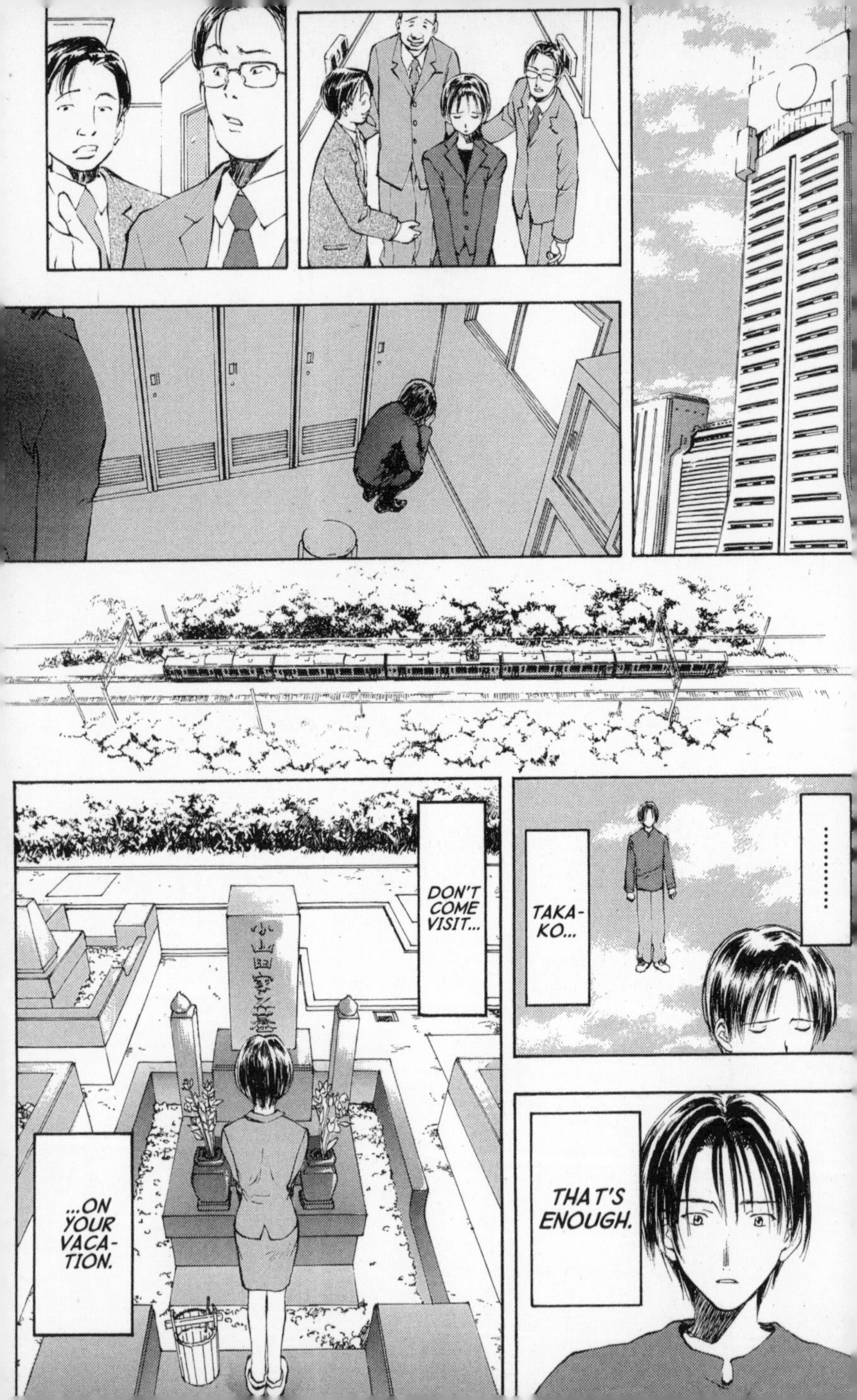

......
TAKA-KO...
THAT'S ENOUGH.
DON'T COME VISIT...
...ON YOUR VACA-TION.

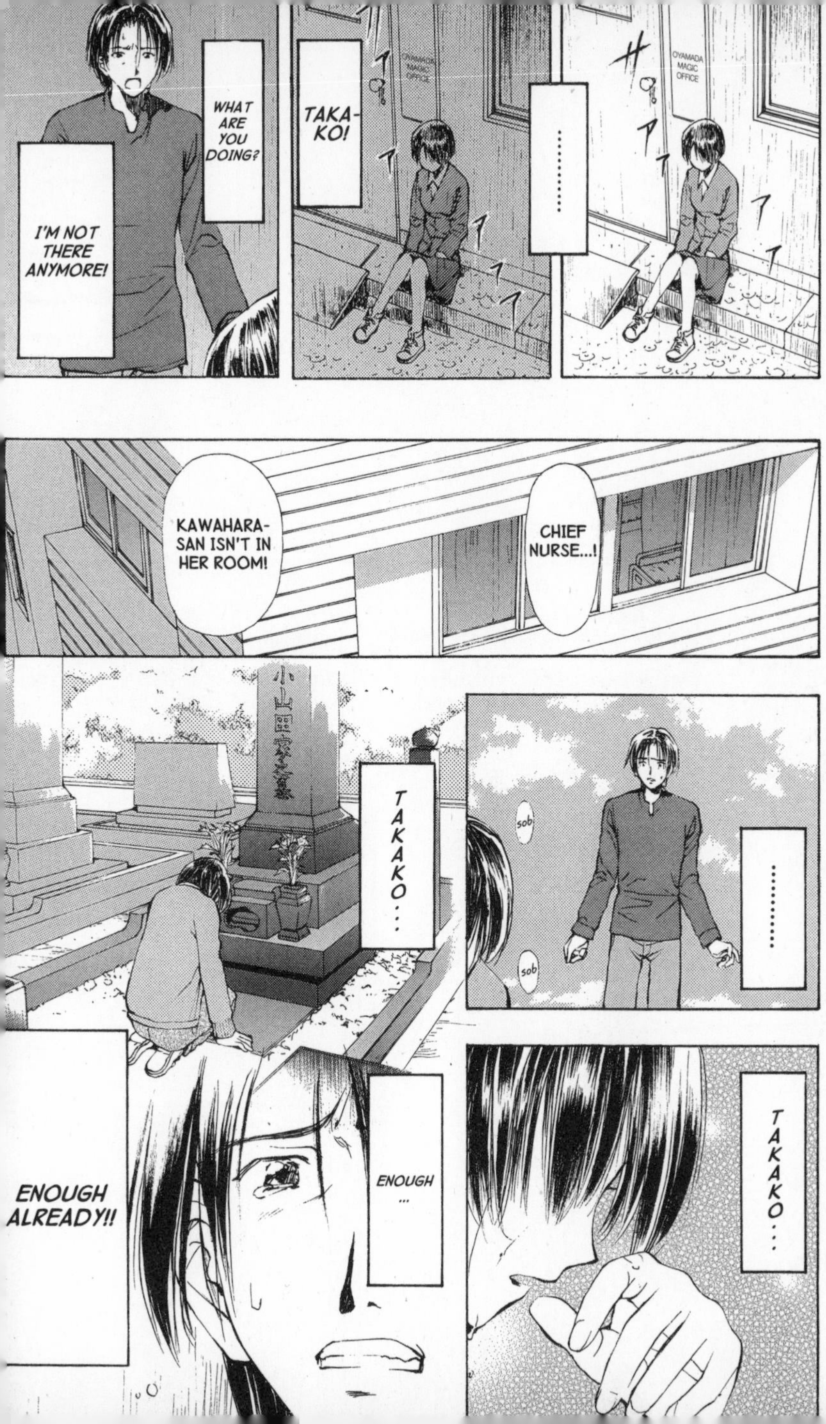
OYAMADA MAGIC OFFICE
……
OYAMADA MAGIC OFFICE
TAKAKO!
WHAT ARE YOU DOING?
I'M NOT THERE ANYMORE!
CHIEF NURSE...!
KAWAHARA-SAN ISN'T IN HER ROOM!
……
sob
sob
TAKAKO...
TAKAKO...
ENOUGH ...
ENOUGH ALREADY!!

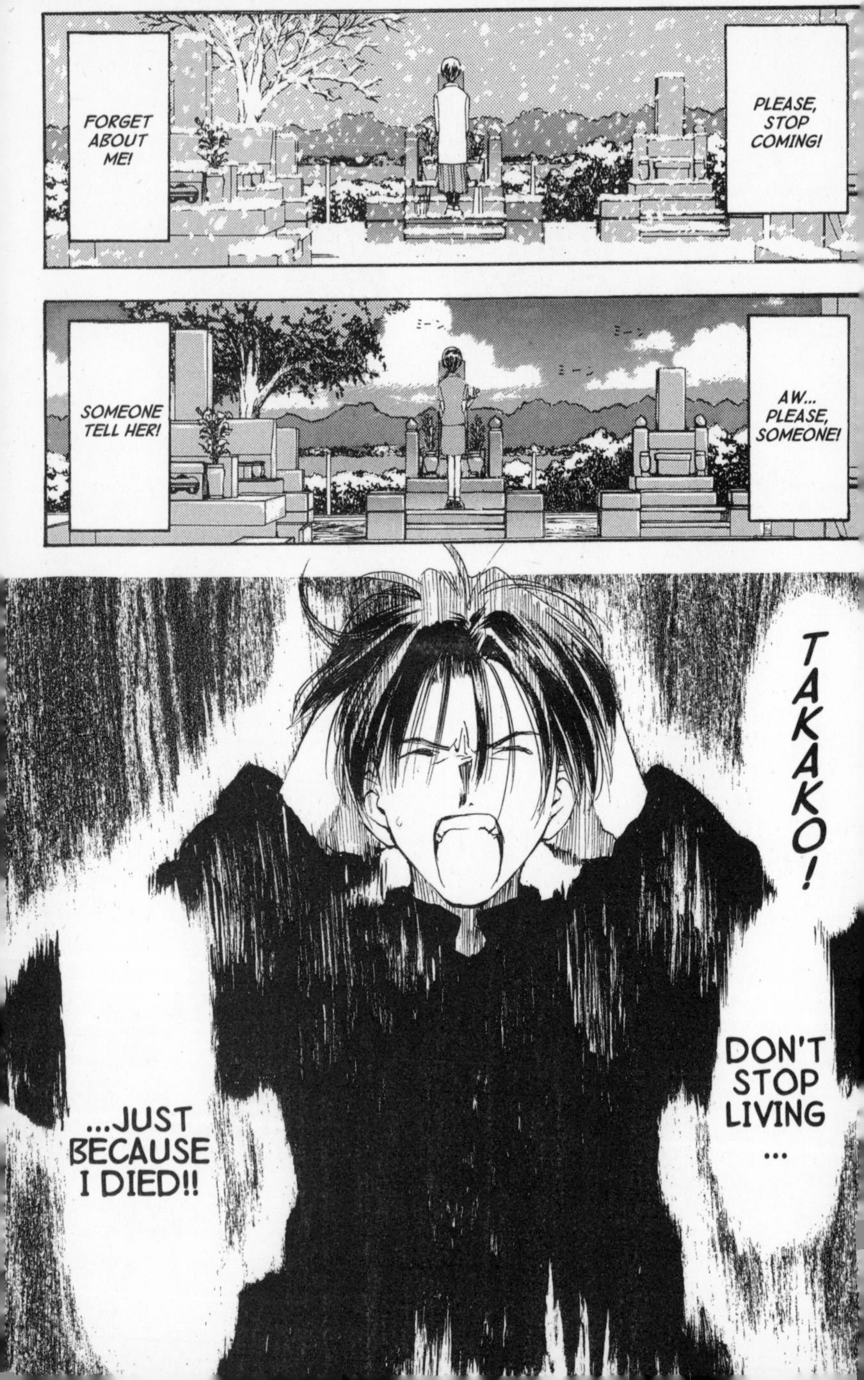
PLEASE, STOP COMING!
FORGET ABOUT ME!
AW... PLEASE, SOMEONE!
SOMEONE TELL HER!
TAKAKO!
DON'T STOP LIVING ...
...JUST BECAUSE I DIED!!

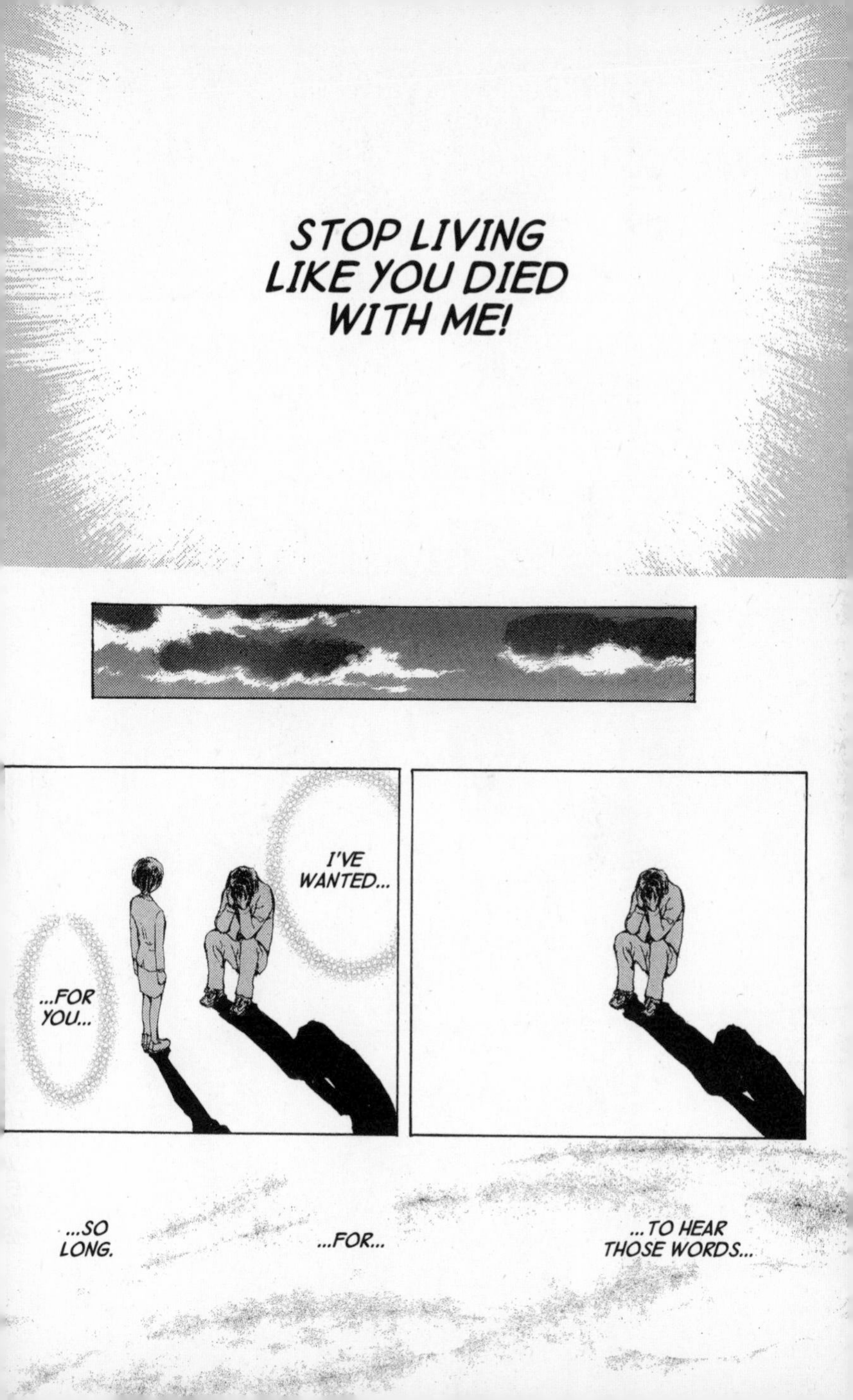
STOP LIVING LIKE YOU DIED WITH ME!
I'VE WANTED...
...FOR YOU...
...TO HEAR THOSE WORDS...
...FOR...
...SO LONG.

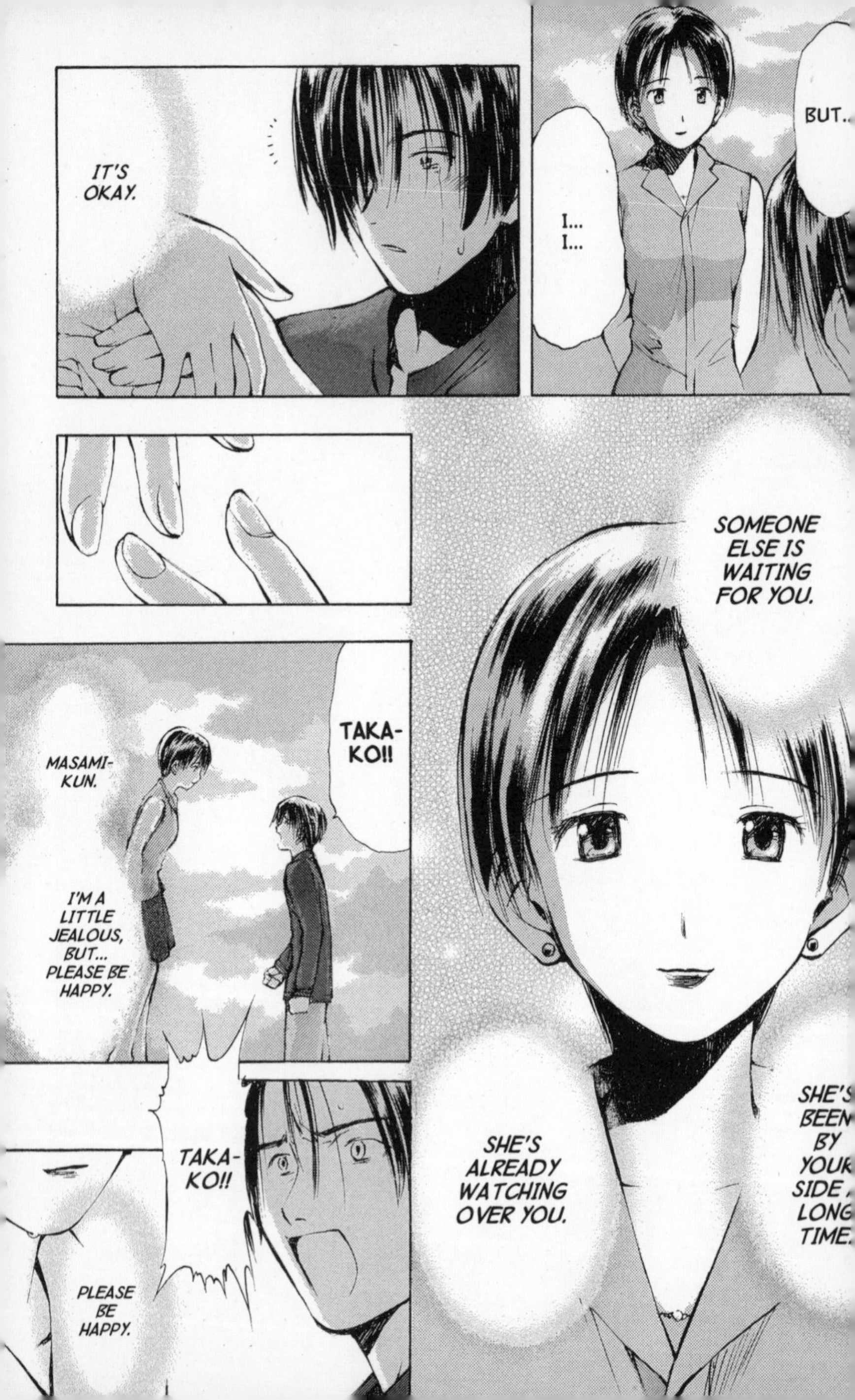
BUT...
I... I...
IT'S OKAY.
SOMEONE ELSE IS WAITING FOR YOU.
SHE'S BEEN BY YOUR SIDE A LONG TIME.
SHE'S ALREADY WATCHING OVER YOU.
TAKA-KO!!
MASAMI-KUN.
I'M A LITTLE JEALOUS, BUT... PLEASE BE HAPPY.
TAKA-KO!!
PLEASE BE HAPPY.

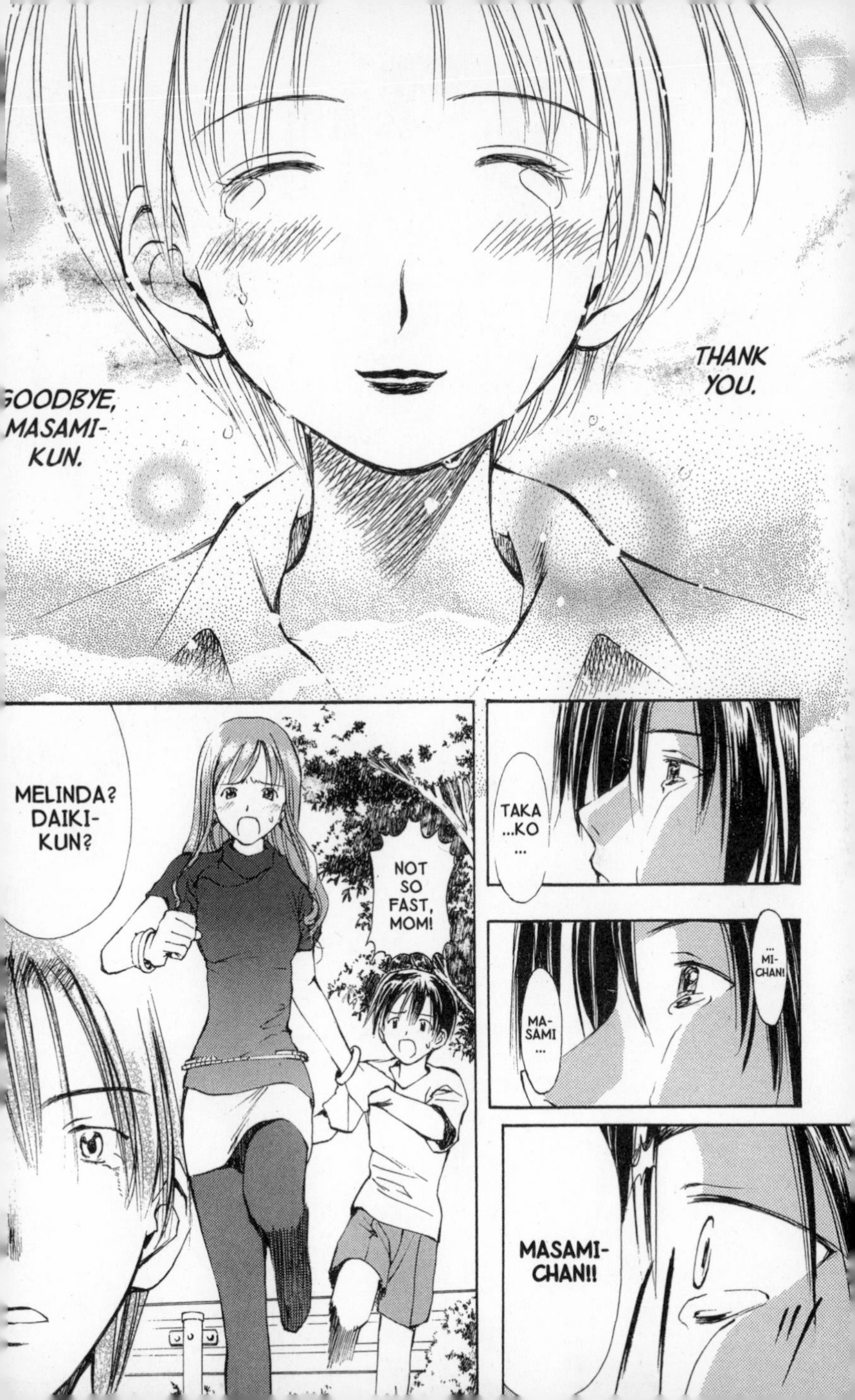
THANK YOU.
GOODBYE, MASAMI-KUN.
TAKA ...KO ...
MASAMI ...
... MI-CHAN!
MASAMI-CHAN!!
NOT SO FAST, MOM!
MELINDA? DAIKI-KUN?

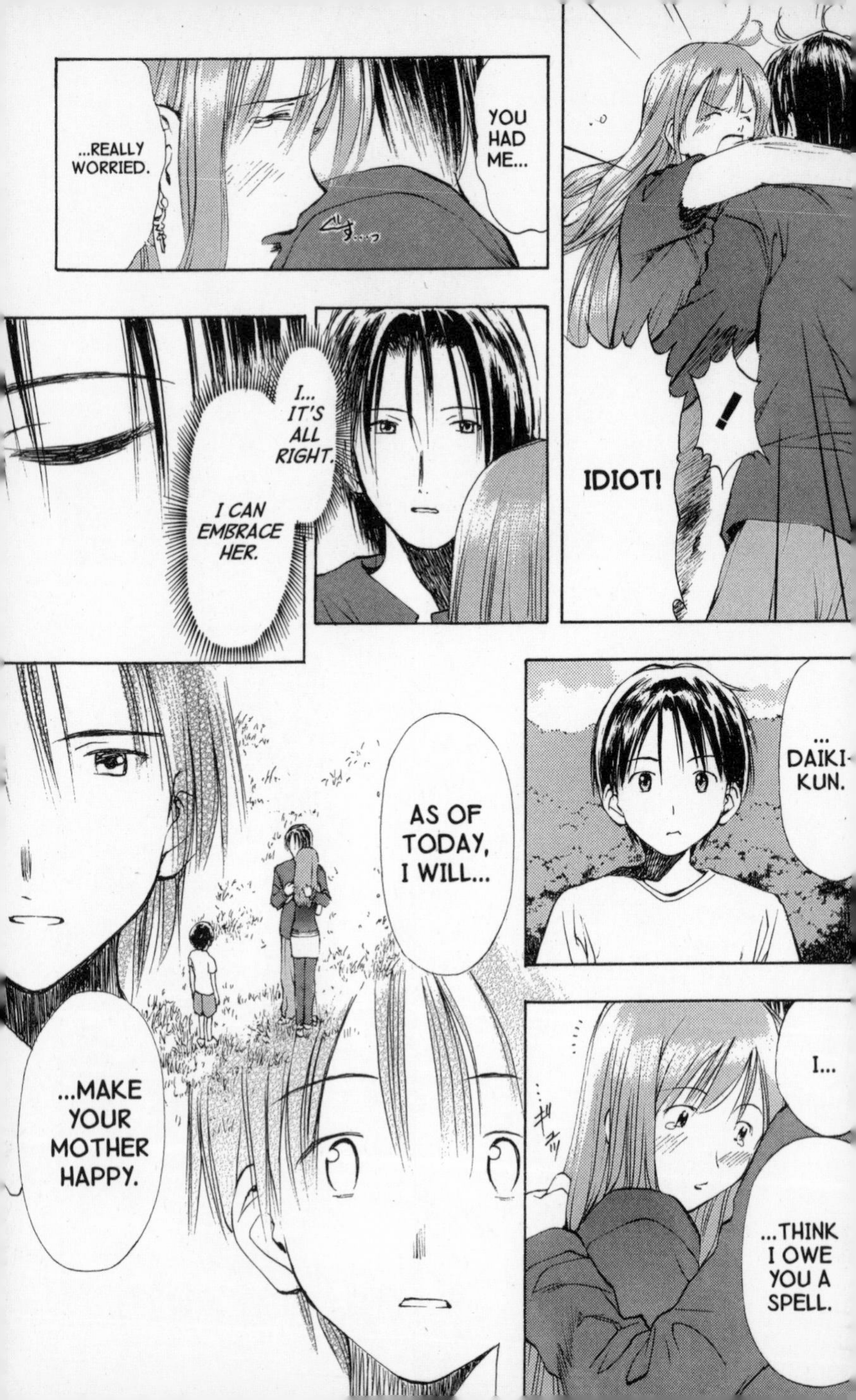
!
IDIOT!
YOU HAD ME...
...REALLY WORRIED.
I... IT'S ALL RIGHT.
I CAN EMBRACE HER.
... DAIKI-KUN.
I...
...THINK I OWE YOU A SPELL.
AS OF TODAY, I WILL...
...MAKE YOUR MOTHER HAPPY.

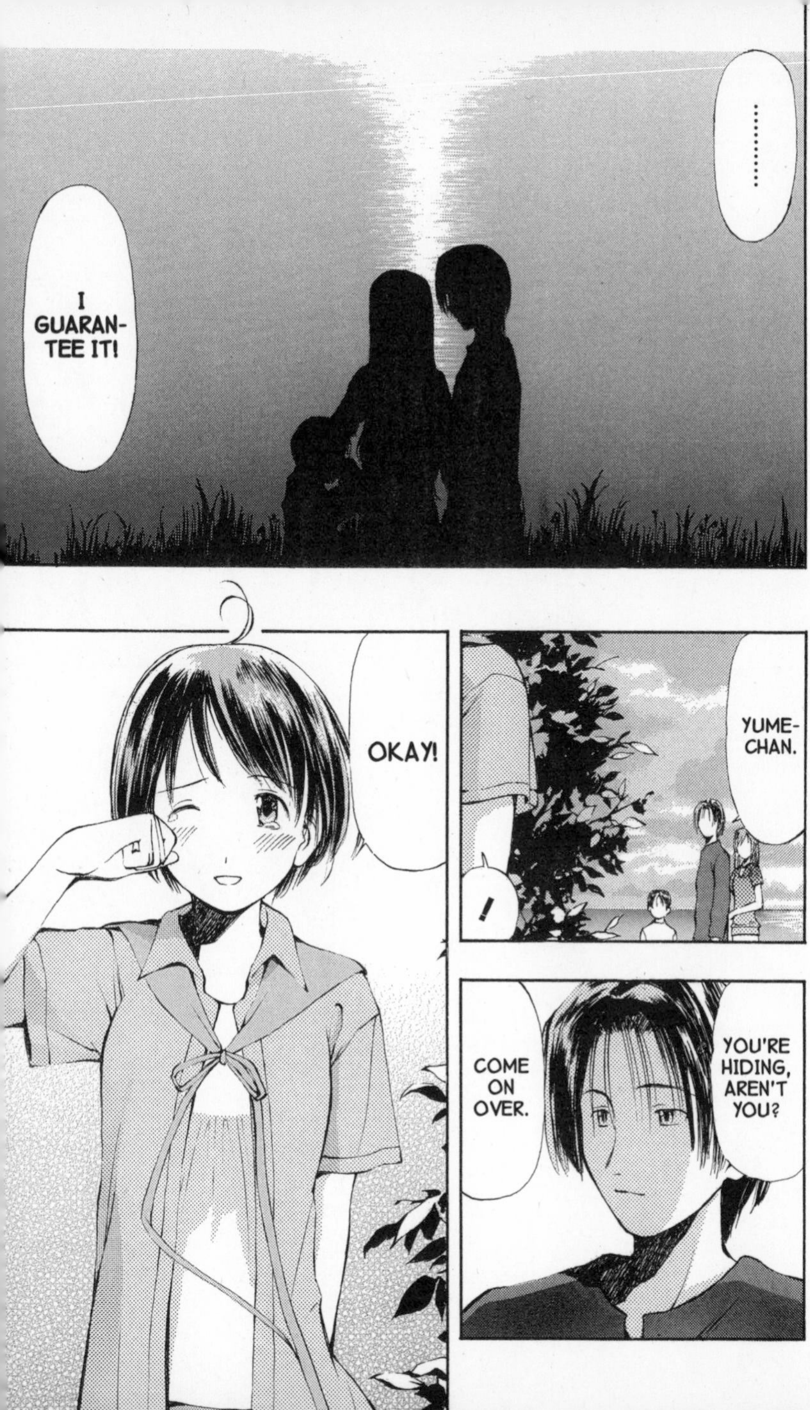
......
I GUARANTEE IT!
YUME-CHAN.
!
YOU'RE HIDING, AREN'T YOU?
COME ON OVER.
OKAY!

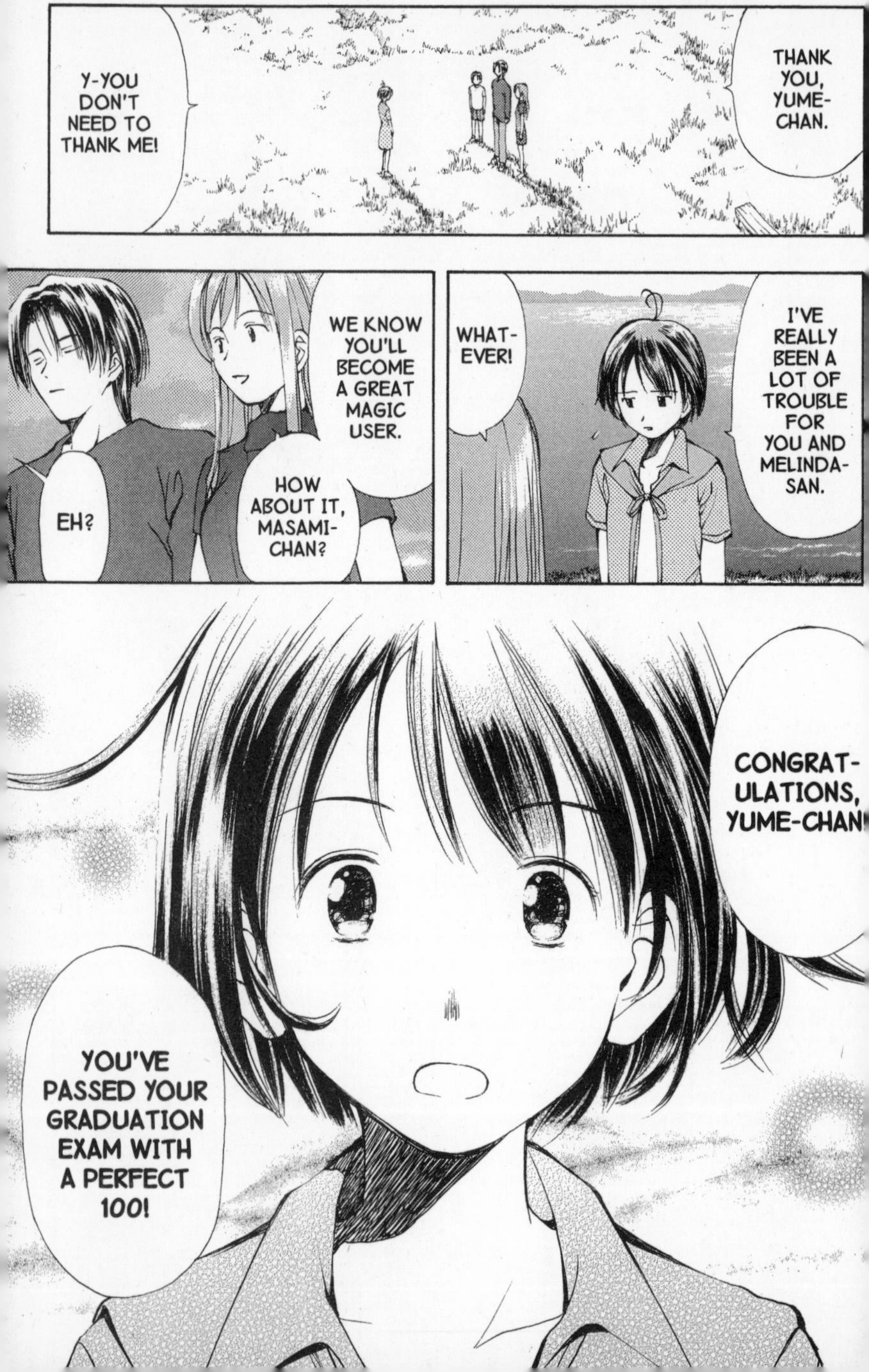
THANK YOU, YUME-CHAN.
Y-YOU DON'T NEED TO THANK ME!
I'VE REALLY BEEN A LOT OF TROUBLE FOR YOU AND MELINDA-SAN.
WHAT-EVER!
WE KNOW YOU'LL BECOME A GREAT MAGIC USER.
HOW ABOUT IT, MASAMI-CHAN?
EH?
CONGRAT-ULATIONS, YUME-CHAN
YOU'VE PASSED YOUR GRADUATION EXAM WITH A PERFECT 100!

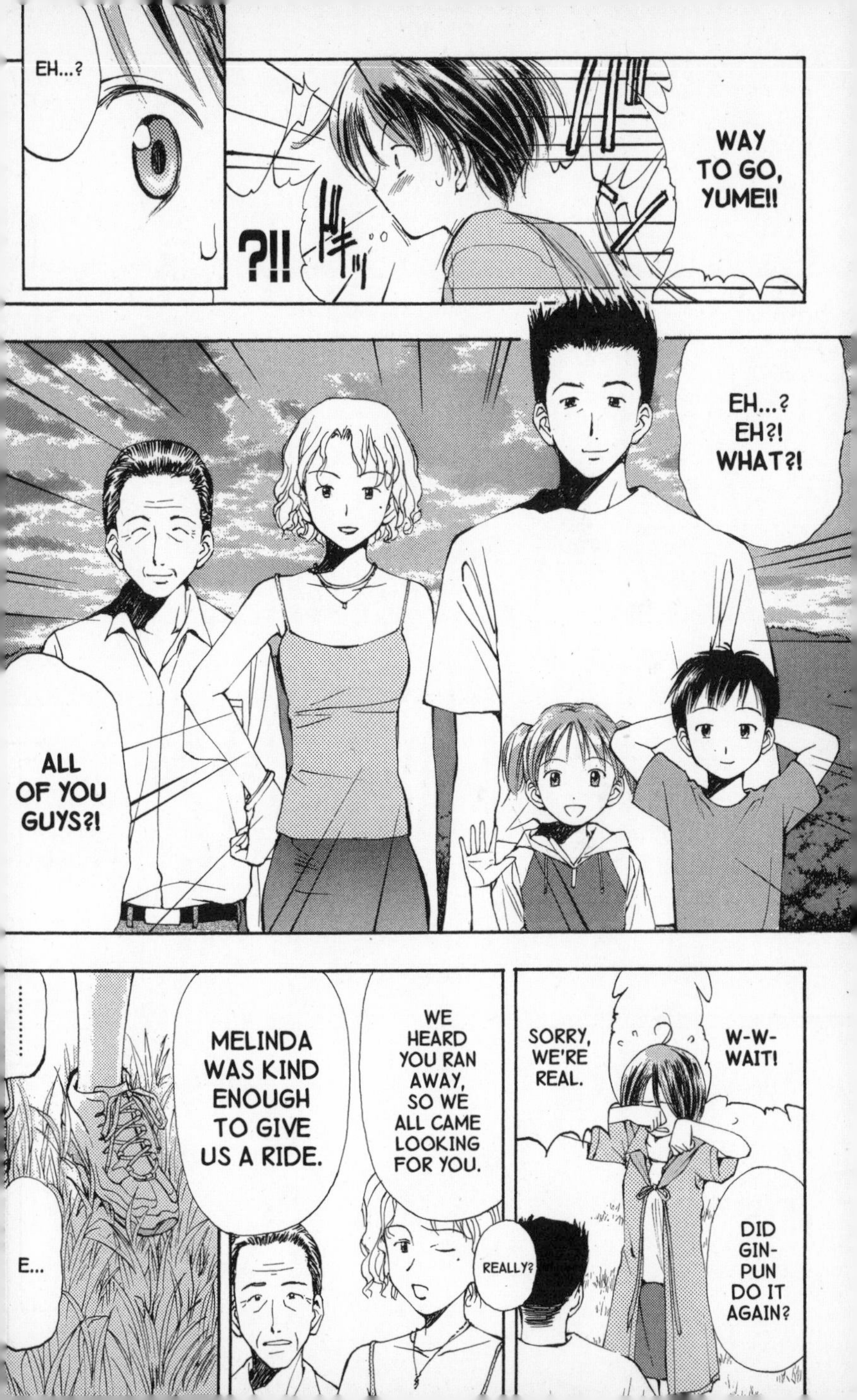
WAY TO GO, YUME!!
?!!
EH...?
EH...? EH?! WHAT?!
ALL OF YOU GUYS?!
W-W-WAIT!
SORRY, WE'RE REAL.
DID GIN-PUN DO IT AGAIN?
REALLY?
WE HEARD YOU RAN AWAY, SO WE ALL CAME LOOKING FOR YOU.
MELINDA WAS KIND ENOUGH TO GIVE US A RIDE.
......
E...

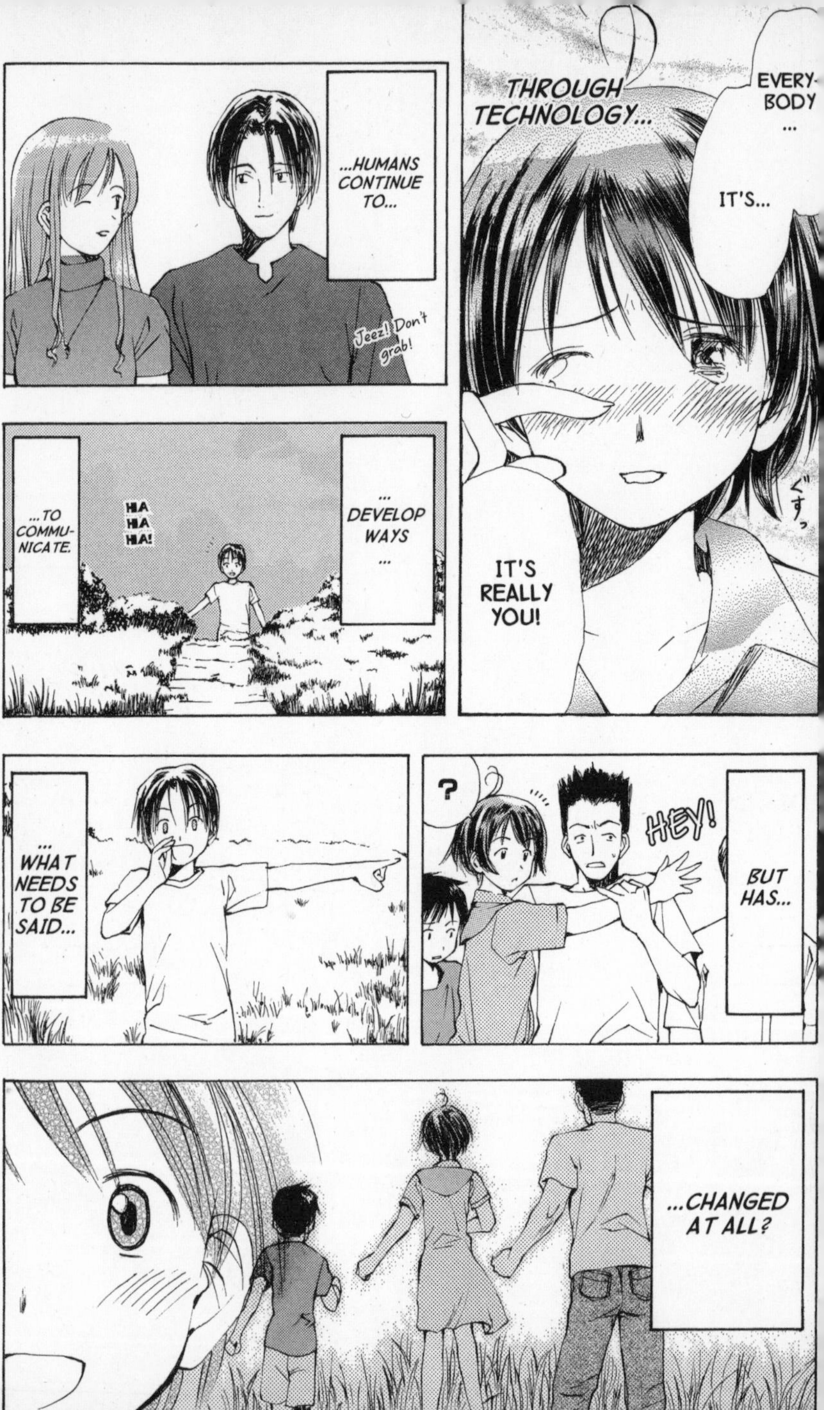
EVERYBODY ...
IT'S...
THROUGH TECHNOLOGY...
ぐすっ
IT'S REALLY YOU!
...HUMANS CONTINUE TO...
Jeez! Don't grab!
... DEVELOP WAYS ...
HA HA HA!
...TO COMMUNICATE.
BUT HAS...
HEY!
?
... WHAT NEEDS TO BE SAID...
...CHANGED AT ALL?

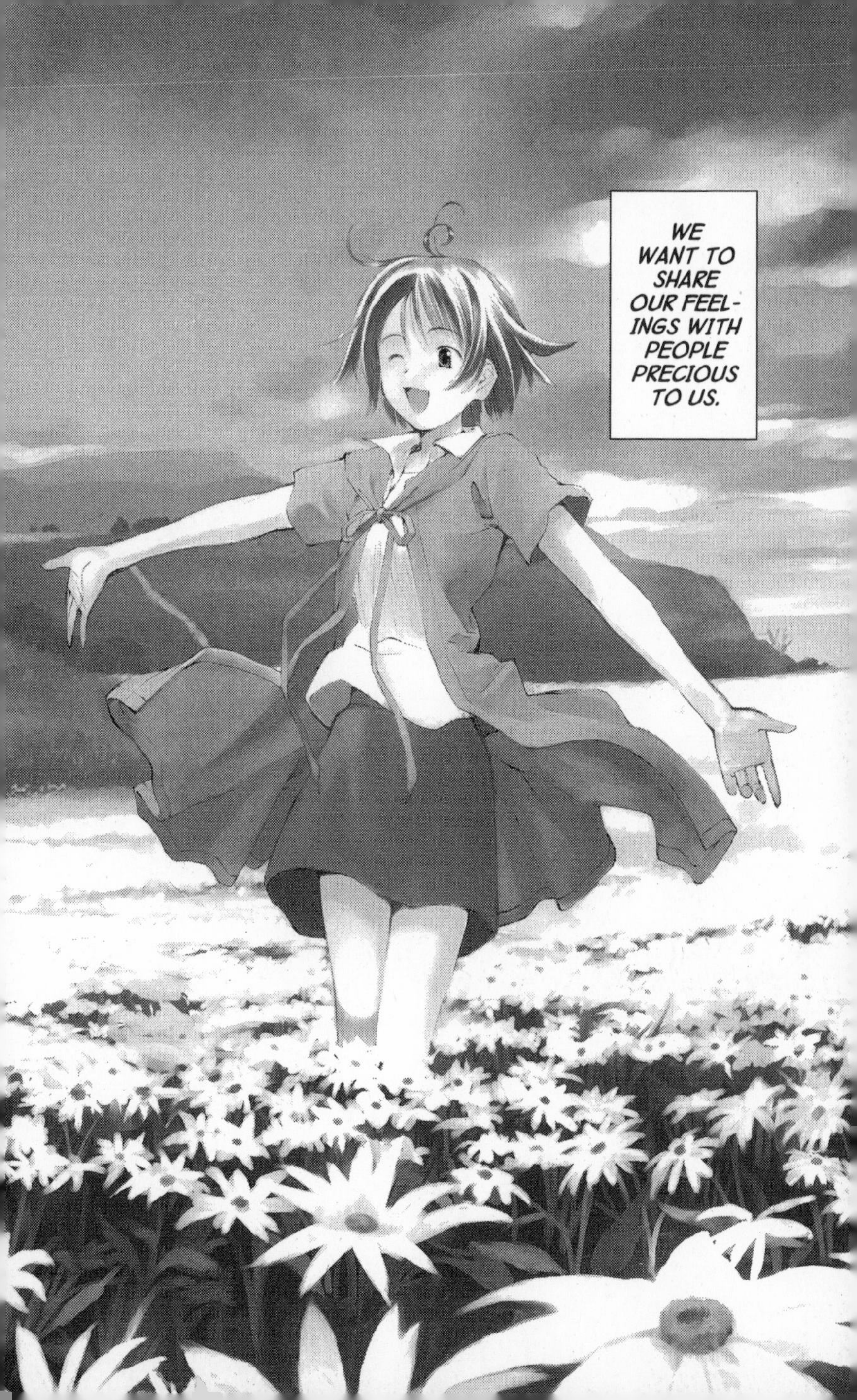
WE WANT TO SHARE OUR FEEL-INGS WITH PEOPLE PRECIOUS TO US.

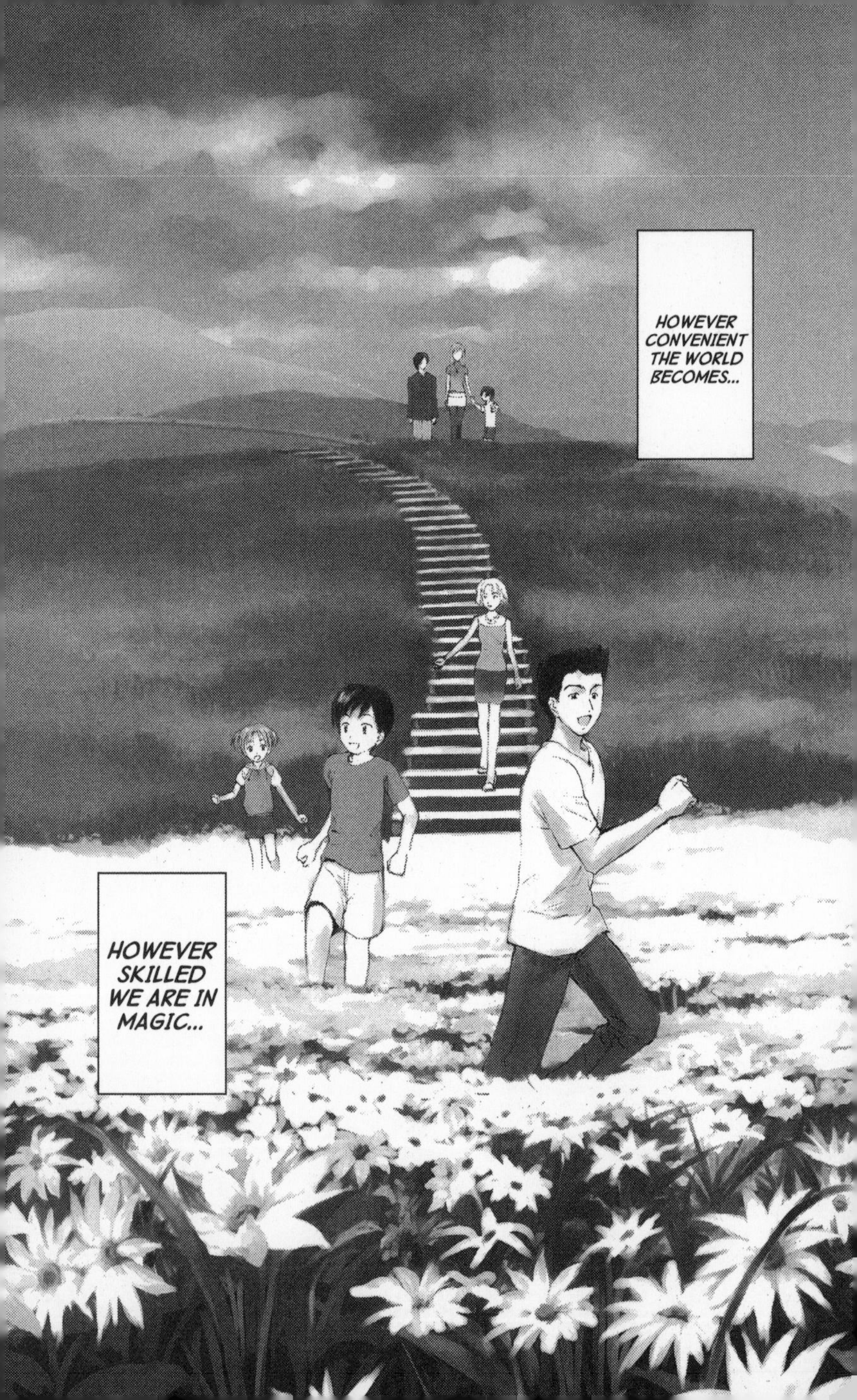
HOWEVER CONVENIENT THE WORLD BECOMES...
HOWEVER SKILLED WE ARE IN MAGIC...

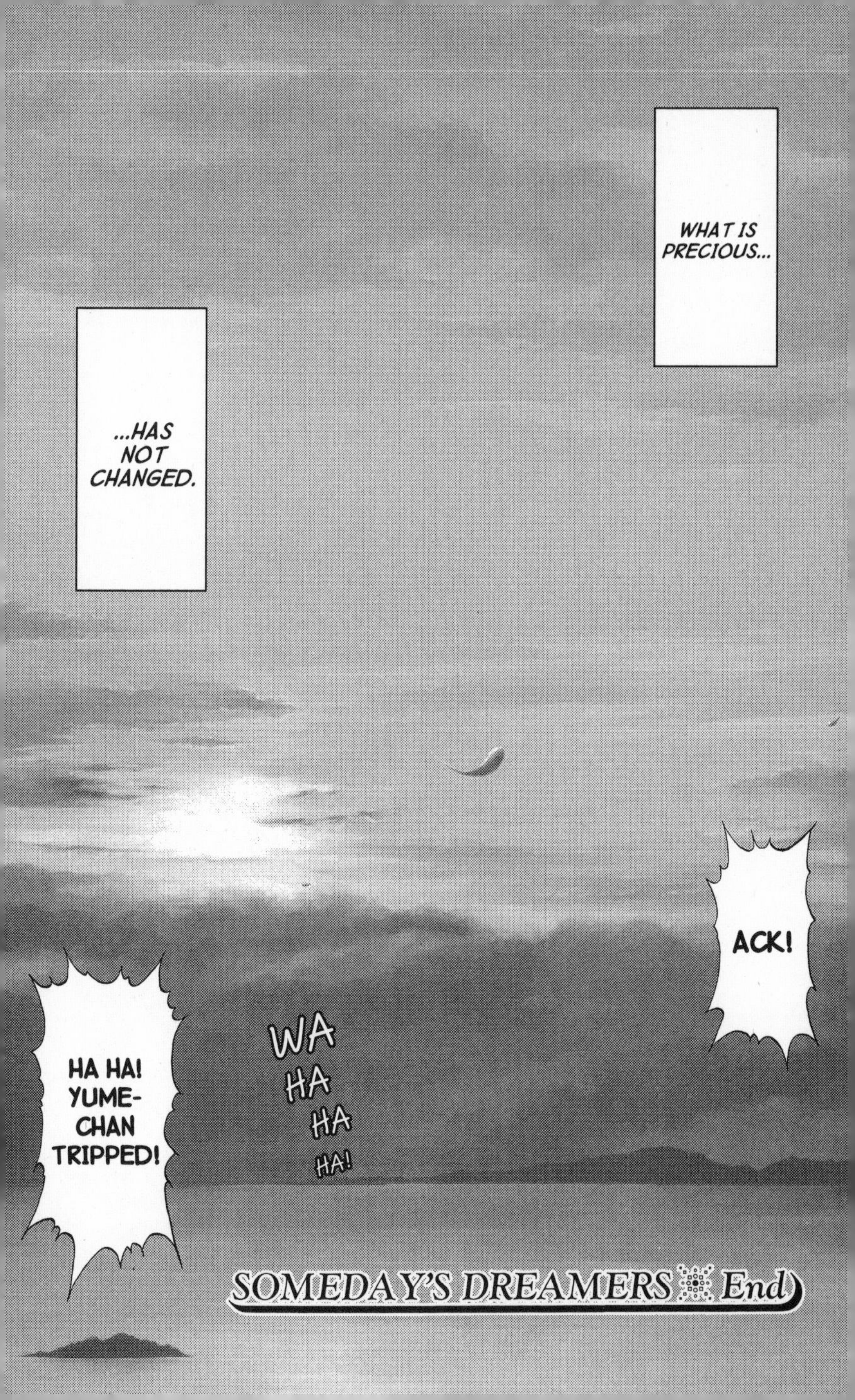
WHAT IS PRECIOUS...
...HAS NOT CHANGED.
ACK!
WA HA HA HA!
HA HA! YUME-CHAN TRIPPED!
SOMEDAY'S DREAMERS End

STAFF

ORIGINAL WORK
NORIE YAMADA

ART
KUMICHI YOSHIZUKI

ART ASSISTANTS
JUNJI IKEDA
MAKOTO KOIZUMI
SHIN HASEGAWA
TAKEHIRO KOTERA

DIALECT CONSULTANT
TSUCCHII

REFERENCED LITERATURE
BEAUTIFUL DEATH, PERFECT PHILOSOPHY
© SHIN OHARA/ CHUUKO LIBRARY

THE INHERITANCE OF LIFE
© SHIN OHARA/ PROTESTANT PUBLICATION CORP.

COOPERATION
SHUN KIYOMI (KADOKAWA DAI-EI FILMS)
SATOSHI TOUDA (KADOKAWA DAI-EI FILMS)

EDITING
GOU SUGUHARA

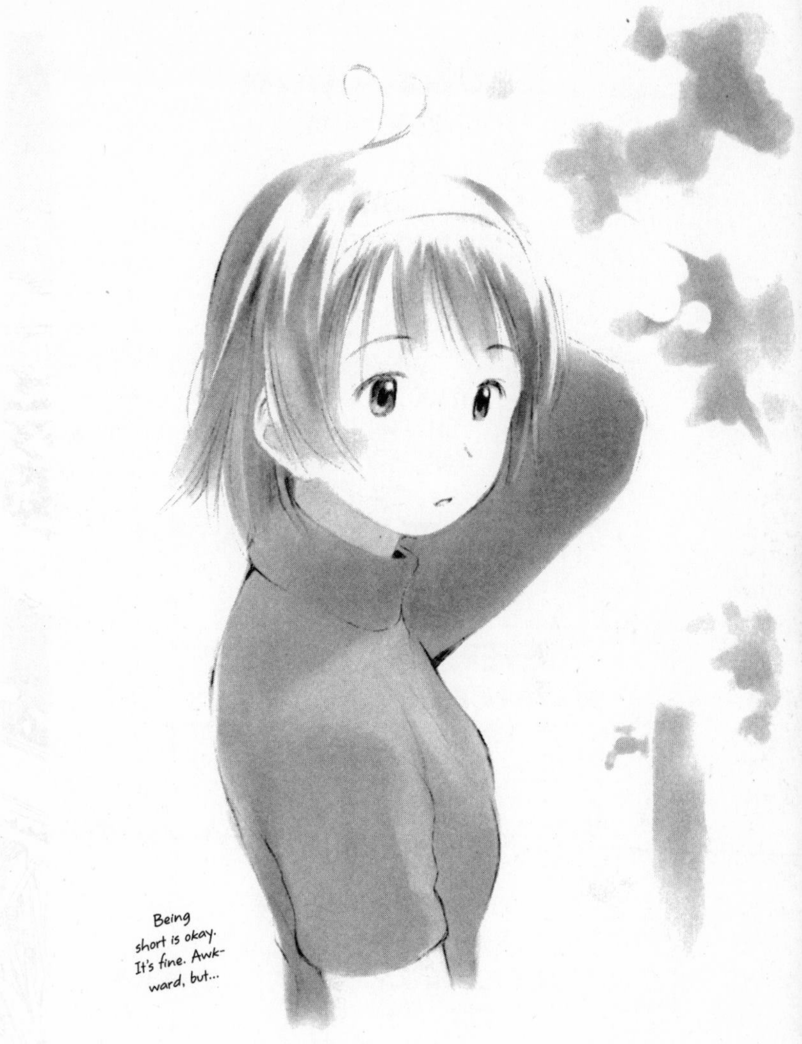
Being short is okay. It's fine. Awk-ward, but...

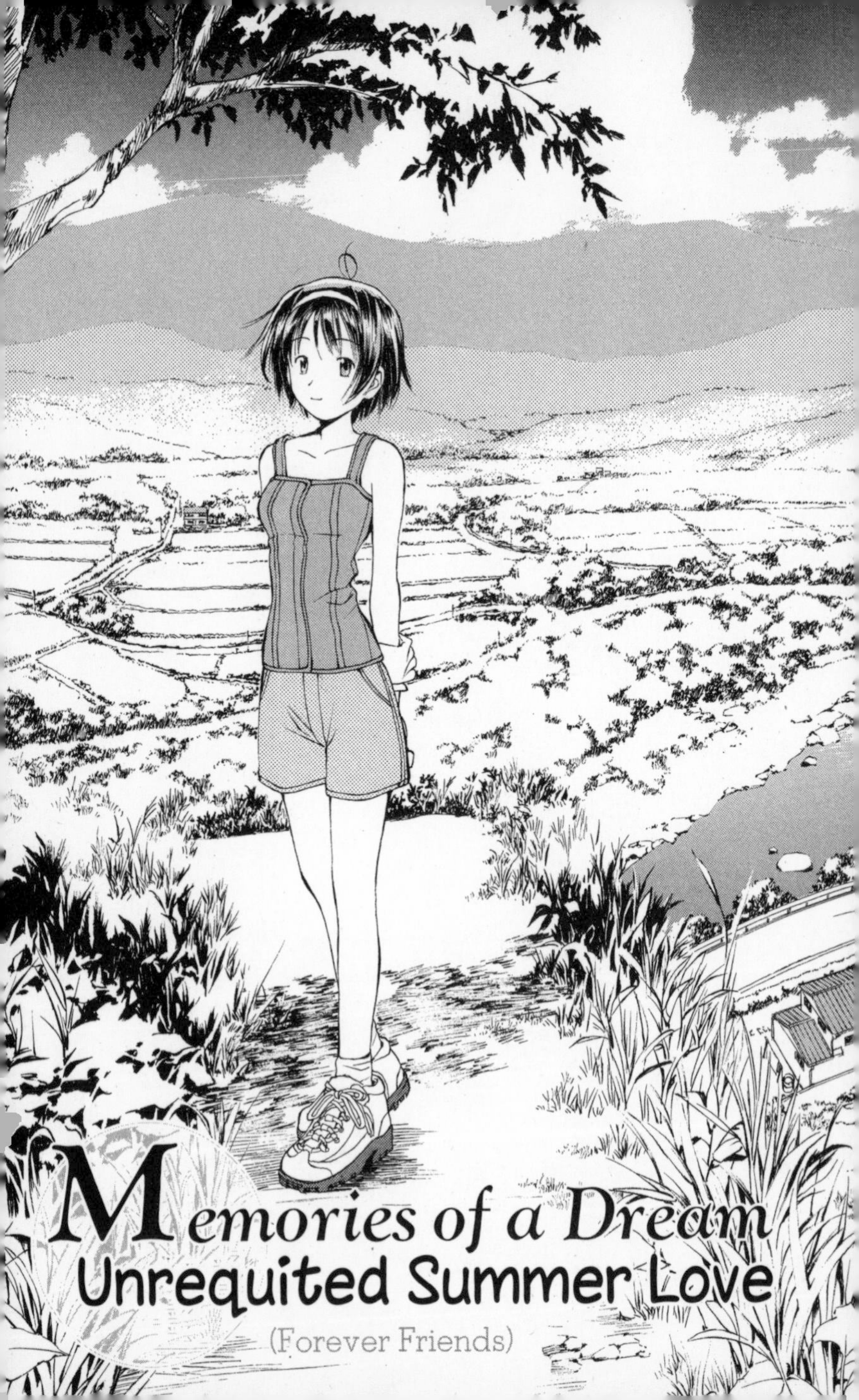
Memories of a Dream
Unrequited Summer Love
(Forever Friends)

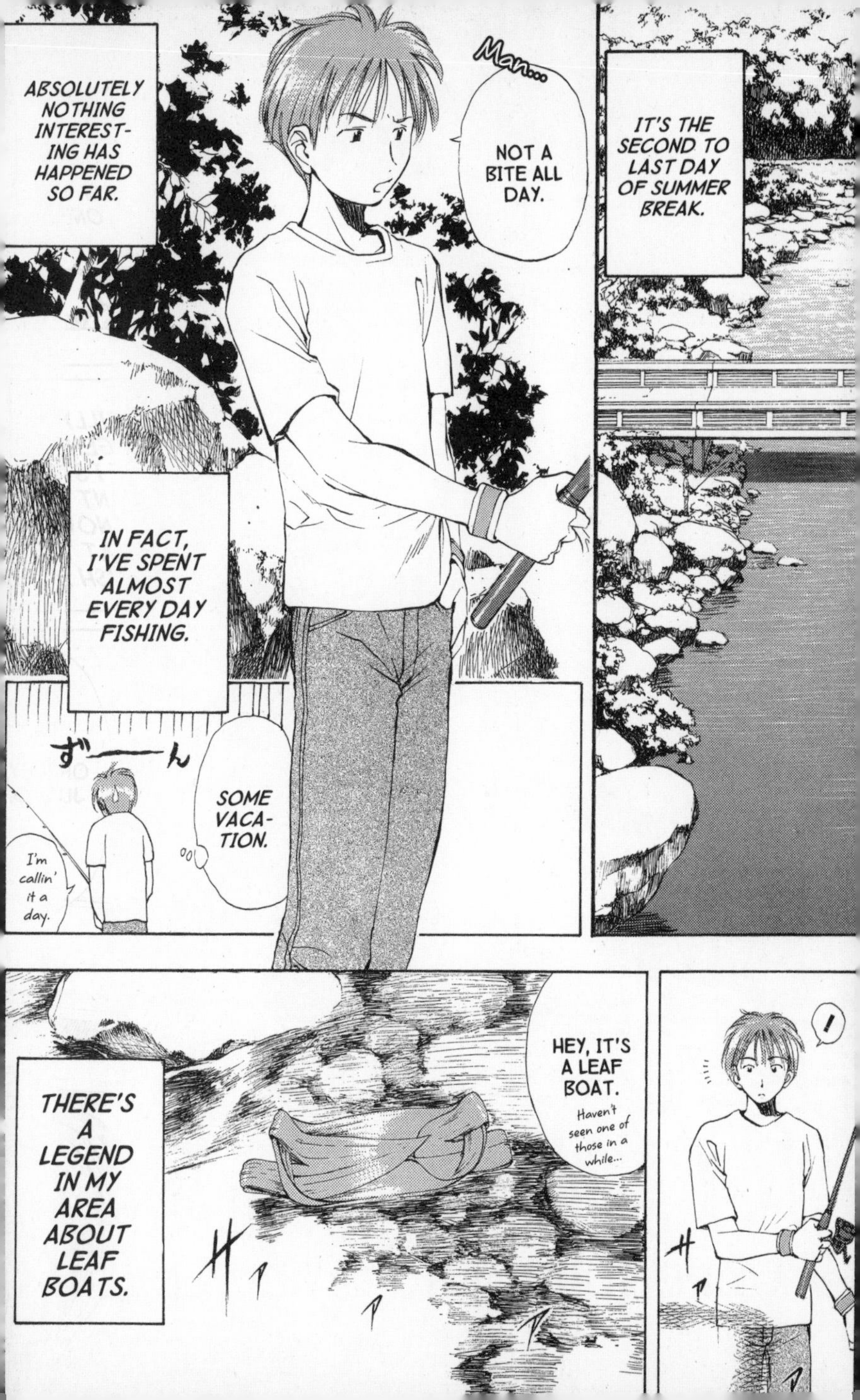
IT'S THE SECOND TO LAST DAY OF SUMMER BREAK.
Man...
NOT A BITE ALL DAY.
ABSOLUTELY NOTHING INTEREST-ING HAS HAPPENED SO FAR.
IN FACT, I'VE SPENT ALMOST EVERY DAY FISHING.
ずーーん
SOME VACA-TION.
I'm callin' it a day.
!
HEY, IT'S A LEAF BOAT.
Haven't seen one of those in a while...
THERE'S A LEGEND IN MY AREA ABOUT LEAF BOATS.

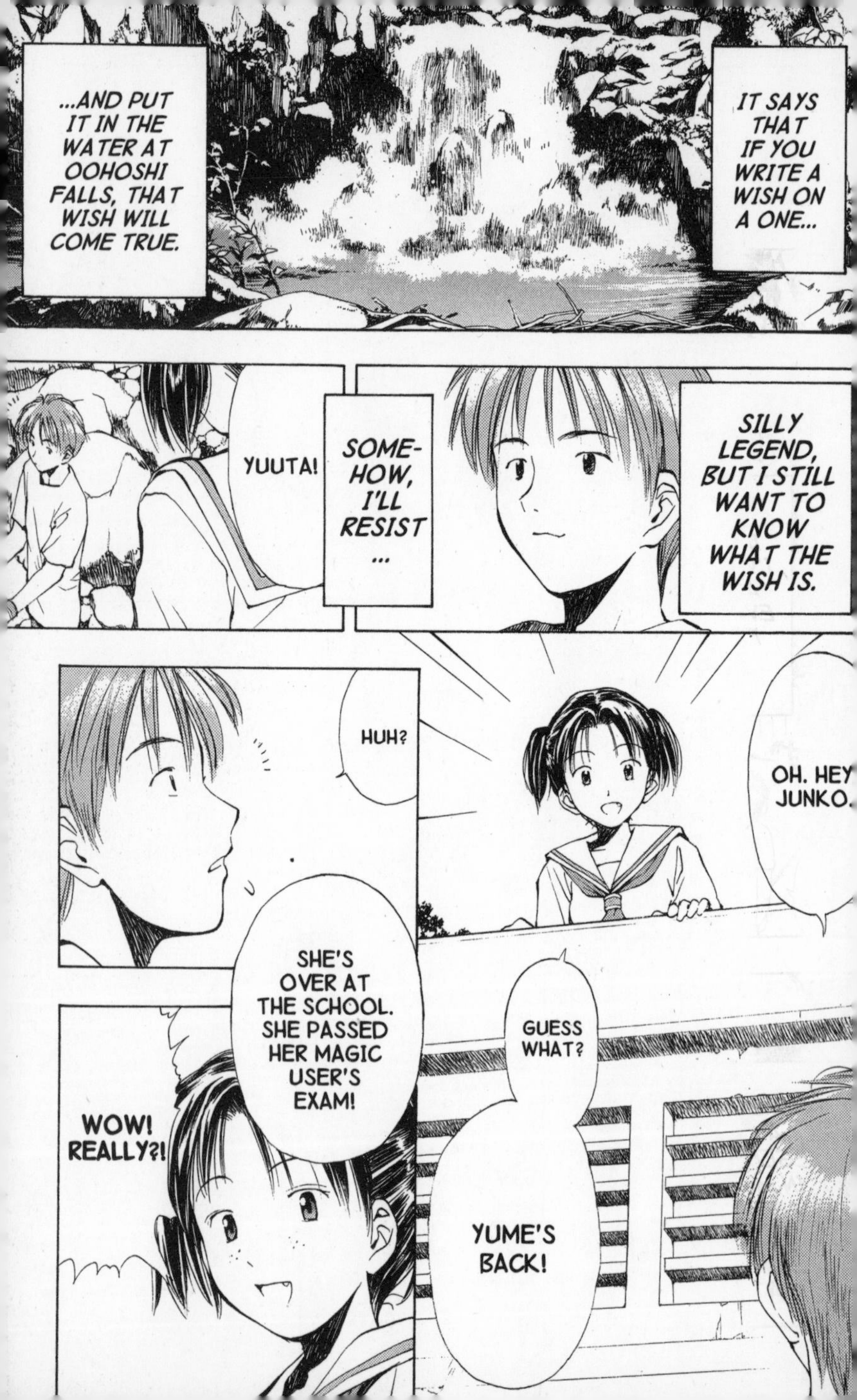
IT SAYS THAT IF YOU WRITE A WISH ON A ONE...
...AND PUT IT IN THE WATER AT OOHOSHI FALLS, THAT WISH WILL COME TRUE.
SILLY LEGEND, BUT I STILL WANT TO KNOW WHAT THE WISH IS.
SOME-HOW, I'LL RESIST ...
YUUTA!
OH. HEY JUNKO.
HUH?
GUESS WHAT?
YUME'S BACK!
SHE'S OVER AT THE SCHOOL. SHE PASSED HER MAGIC USER'S EXAM!
WOW! REALLY?!

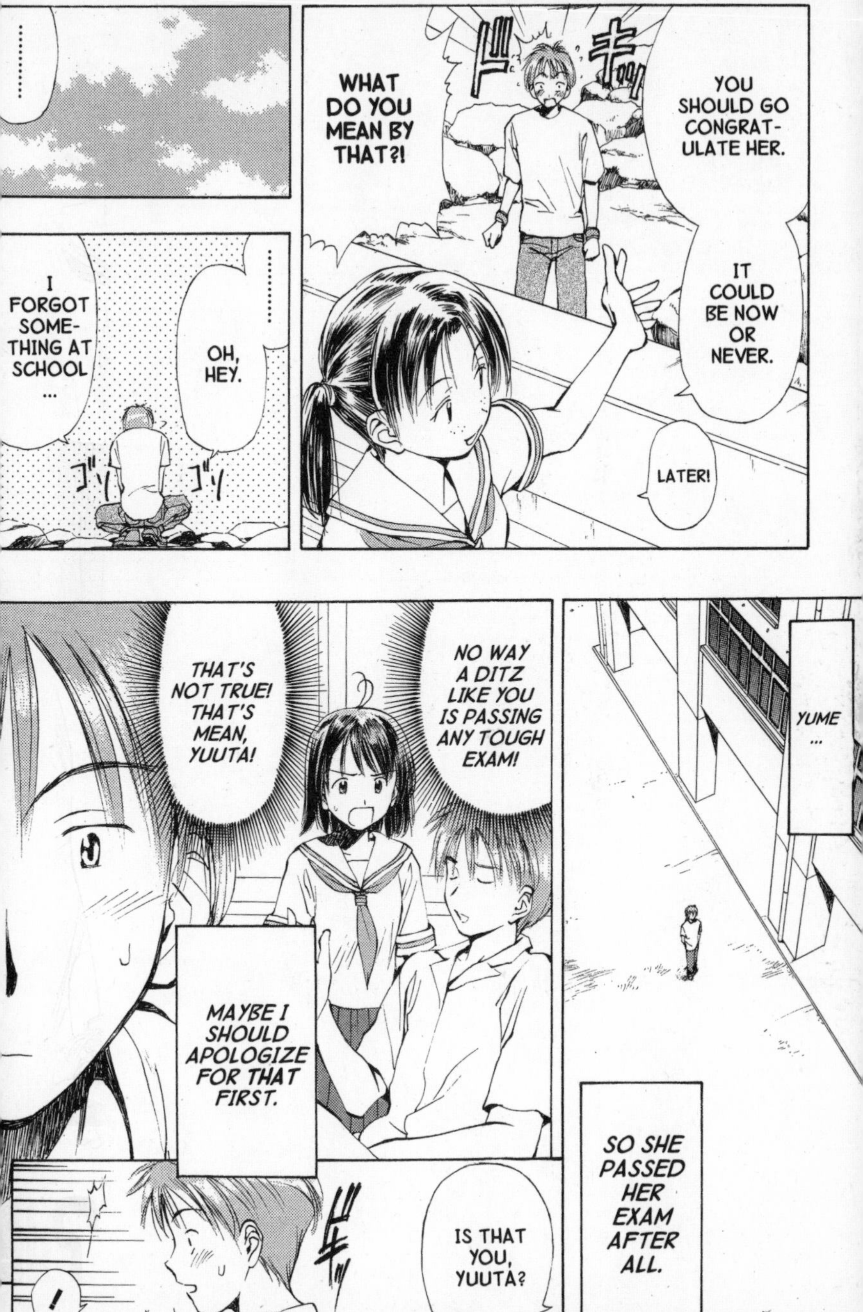
YOU SHOULD GO CONGRAT-ULATE HER.
WHAT DO YOU MEAN BY THAT?!
IT COULD BE NOW OR NEVER.
LATER!
......
......
OH, HEY.
I FORGOT SOME-THING AT SCHOOL ...
YUME ...
SO SHE PASSED HER EXAM AFTER ALL.
NO WAY A DITZ LIKE YOU IS PASSING ANY TOUGH EXAM!
THAT'S NOT TRUE! THAT'S MEAN, YUUTA!
MAYBE I SHOULD APOLOGIZE FOR THAT FIRST.
IS THAT YOU, YUUTA?
!

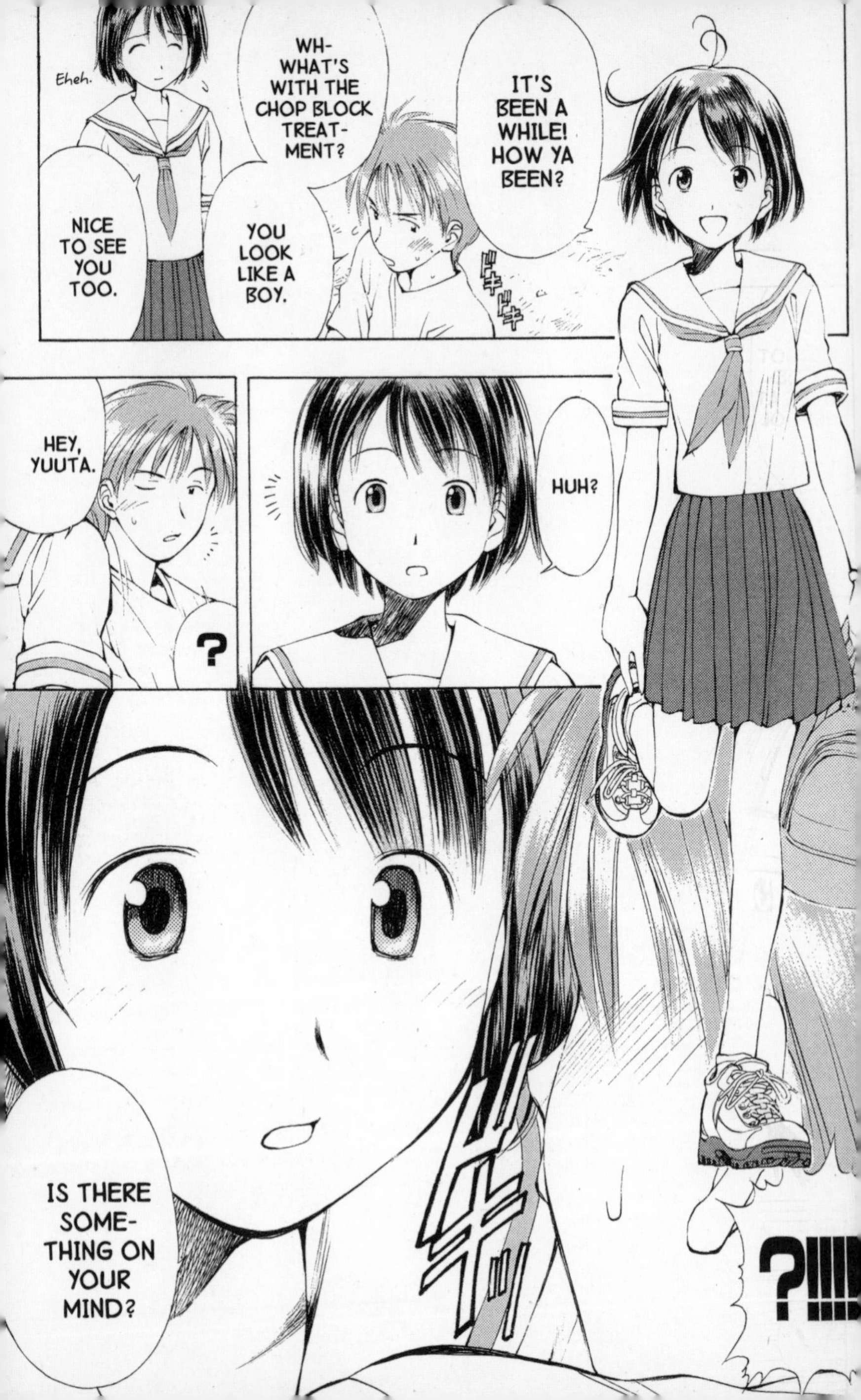
IT'S BEEN A WHILE! HOW YA BEEN?
WH- WHAT'S WITH THE CHOP BLOCK TREAT- MENT?
Eheh.
YOU LOOK LIKE A BOY.
NICE TO SEE YOU TOO.
HUH?
HEY, YUUTA.
?
IS THERE SOME- THING ON YOUR MIND?
?!!!!

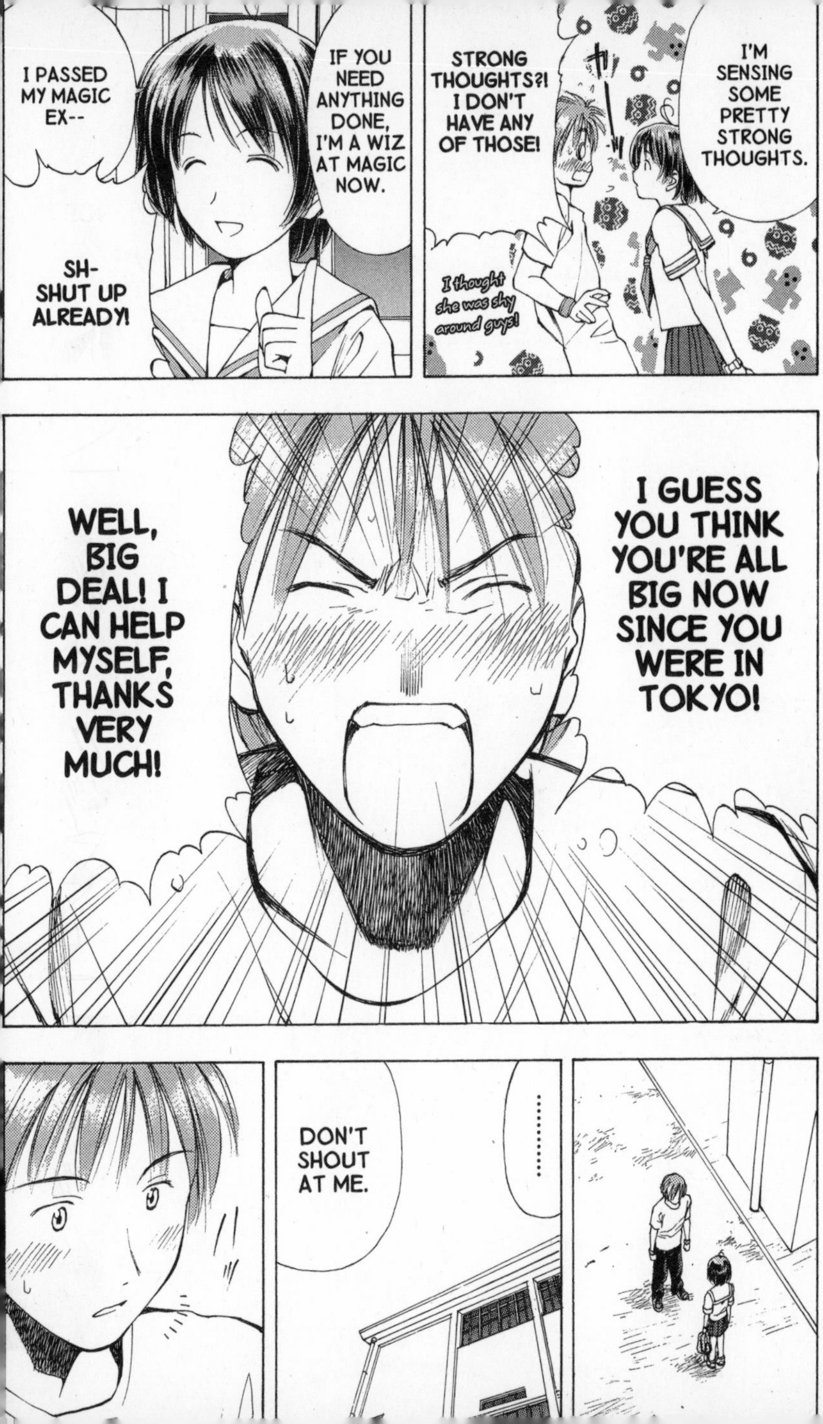
I'M SENSING SOME PRETTY STRONG THOUGHTS.
STRONG THOUGHTS?! I DON'T HAVE ANY OF THOSE!
I thought she was shy around guys!
IF YOU NEED ANYTHING DONE, I'M A WIZ AT MAGIC NOW.
I PASSED MY MAGIC EX--
SH- SHUT UP ALREADY!
I GUESS YOU THINK YOU'RE ALL BIG NOW SINCE YOU WERE IN TOKYO!
WELL, BIG DEAL! I CAN HELP MYSELF, THANKS VERY MUCH!
....
DON'T SHOUT AT ME.

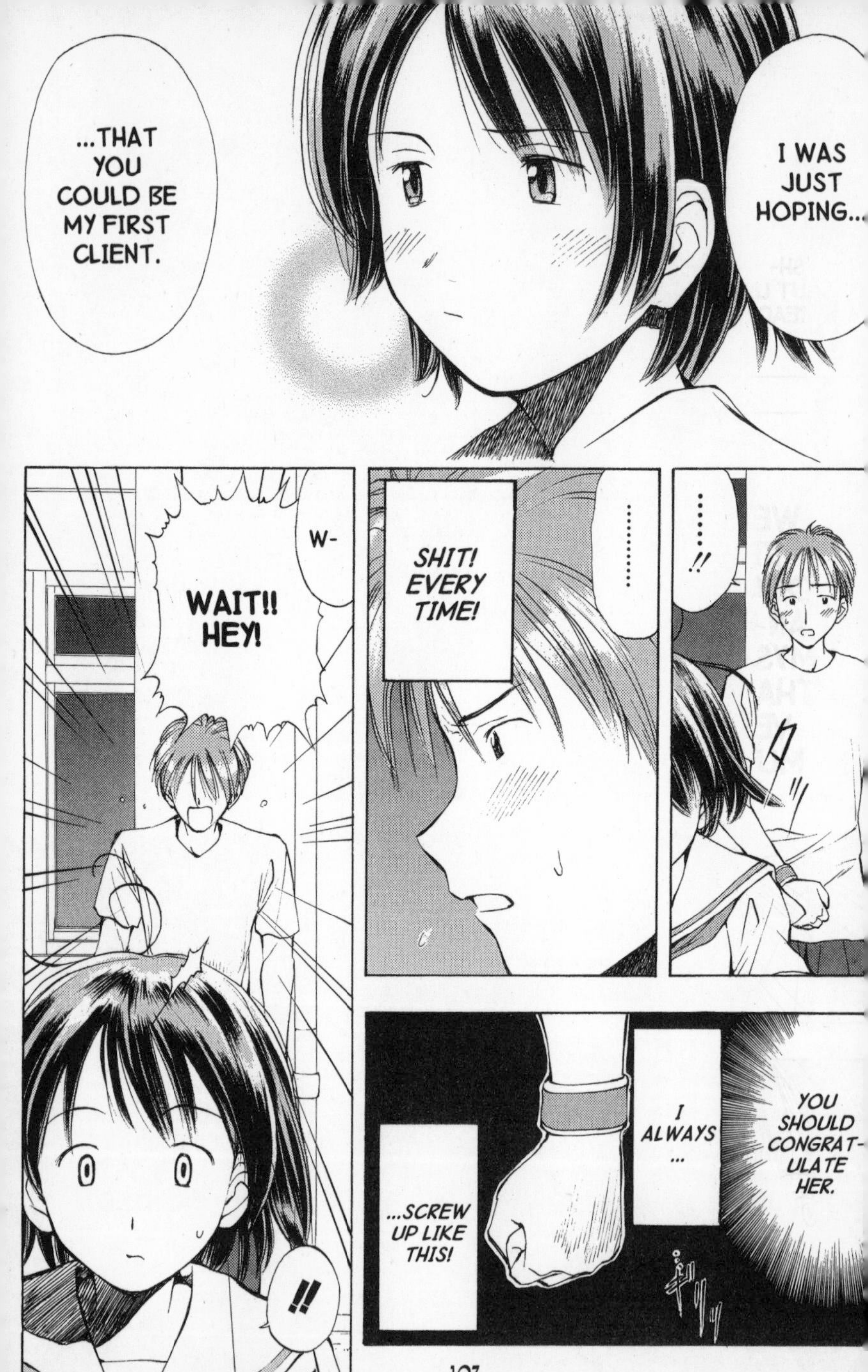
I WAS JUST HOPING...
...THAT YOU COULD BE MY FIRST CLIENT.
......!!
......
SHIT! EVERY TIME!
YOU SHOULD CONGRAT-ULATE HER.
I ALWAYS...
...SCREW UP LIKE THIS!
W-
WAIT!! HEY!
!!

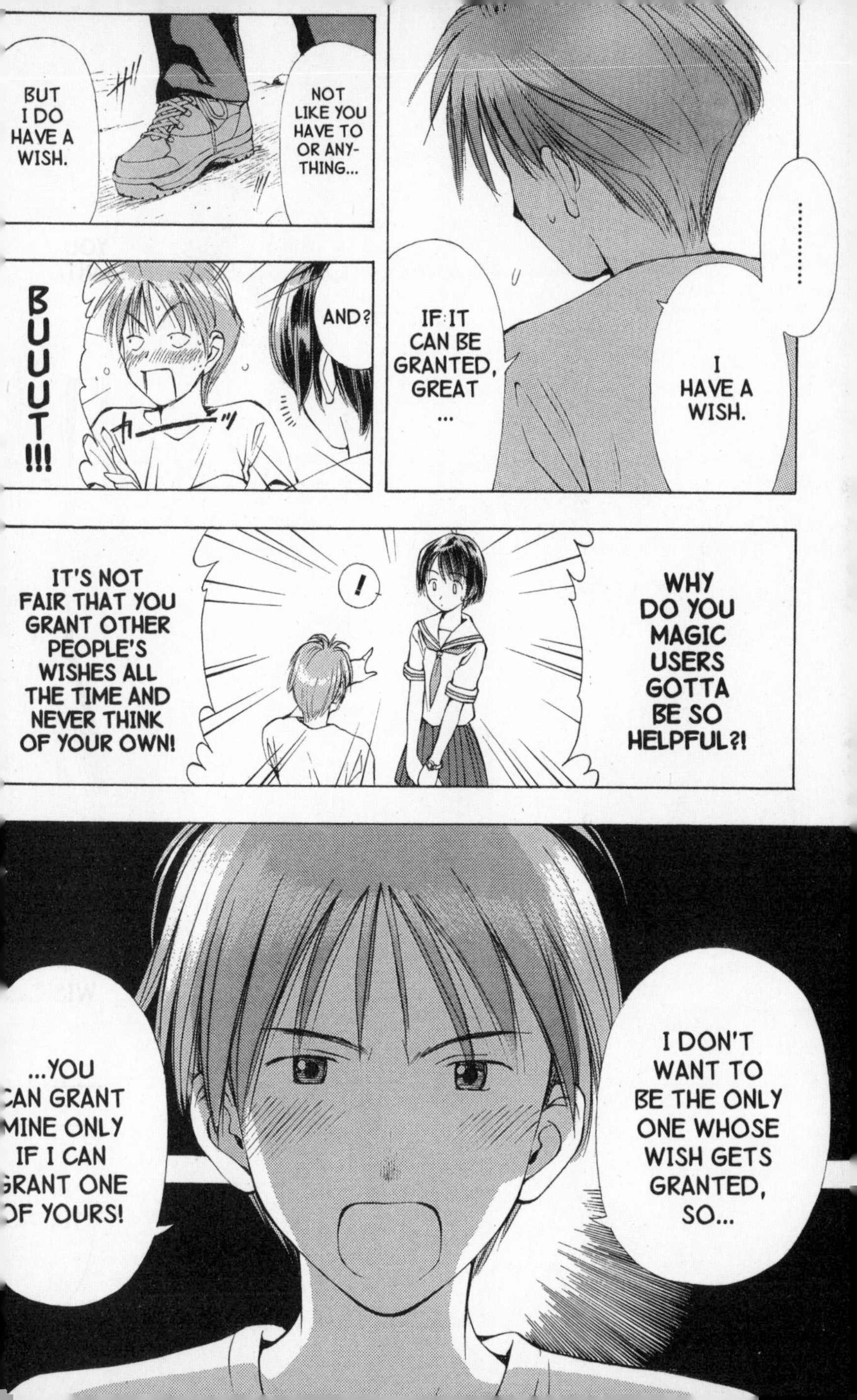

......
I HAVE A WISH.
IF IT CAN BE GRANTED, GREAT...
NOT LIKE YOU HAVE TO OR ANYTHING...
BUT I DO HAVE A WISH.
AND?
BUUUT!!!
WHY DO YOU MAGIC USERS GOTTA BE SO HELPFUL?!
!
IT'S NOT FAIR THAT YOU GRANT OTHER PEOPLE'S WISHES ALL THE TIME AND NEVER THINK OF YOUR OWN!
I DON'T WANT TO BE THE ONLY ONE WHOSE WISH GETS GRANTED, SO...
...YOU CAN GRANT MINE ONLY IF I CAN GRANT ONE OF YOURS!

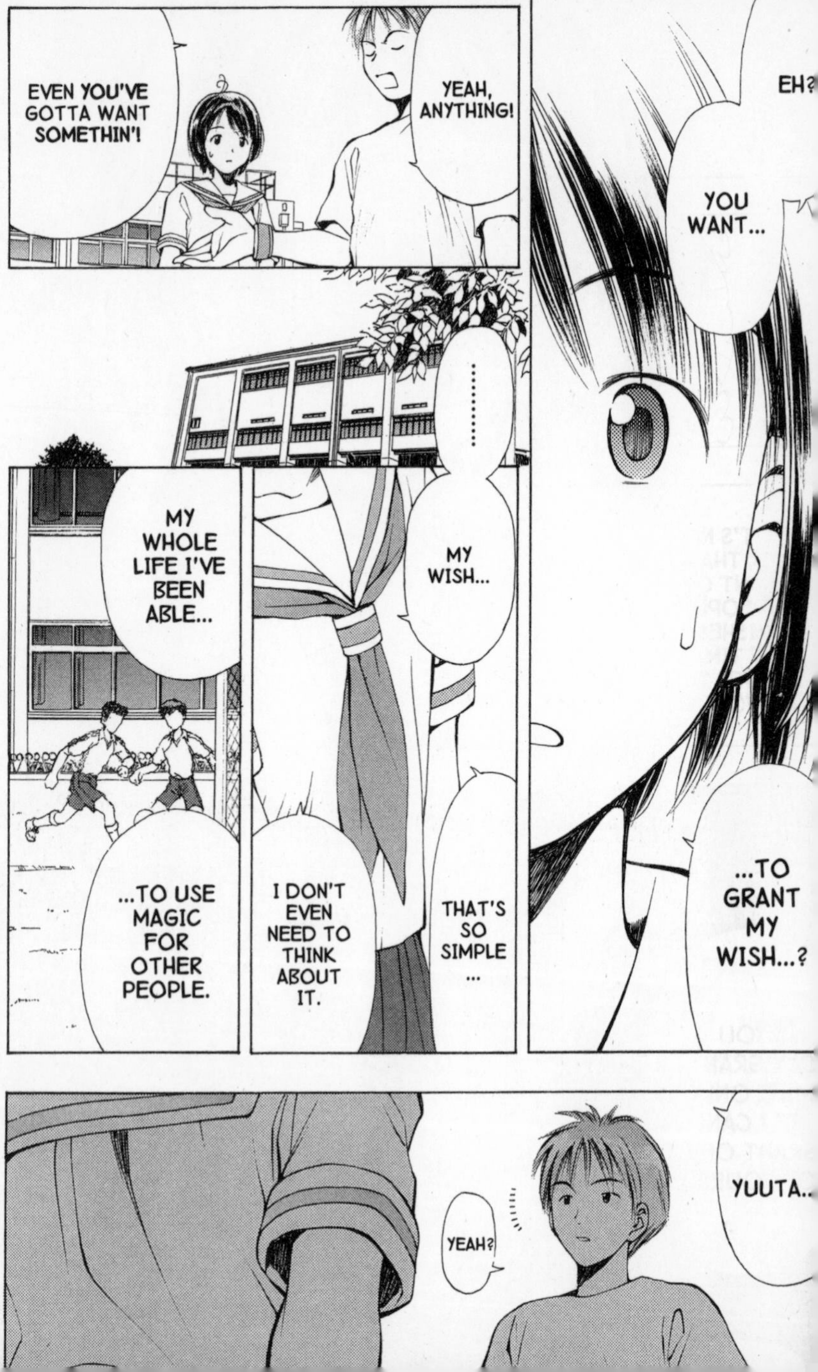
EH?
YOU WANT...
...TO GRANT MY WISH...?
YEAH, ANYTHING!
EVEN YOU'VE GOTTA WANT SOMETHIN'!
......
MY WISH...
THAT'S SO SIMPLE...
I DON'T EVEN NEED TO THINK ABOUT IT.
MY WHOLE LIFE I'VE BEEN ABLE...
...TO USE MAGIC FOR OTHER PEOPLE.
YUUTA...
YEAH?

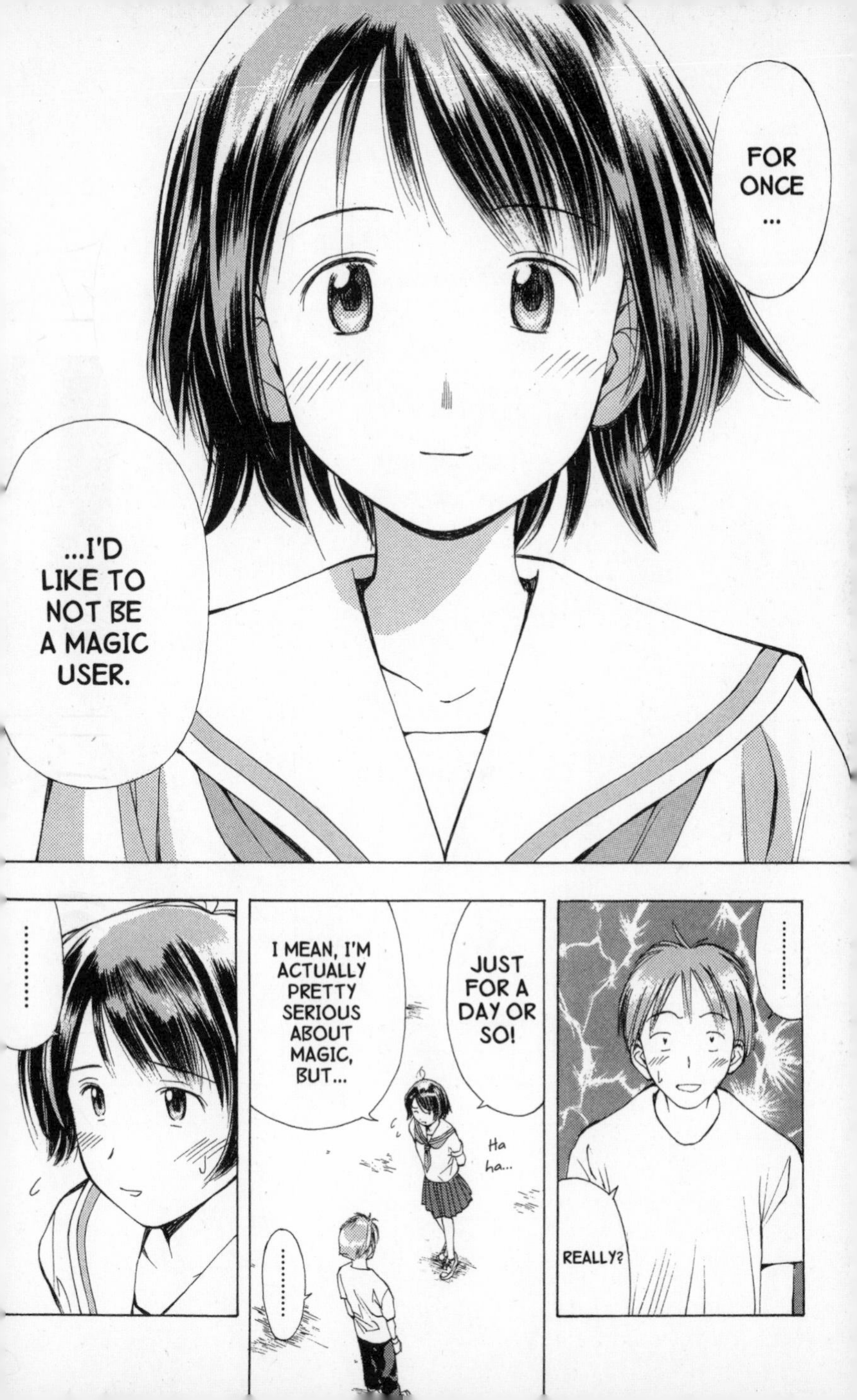
FOR ONCE ...
...I'D LIKE TO NOT BE A MAGIC USER.
....
REALLY?
JUST FOR A DAY OR SO!
I MEAN, I'M ACTUALLY PRETTY SERIOUS ABOUT MAGIC, BUT...
Ha ha...
....
....

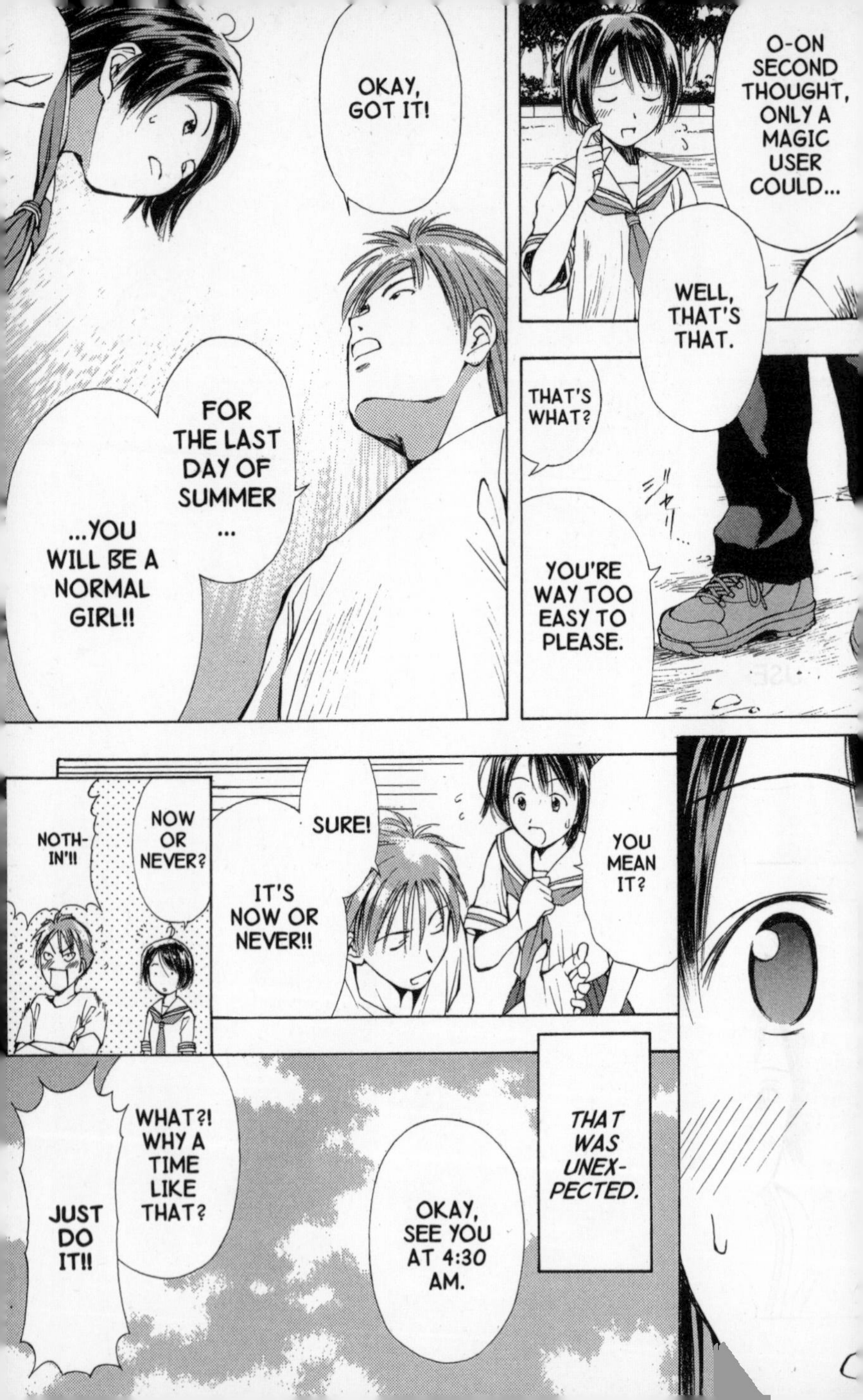
O-ON SECOND THOUGHT, ONLY A MAGIC USER COULD...
WELL, THAT'S THAT.
THAT'S WHAT?
YOU'RE WAY TOO EASY TO PLEASE.
OKAY, GOT IT!
FOR THE LAST DAY OF SUMMER ...
...YOU WILL BE A NORMAL GIRL!!
YOU MEAN IT?
SURE!
IT'S NOW OR NEVER!!
NOW OR NEVER?
NOTH-IN'!!
THAT WAS UNEXPECTED.
OKAY, SEE YOU AT 4:30 AM.
WHAT?! WHY A TIME LIKE THAT?
JUST DO IT!!

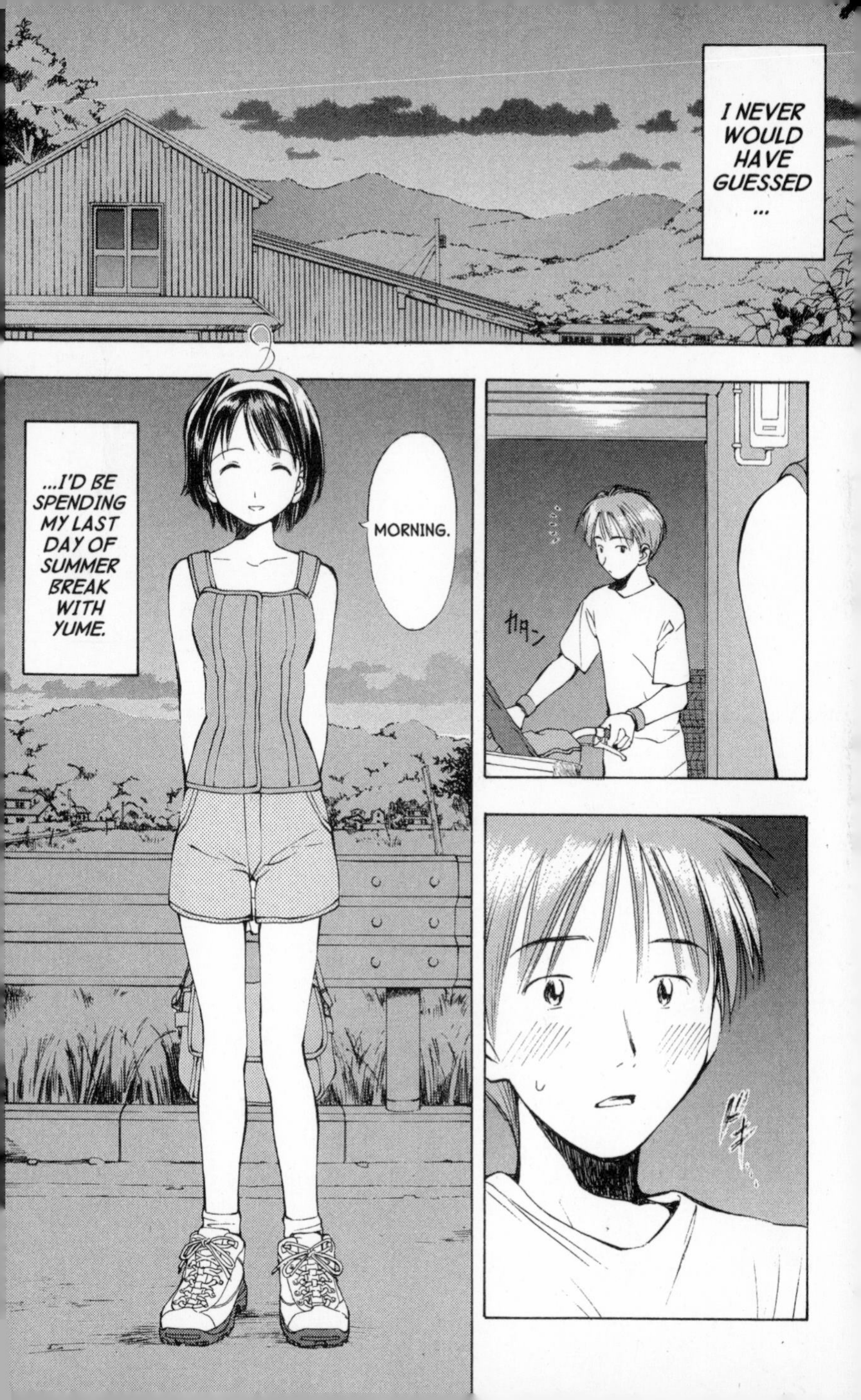
I NEVER WOULD HAVE GUESSED ...
...I'D BE SPENDING MY LAST DAY OF SUMMER BREAK WITH YUME.
MORNING.

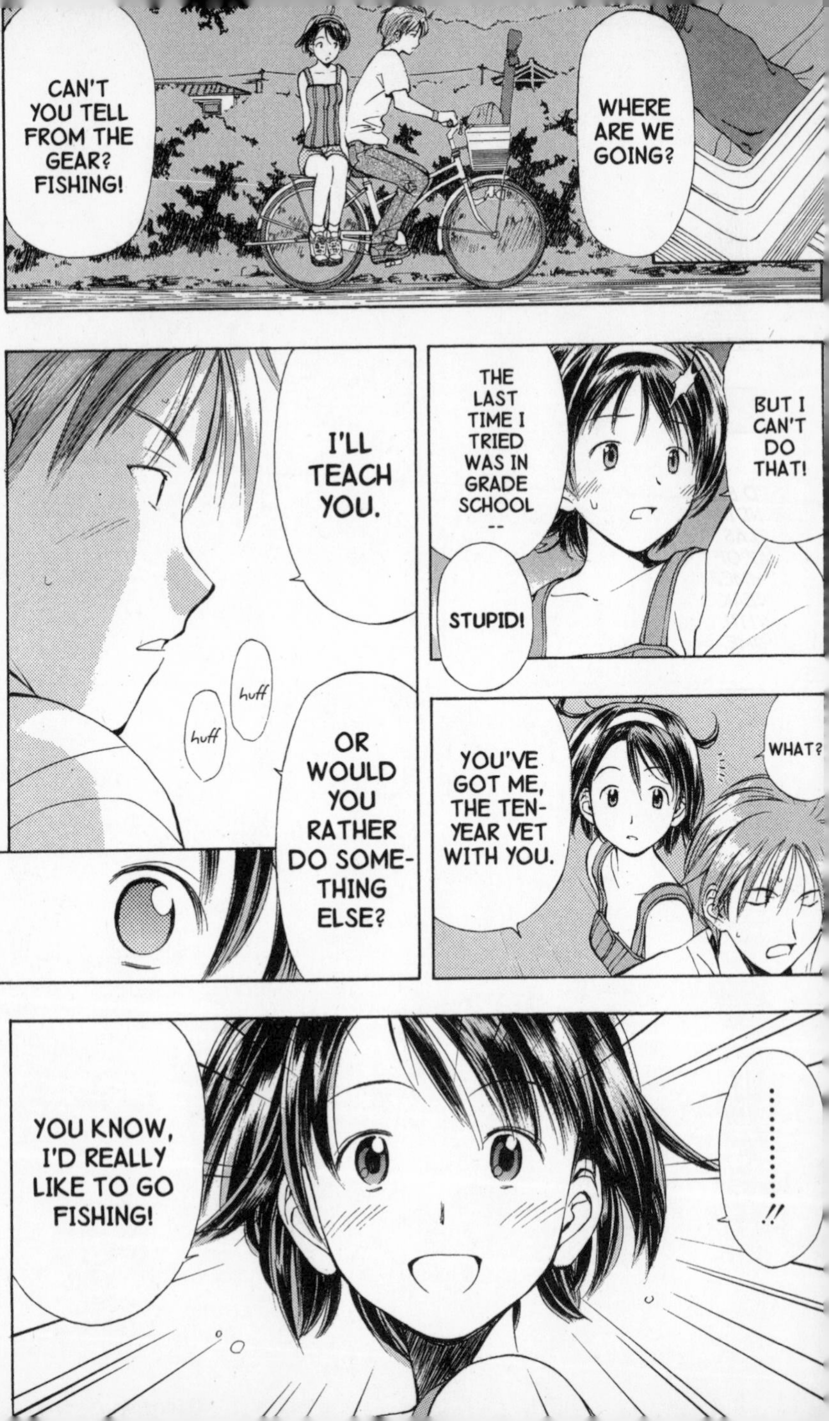
WHERE ARE WE GOING?
CAN'T YOU TELL FROM THE GEAR? FISHING!
BUT I CAN'T DO THAT!
THE LAST TIME I TRIED WAS IN GRADE SCHOOL --
STUPID!
WHAT?
YOU'VE GOT ME, THE TEN-YEAR VET WITH YOU.
I'LL TEACH YOU.
huff
huff
OR WOULD YOU RATHER DO SOME-THING ELSE?
......!!
YOU KNOW, I'D REALLY LIKE TO GO FISHING!

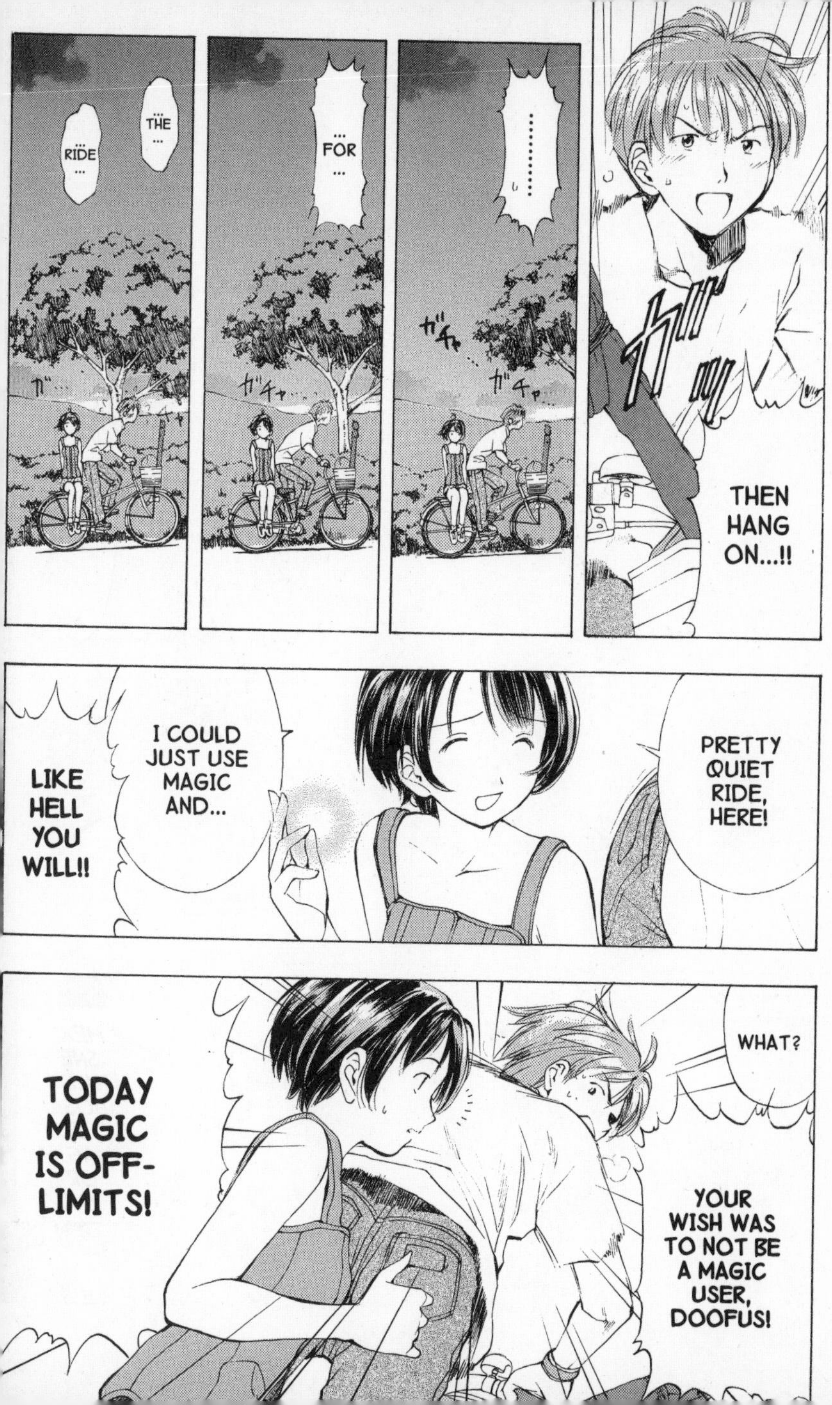
THEN HANG ON...!!
....
ガチャ...
ガチャ...
... FOR ...
ガチャ...
... THE ...
... RIDE ...
ガ...
PRETTY QUIET RIDE, HERE!
I COULD JUST USE MAGIC AND...
LIKE HELL YOU WILL!!
WHAT?
YOUR WISH WAS TO NOT BE A MAGIC USER, DOOFUS!
TODAY MAGIC IS OFF-LIMITS!

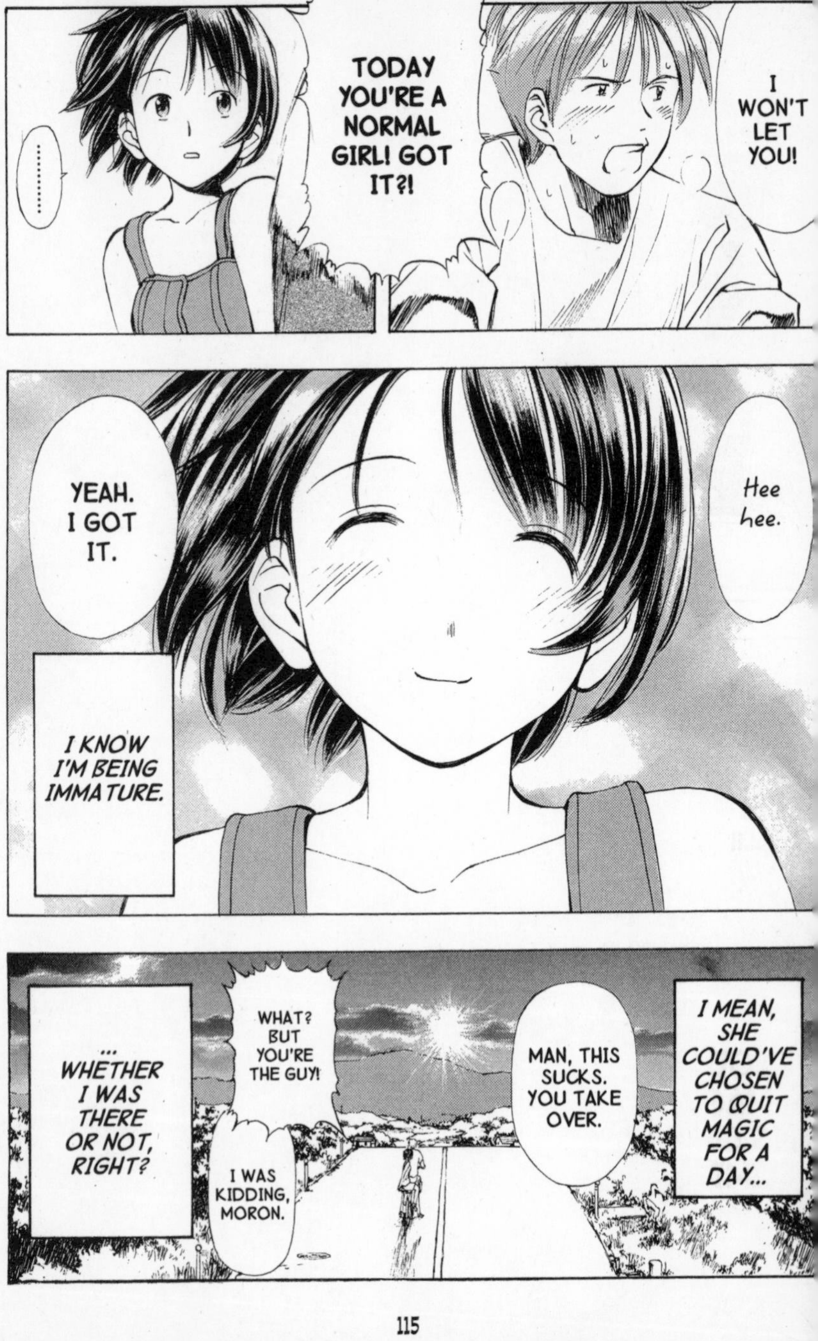
I WON'T LET YOU!
TODAY YOU'RE A NORMAL GIRL! GOT IT?!
....
Hee hee.
YEAH. I GOT IT.
I KNOW I'M BEING IMMATURE.
I MEAN, SHE COULD'VE CHOSEN TO QUIT MAGIC FOR A DAY...
MAN, THIS SUCKS. YOU TAKE OVER.
WHAT? BUT YOU'RE THE GUY!
I WAS KIDDING, MORON.
... WHETHER I WAS THERE OR NOT, RIGHT?

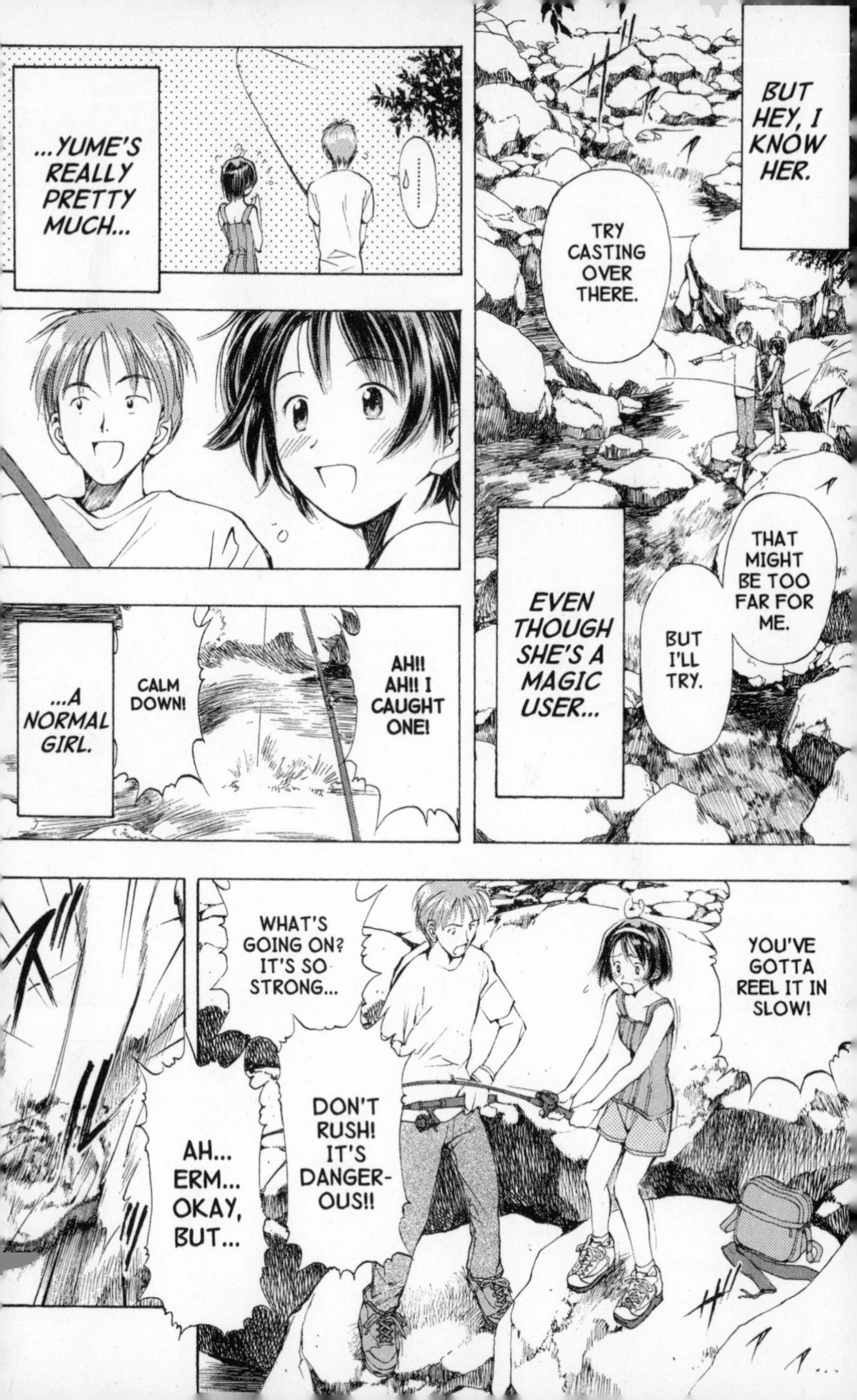
BUT HEY, I KNOW HER.
TRY CASTING OVER THERE.
THAT MIGHT BE TOO FAR FOR ME.
BUT I'LL TRY.
EVEN THOUGH SHE'S A MAGIC USER...
...YUME'S REALLY PRETTY MUCH...
AH!! AH!! I CAUGHT ONE!
CALM DOWN!
...A NORMAL GIRL.
YOU'VE GOTTA REEL IT IN SLOW!
WHAT'S GOING ON? IT'S SO STRONG...
DON'T RUSH! IT'S DANGER-OUS!!
AH... ERM... OKAY, BUT...

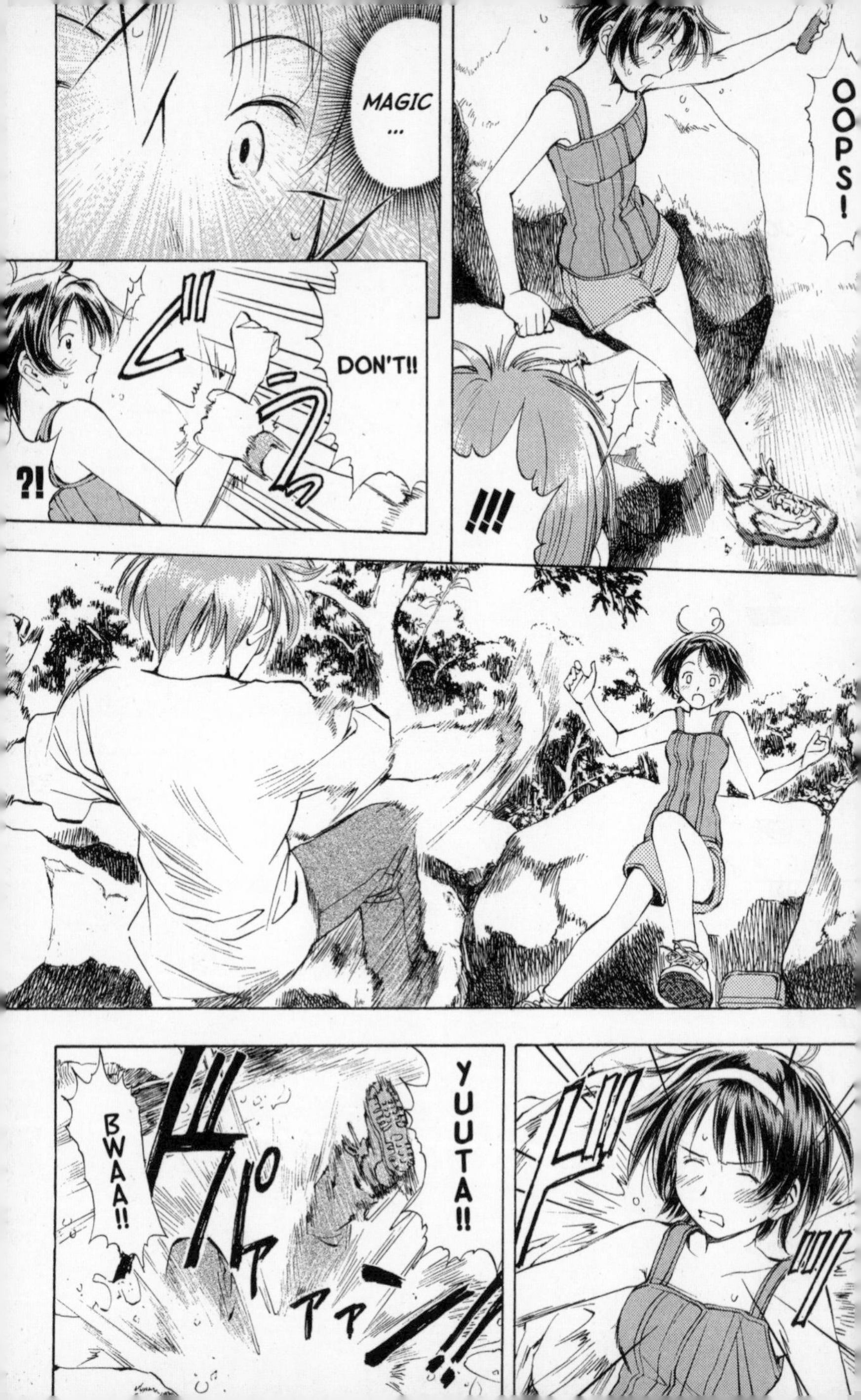
OOPS!
MAGIC ...
DON'T!!
?!
!!!
YUUTA!!
BWAA!!

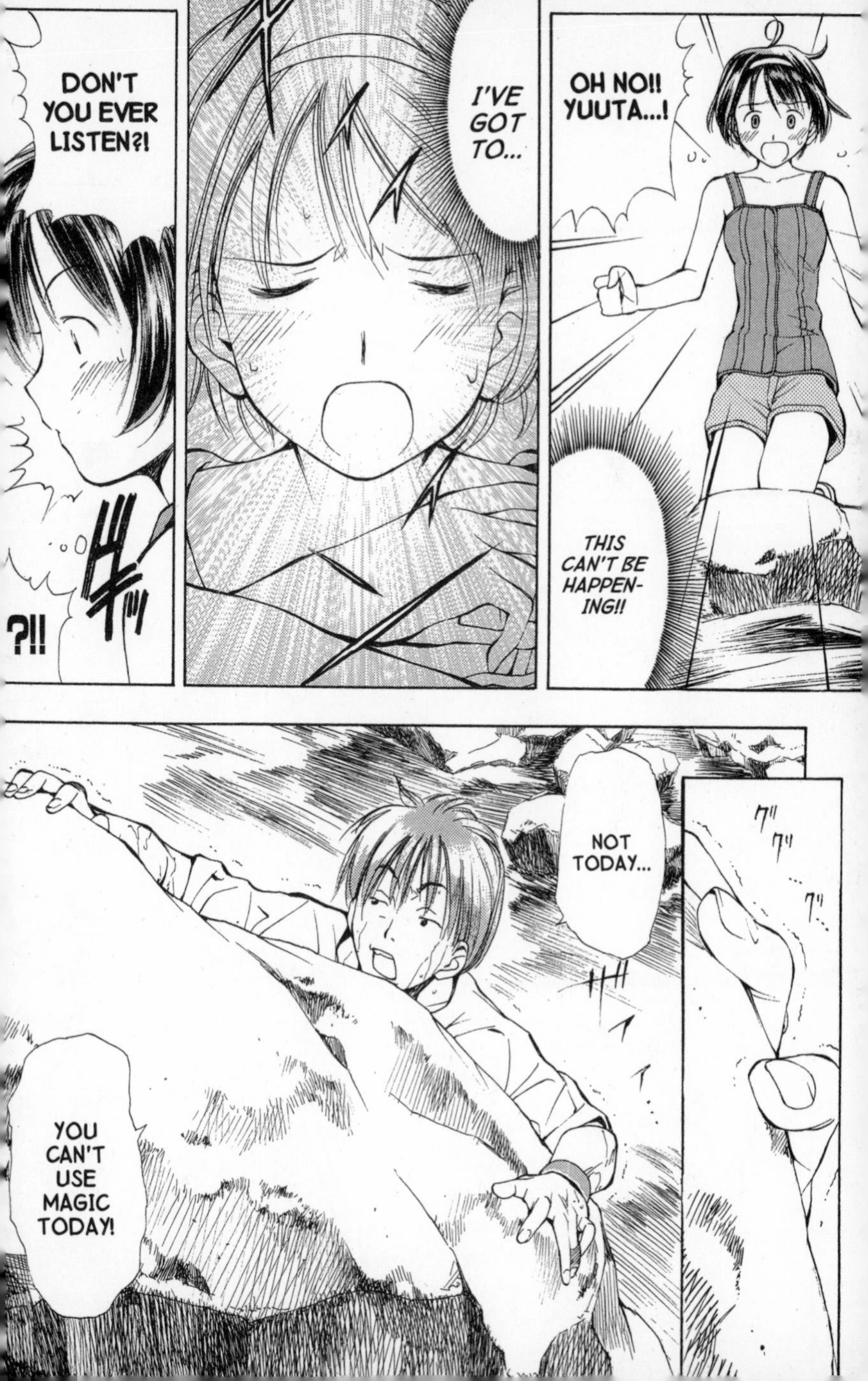
OH NO!! YUUTA...!
THIS CAN'T BE HAPPEN-ING!!
I'VE GOT TO...
DON'T YOU EVER LISTEN?!
?!!
NOT TODAY...
YOU CAN'T USE MAGIC TODAY!

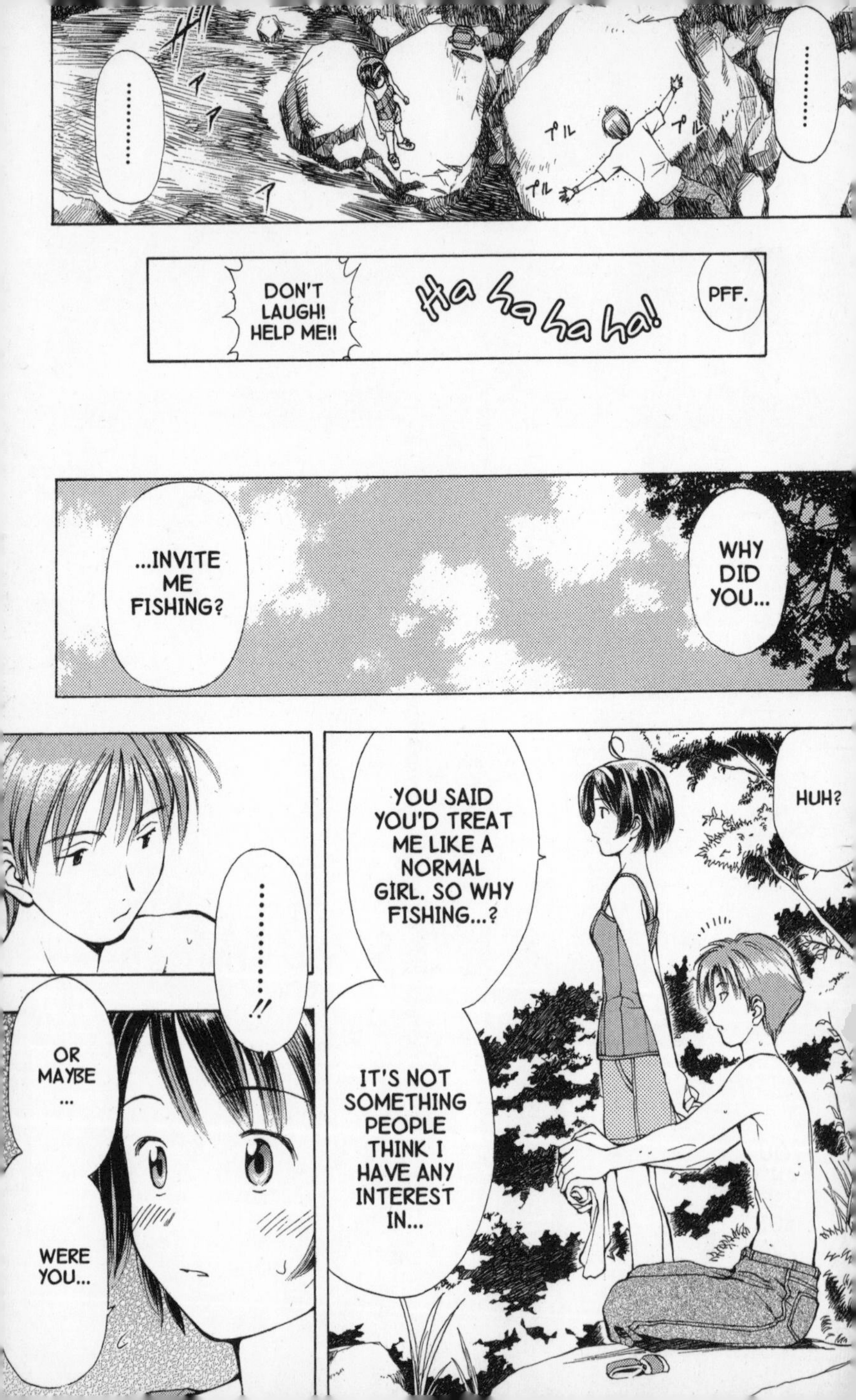
......
プル
プル
プル
......
PFF.
Ha ha ha ha!
DON'T LAUGH! HELP ME!!
WHY DID YOU...
...INVITE ME FISHING?
HUH?
YOU SAID YOU'D TREAT ME LIKE A NORMAL GIRL. SO WHY FISHING...?
IT'S NOT SOMETHING PEOPLE THINK I HAVE ANY INTEREST IN...
......!!
OR MAYBE ...
WERE YOU...

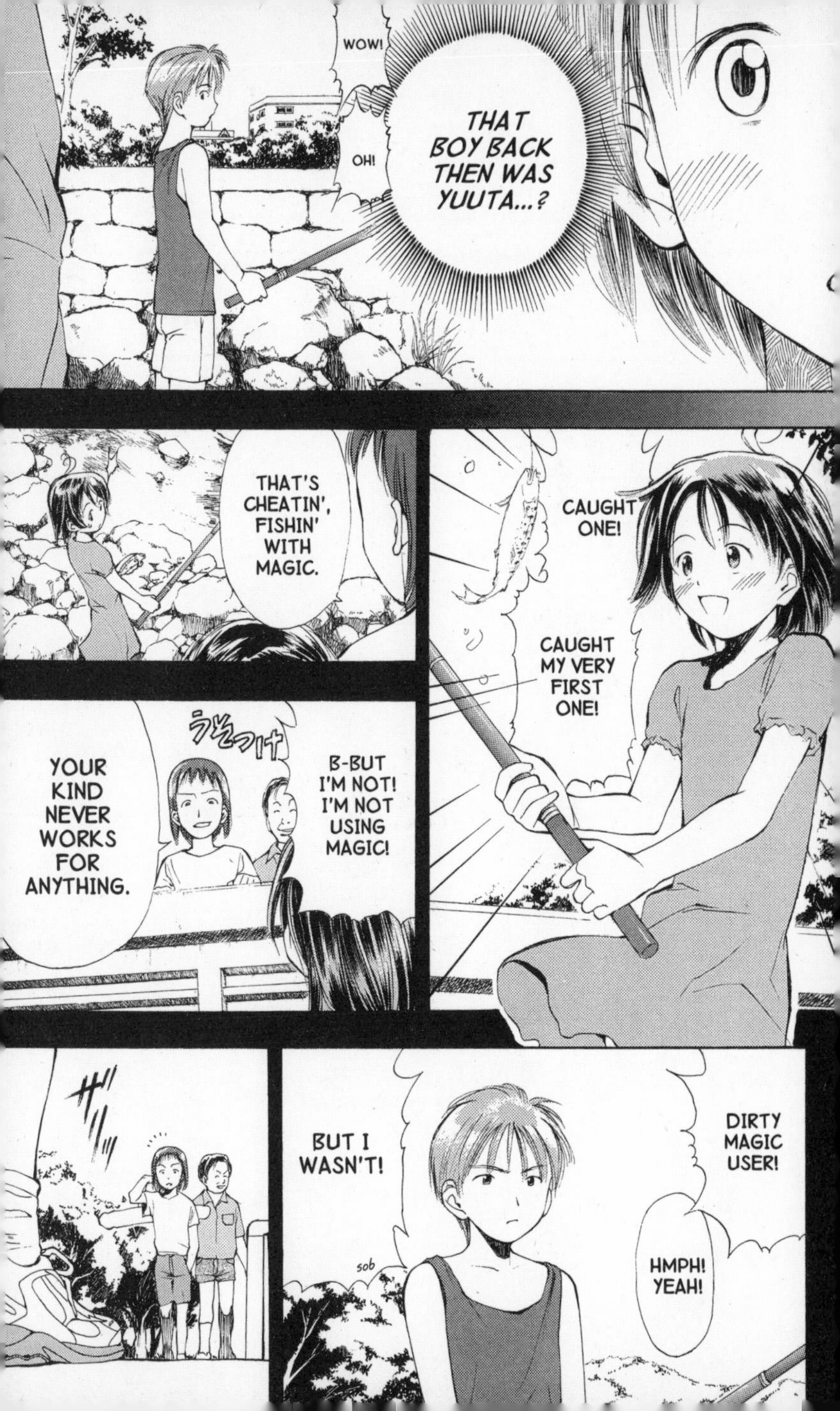
THAT BOY BACK THEN WAS YUUTA...?
WOW!
OH!
CAUGHT ONE!
CAUGHT MY VERY FIRST ONE!
THAT'S CHEATIN', FISHIN' WITH MAGIC.
B-BUT I'M NOT! I'M NOT USING MAGIC!
うそつけ
YOUR KIND NEVER WORKS FOR ANYTHING.
DIRTY MAGIC USER!
BUT I WASN'T!
HMPH! YEAH!
sob

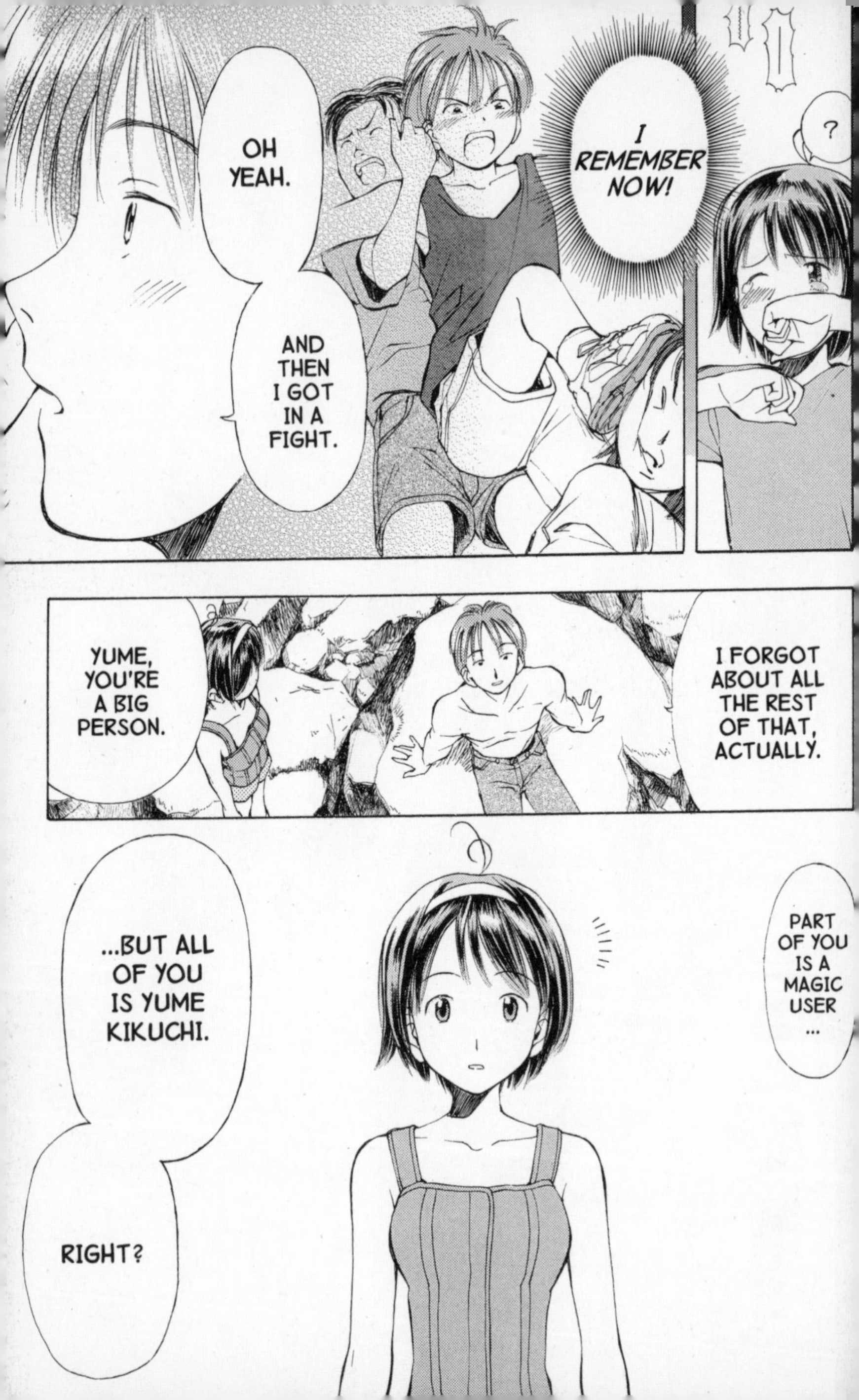
?
I REMEMBER NOW!
OH YEAH.
AND THEN I GOT IN A FIGHT.
I FORGOT ABOUT ALL THE REST OF THAT, ACTUALLY.
YUME, YOU'RE A BIG PERSON.
PART OF YOU IS A MAGIC USER ...
...BUT ALL OF YOU IS YUME KIKUCHI.
RIGHT?

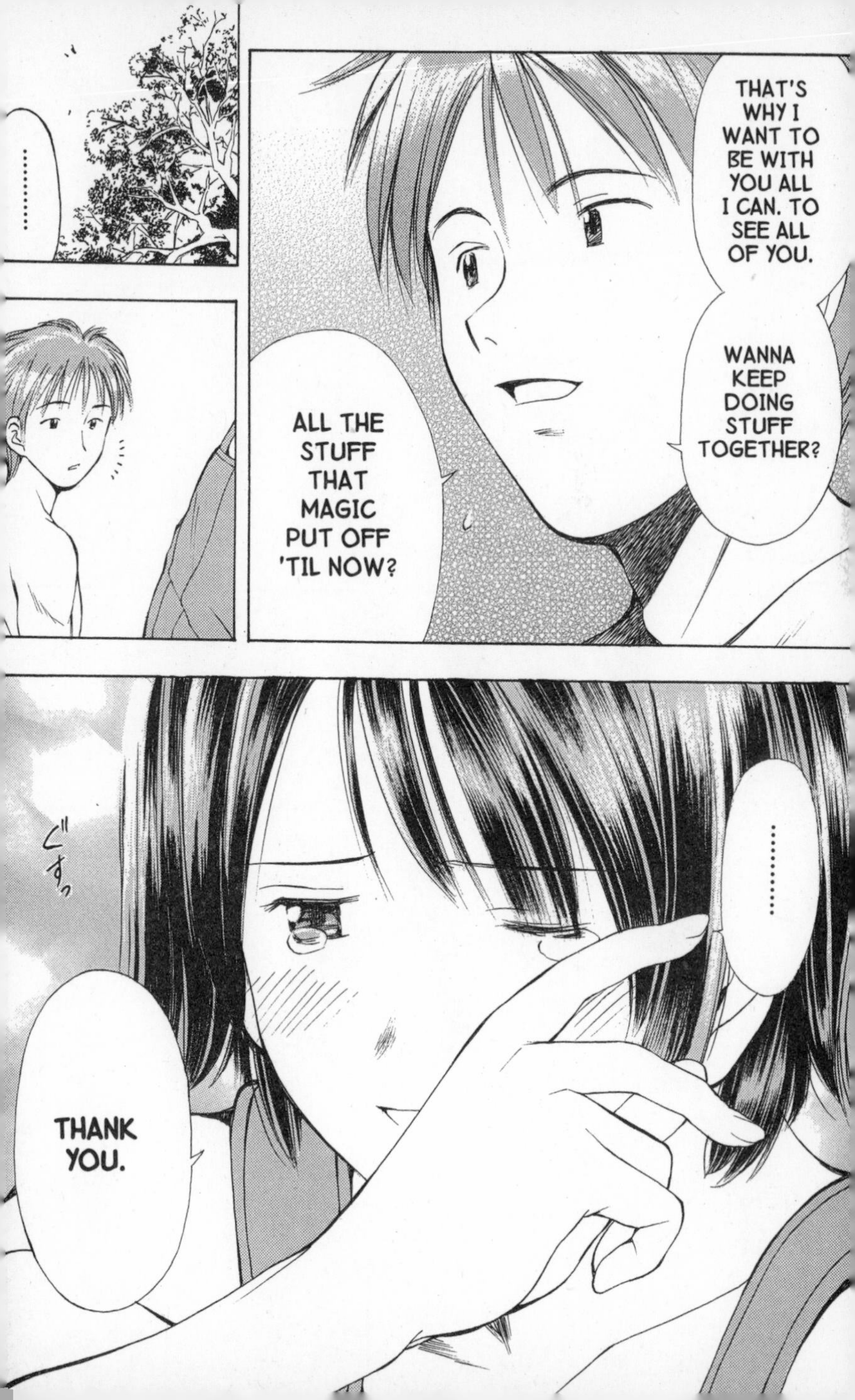
THAT'S WHY I WANT TO BE WITH YOU ALL I CAN. TO SEE ALL OF YOU.
WANNA KEEP DOING STUFF TOGETHER?
ALL THE STUFF THAT MAGIC PUT OFF 'TIL NOW?
....
....
ぐすっ
THANK YOU.

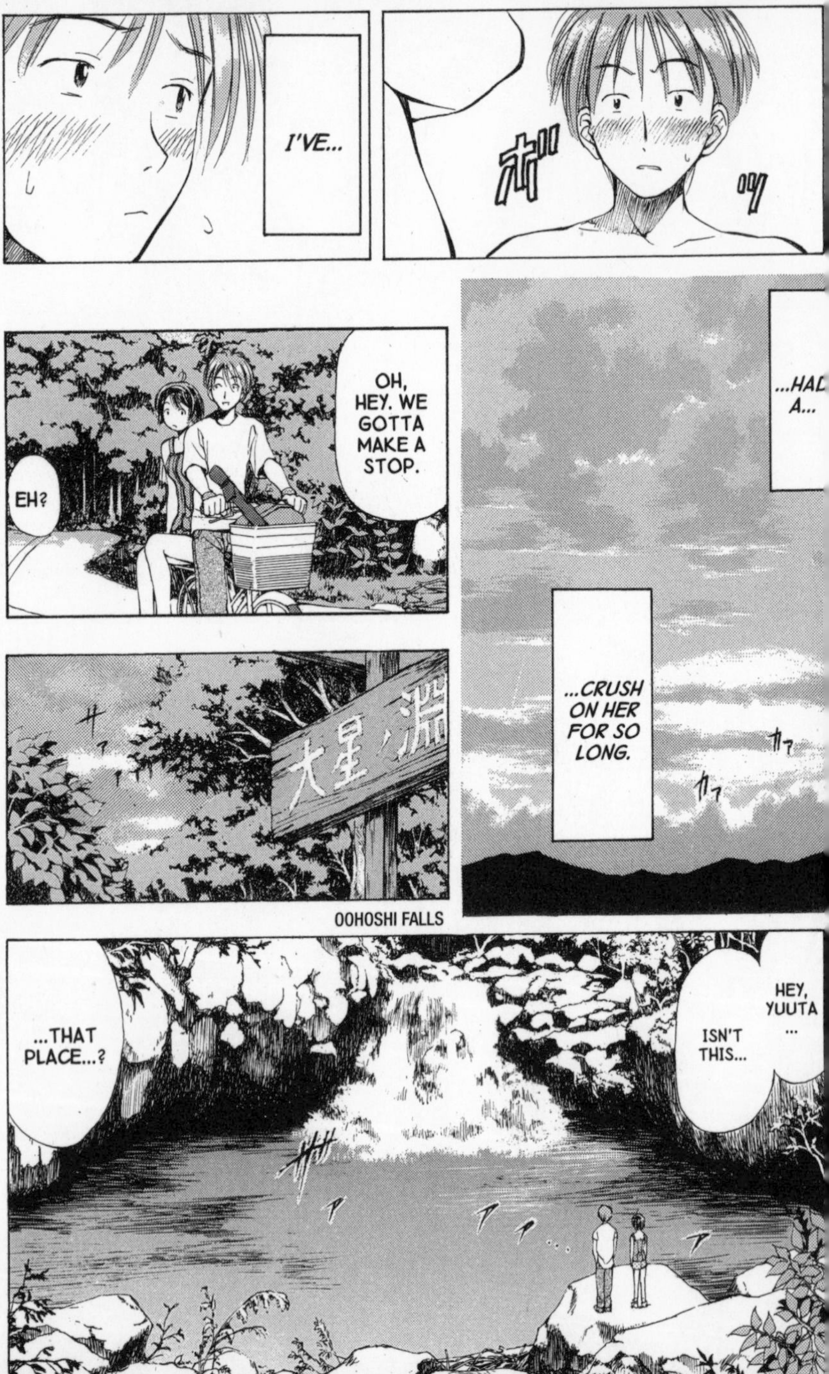
ボッ
I'VE...
...HAD A...
...CRUSH ON HER FOR SO LONG.
カァ
カァ
OH, HEY. WE GOTTA MAKE A STOP.
EH?
大星ノ
OOHOSHI FALLS
HEY, YUUTA...
ISN'T THIS...
...THAT PLACE...?

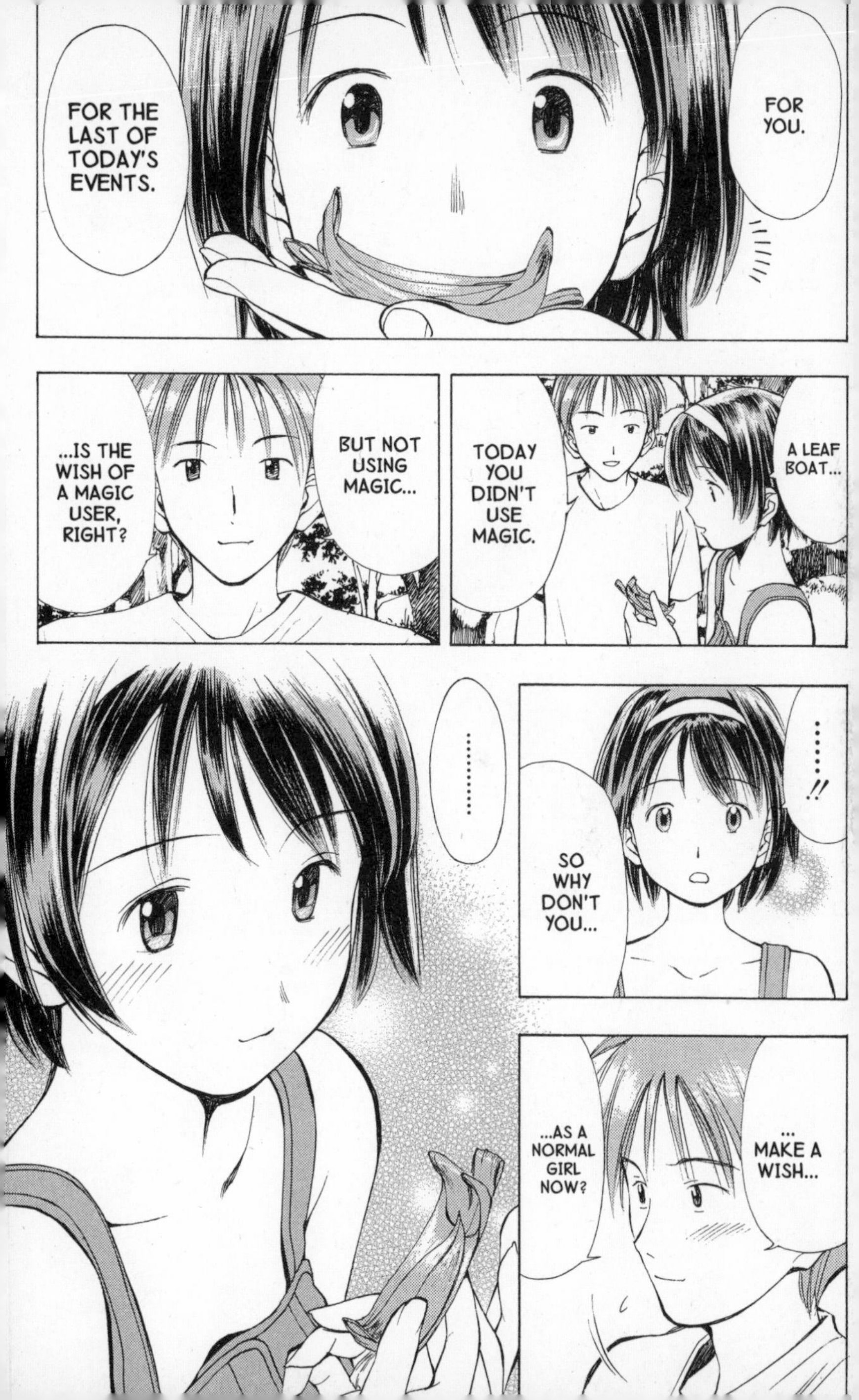
FOR YOU.
FOR THE LAST OF TODAY'S EVENTS.
A LEAF BOAT...
TODAY YOU DIDN'T USE MAGIC.
BUT NOT USING MAGIC...
...IS THE WISH OF A MAGIC USER, RIGHT?
......!!
SO WHY DON'T YOU...
... MAKE A WISH...
...AS A NORMAL GIRL NOW?
....

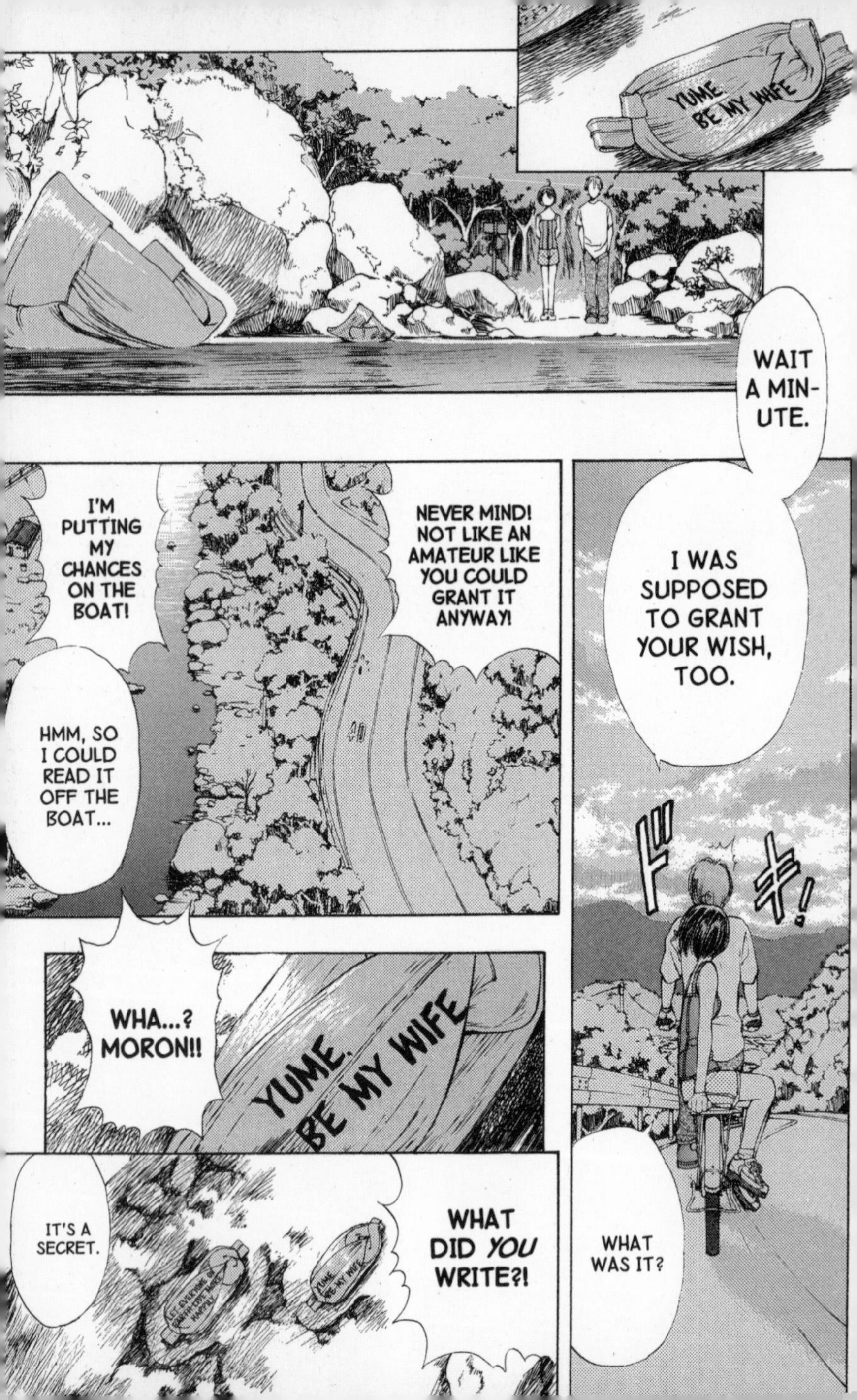
YUME, BE MY WIFE
WAIT A MIN- UTE.
I WAS SUPPOSED TO GRANT YOUR WISH, TOO.
ドキ!
WHAT WAS IT?
NEVER MIND! NOT LIKE AN AMATEUR LIKE YOU COULD GRANT IT ANYWAY!
I'M PUTTING MY CHANCES ON THE BOAT!
HMM, SO I COULD READ IT OFF THE BOAT...
YUME, BE MY WIFE
WHA...? MORON!!
WHAT DID *YOU* WRITE?!
YUME, BE MY WIFE
LET EVERYONE ON EARTH LIVE MORE HAPPILY
IT'S A SECRET.

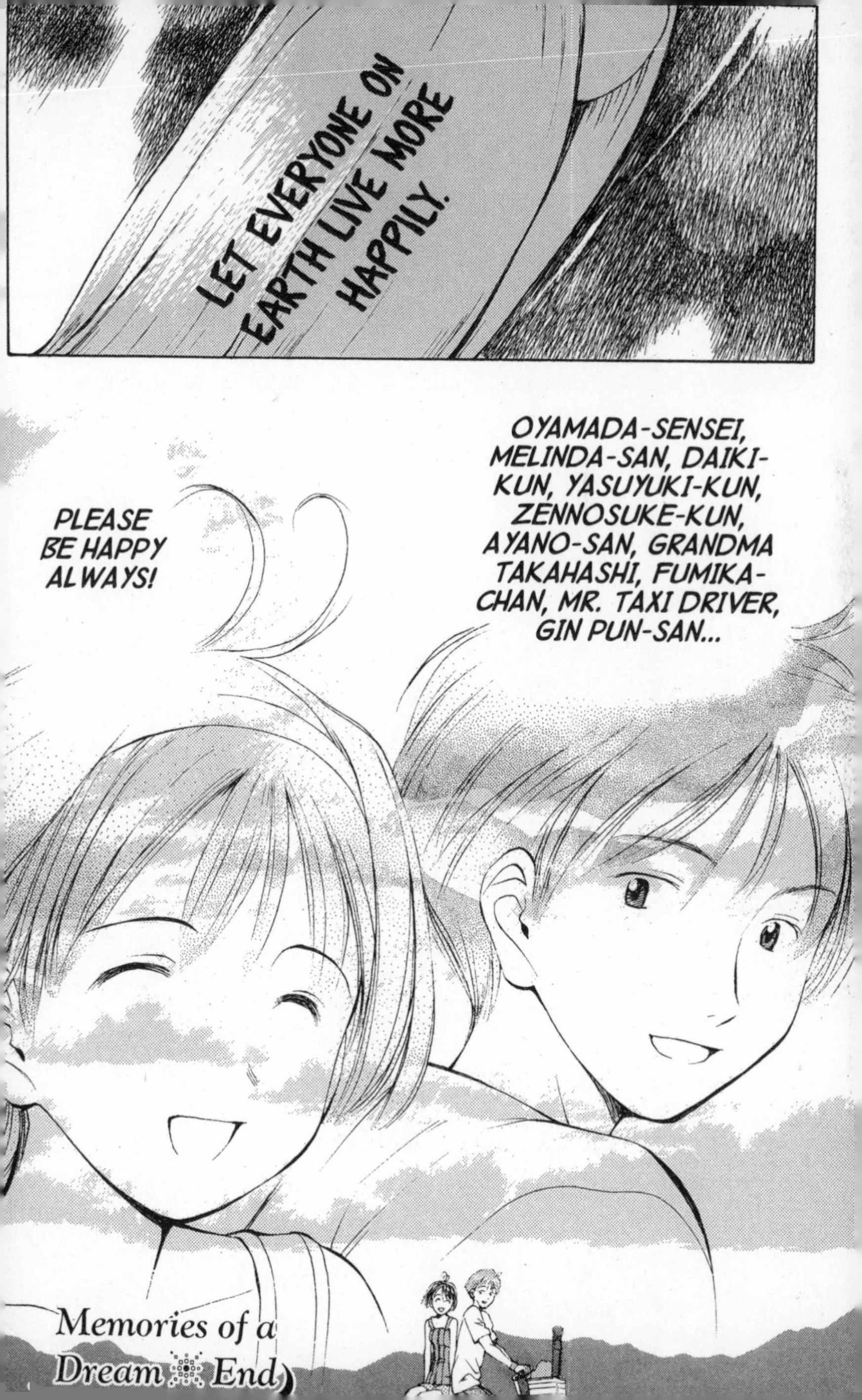
LET EVERYONE ON EARTH LIVE MORE HAPPILY.
OYAMADA-SENSEI, MELINDA-SAN, DAIKI-KUN, YASUYUKI-KUN, ZENNOSUKE-KUN, AYANO-SAN, GRANDMA TAKAHASHI, FUMIKA-CHAN, MR. TAXI DRIVER, GIN PUN-SAN...
PLEASE BE HAPPY ALWAYS!
Memories of a Dream End

One Night Dream Stardust Stage

(Stand by Me)

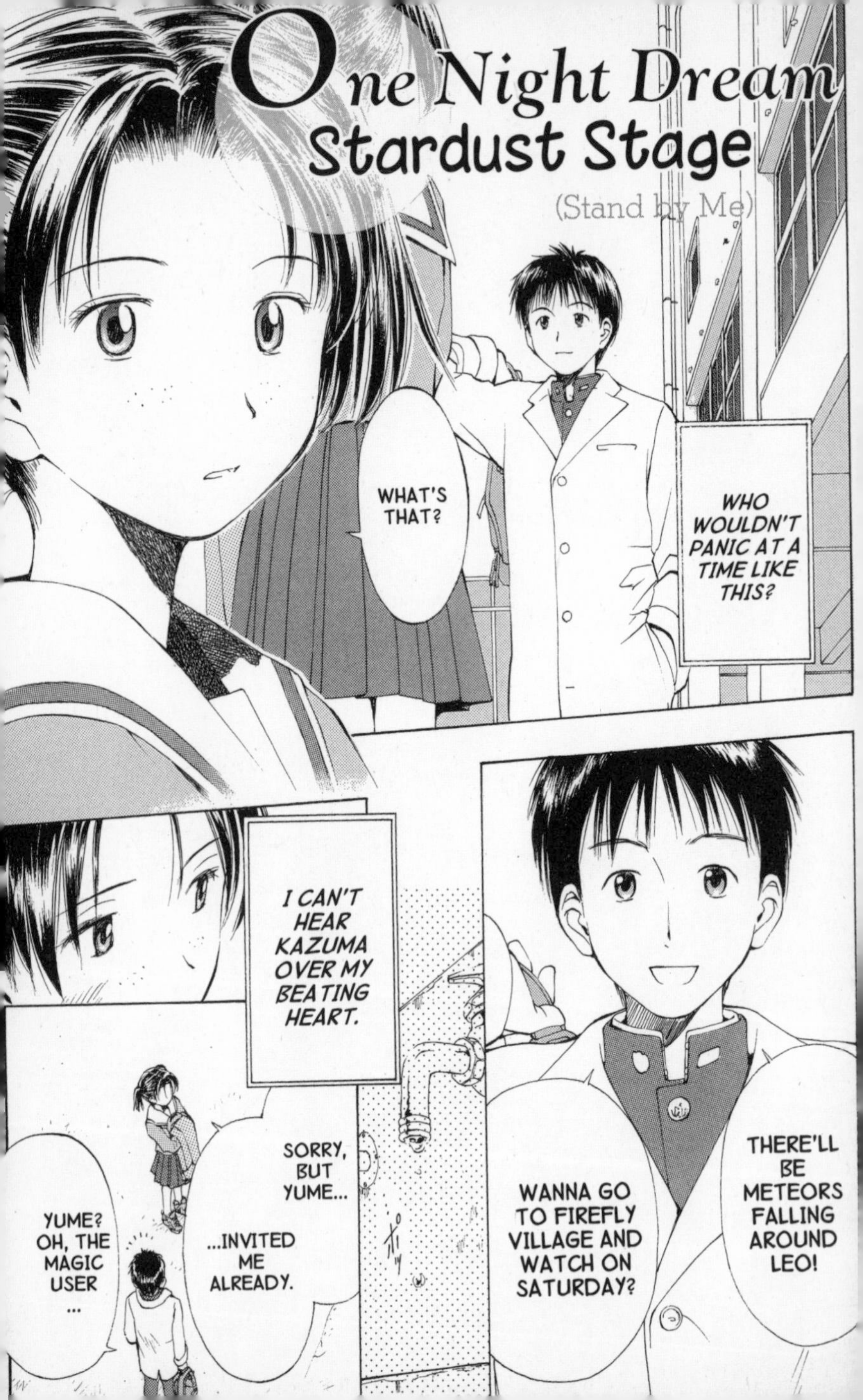
WHO WOULDN'T PANIC AT A TIME LIKE THIS?
WHAT'S THAT?
THERE'LL BE METEORS FALLING AROUND LEO!
WANNA GO TO FIREFLY VILLAGE AND WATCH ON SATURDAY?
I CAN'T HEAR KAZUMA OVER MY BEATING HEART.
SORRY, BUT YUME...
...INVITED ME ALREADY.
YUME? OH, THE MAGIC USER ...

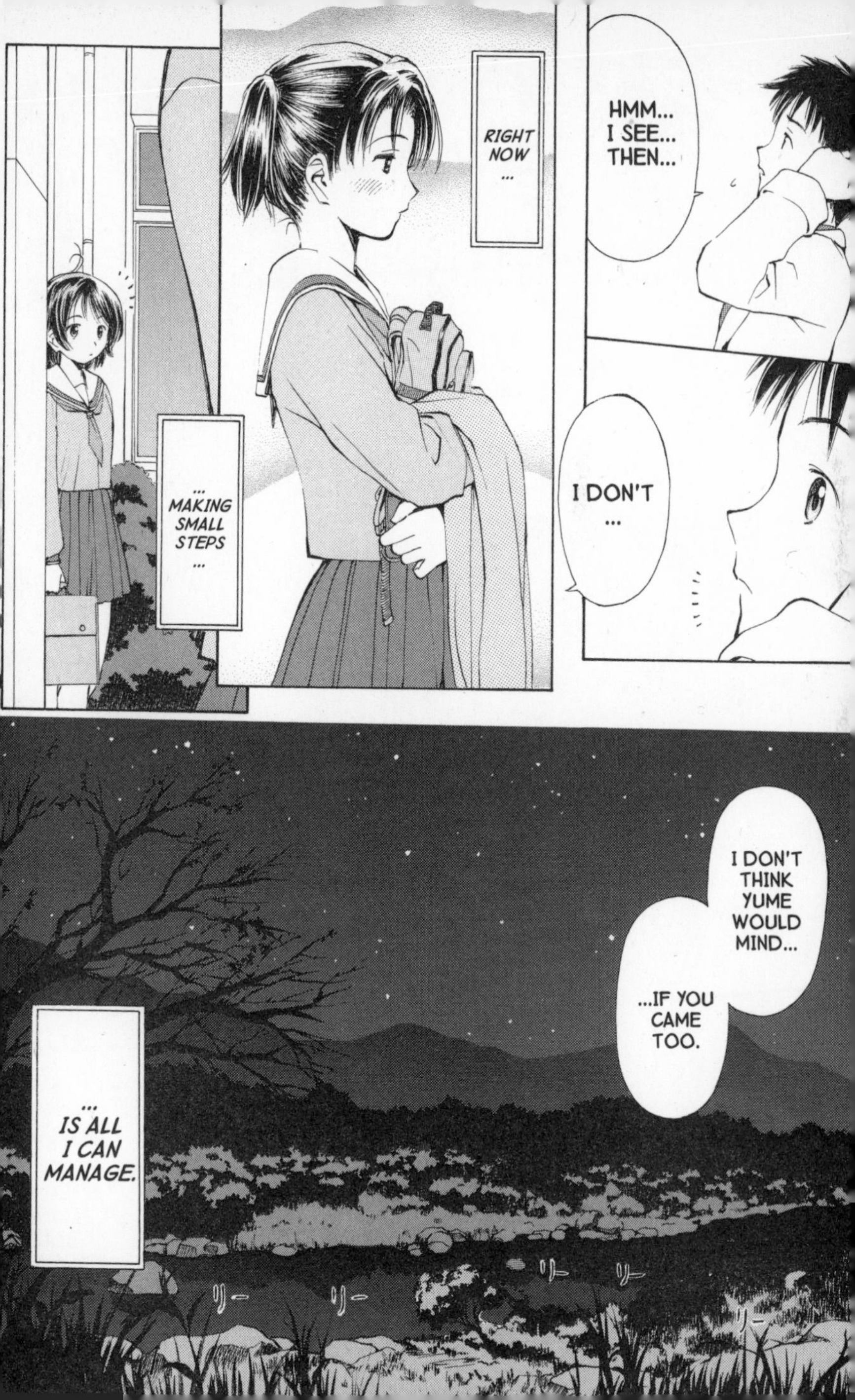

HMM... I SEE... THEN...
I DON'T ...
RIGHT NOW ...
... MAKING SMALL STEPS ...
I DON'T THINK YUME WOULD MIND...
...IF YOU CAME TOO.
... IS ALL I CAN MANAGE.

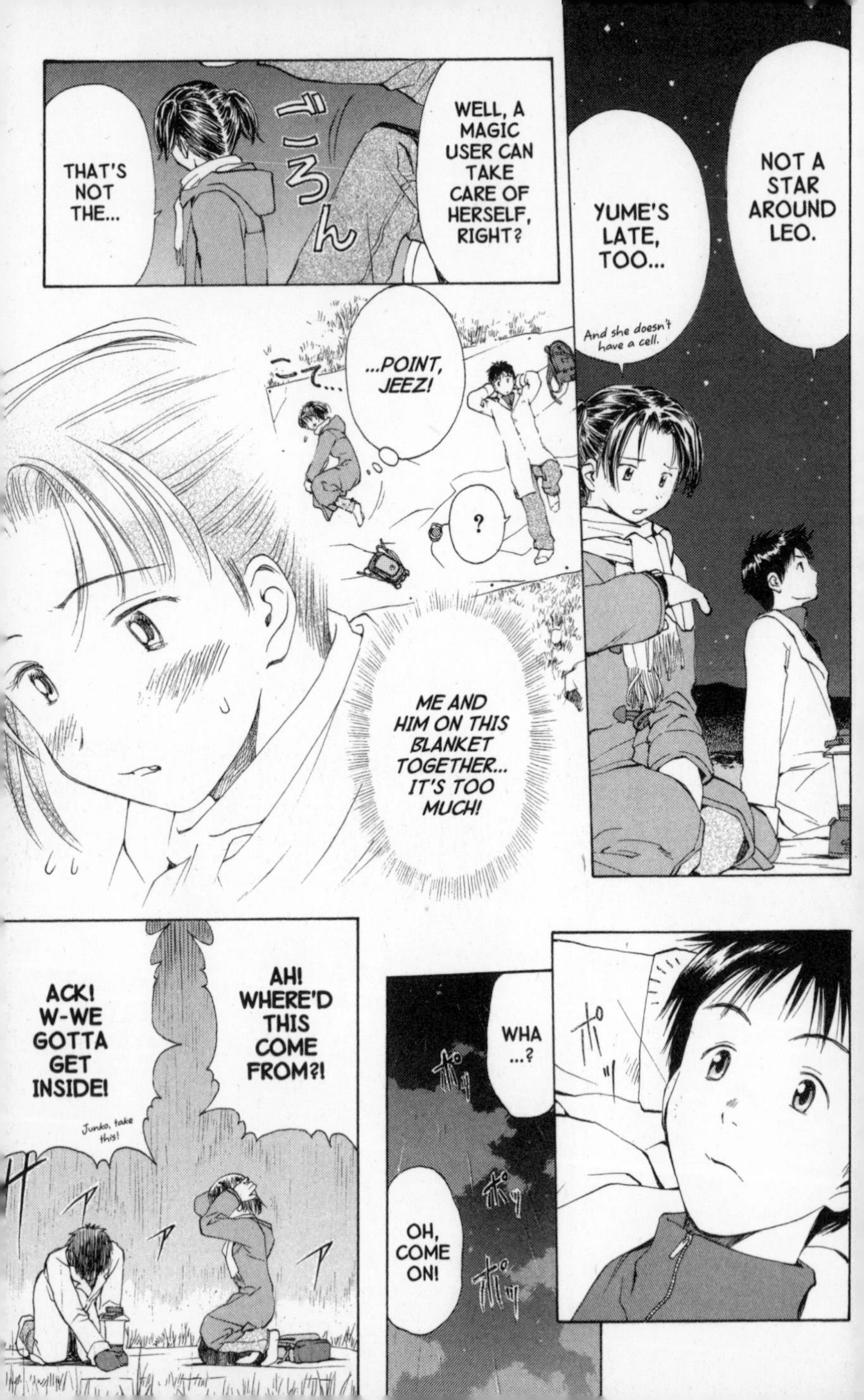
NOT A STAR AROUND LEO.
YUME'S LATE, TOO...
And she doesn't have a cell.
WELL, A MAGIC USER CAN TAKE CARE OF HERSELF, RIGHT?
ごろん
THAT'S NOT THE...
...POINT, JEEZ!
こて...
?
ME AND HIM ON THIS BLANKET TOGETHER... IT'S TOO MUCH!
WHA ...?
OH, COME ON!
AH! WHERE'D THIS COME FROM?!
ACK! W-WE GOTTA GET INSIDE!
Junko, take this!

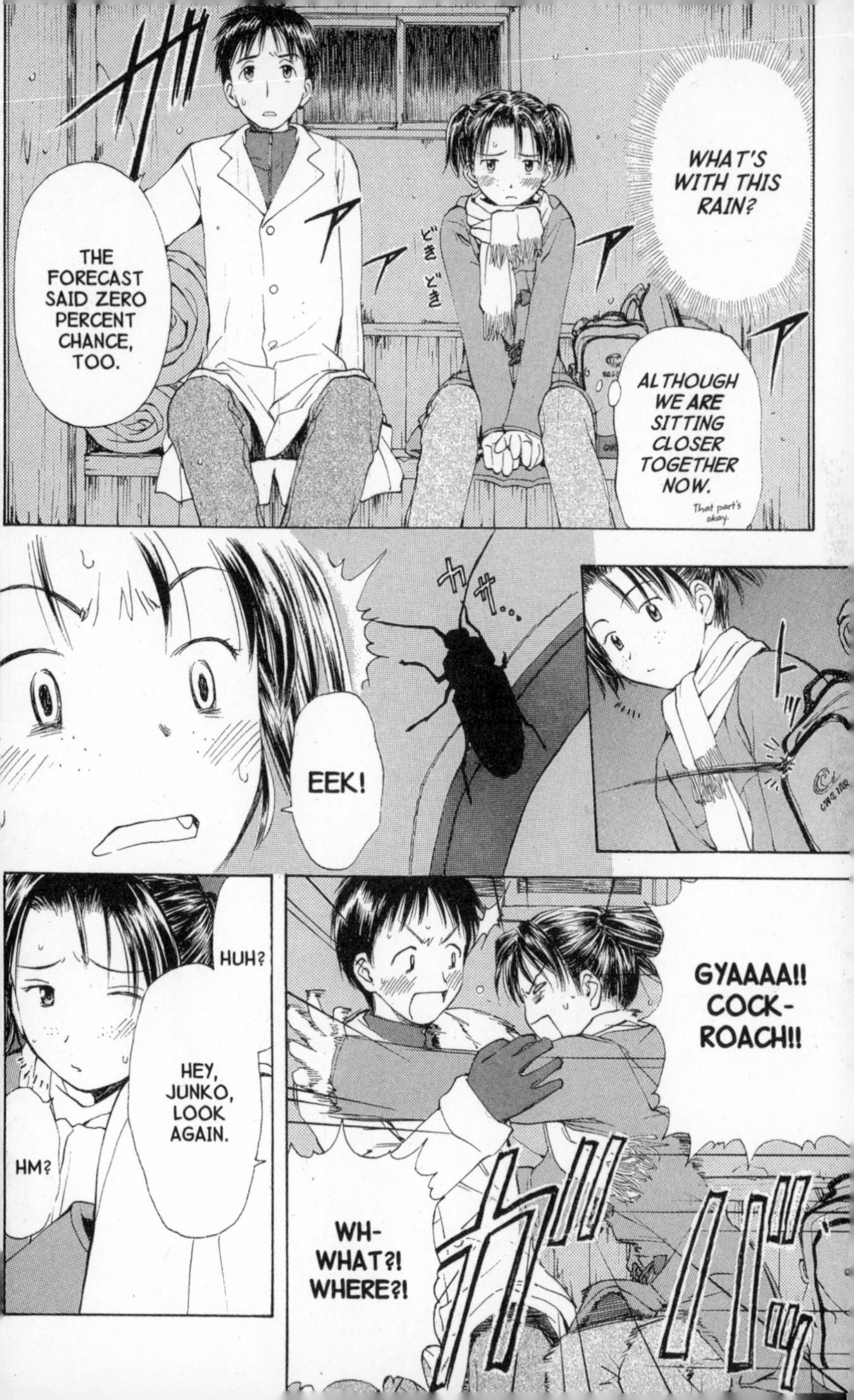
WHAT'S WITH THIS RAIN?
THE FORECAST SAID ZERO PERCENT CHANCE, TOO.
どき どき
ALTHOUGH WE ARE SITTING CLOSER TOGETHER NOW.
That part's okay.
EEK!
GYAAAA!! COCK-ROACH!!
WH-WHAT?! WHERE?!
HUH?
HEY, JUNKO, LOOK AGAIN.
HM?

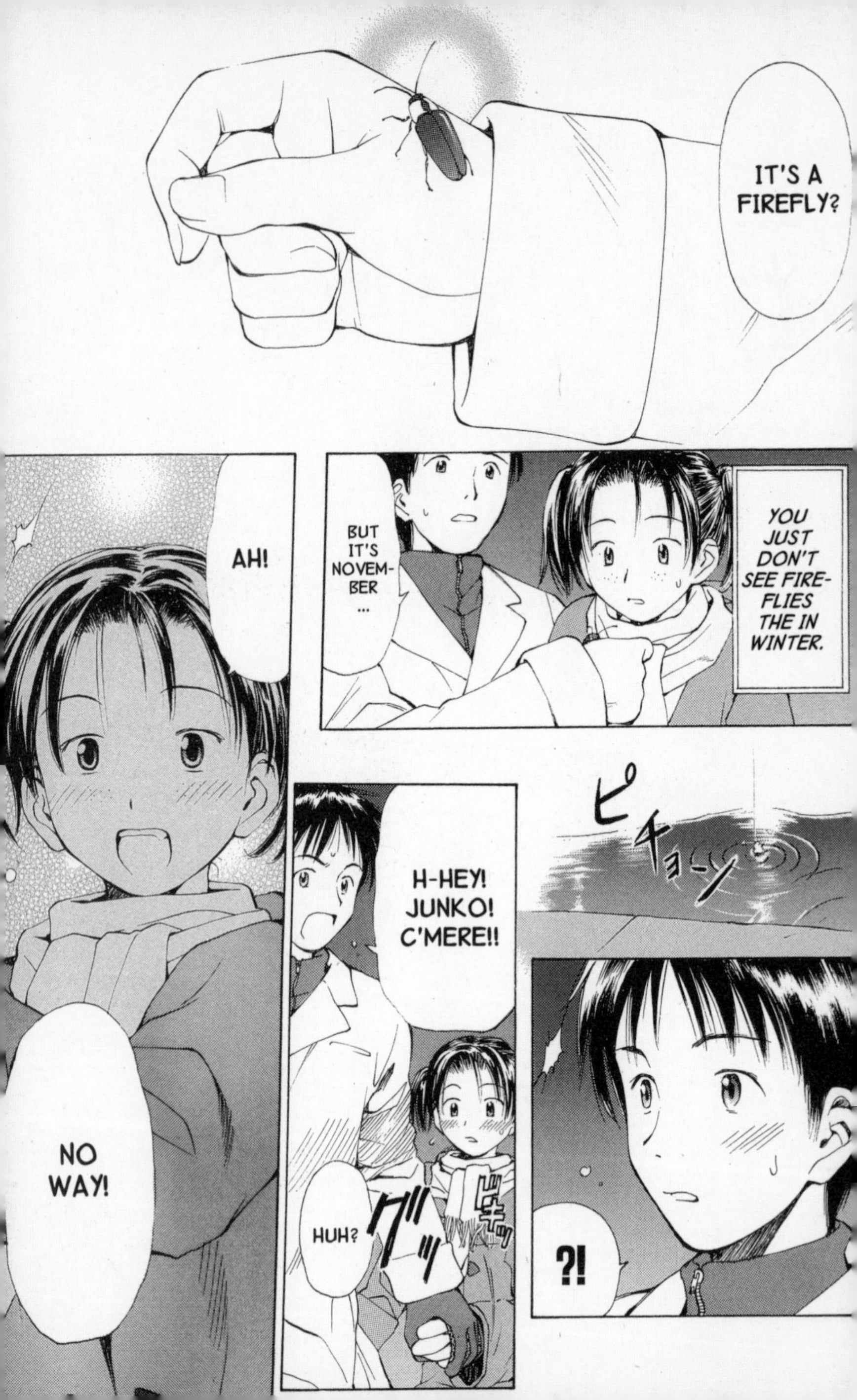
IT'S A FIREFLY?
YOU JUST DON'T SEE FIRE-FLIES THE IN WINTER.
BUT IT'S NOVEMBER ...
ピチョーン
?!
H-HEY! JUNKO! C'MERE!!
グッ
HUH?
AH!
NO WAY!

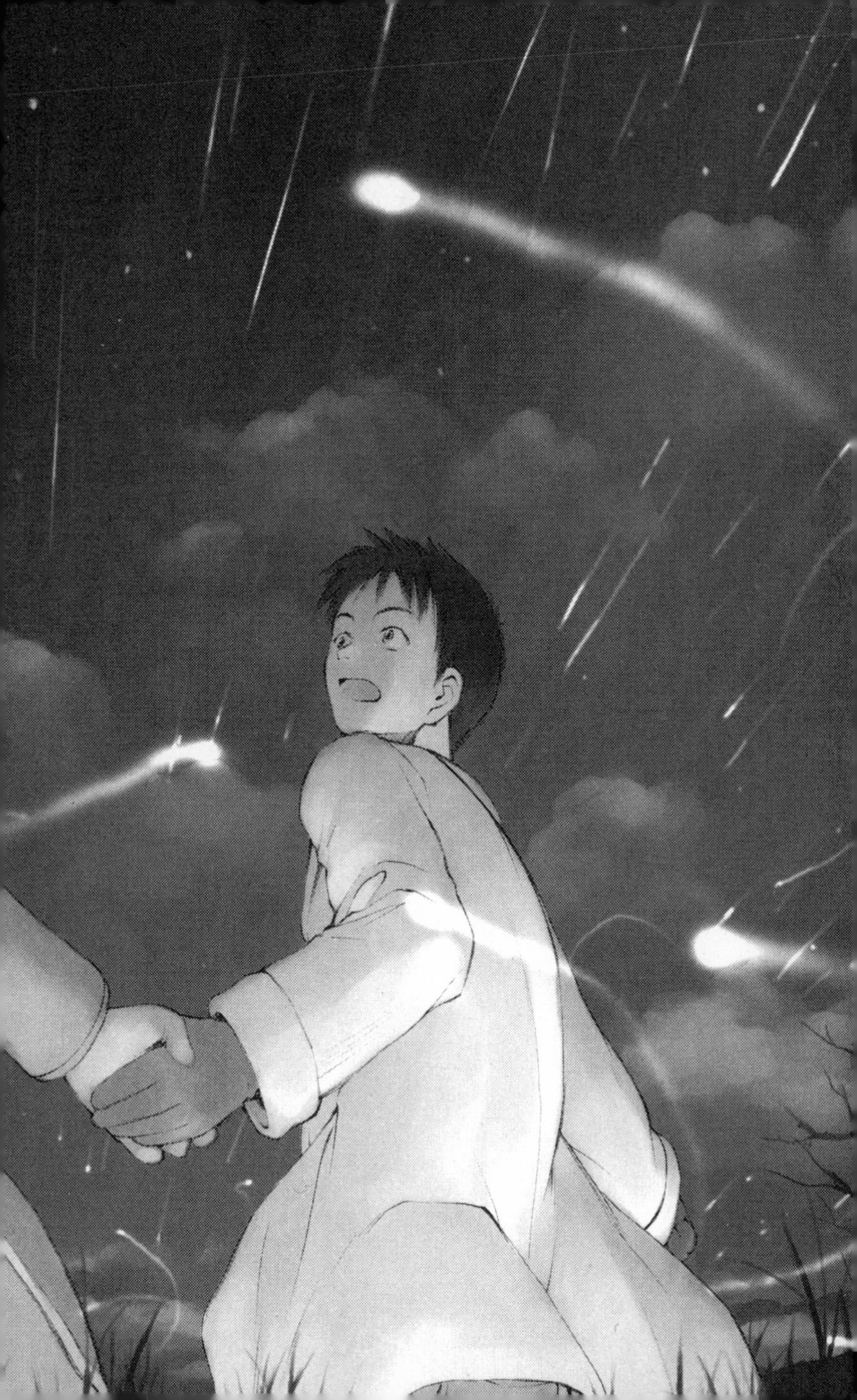

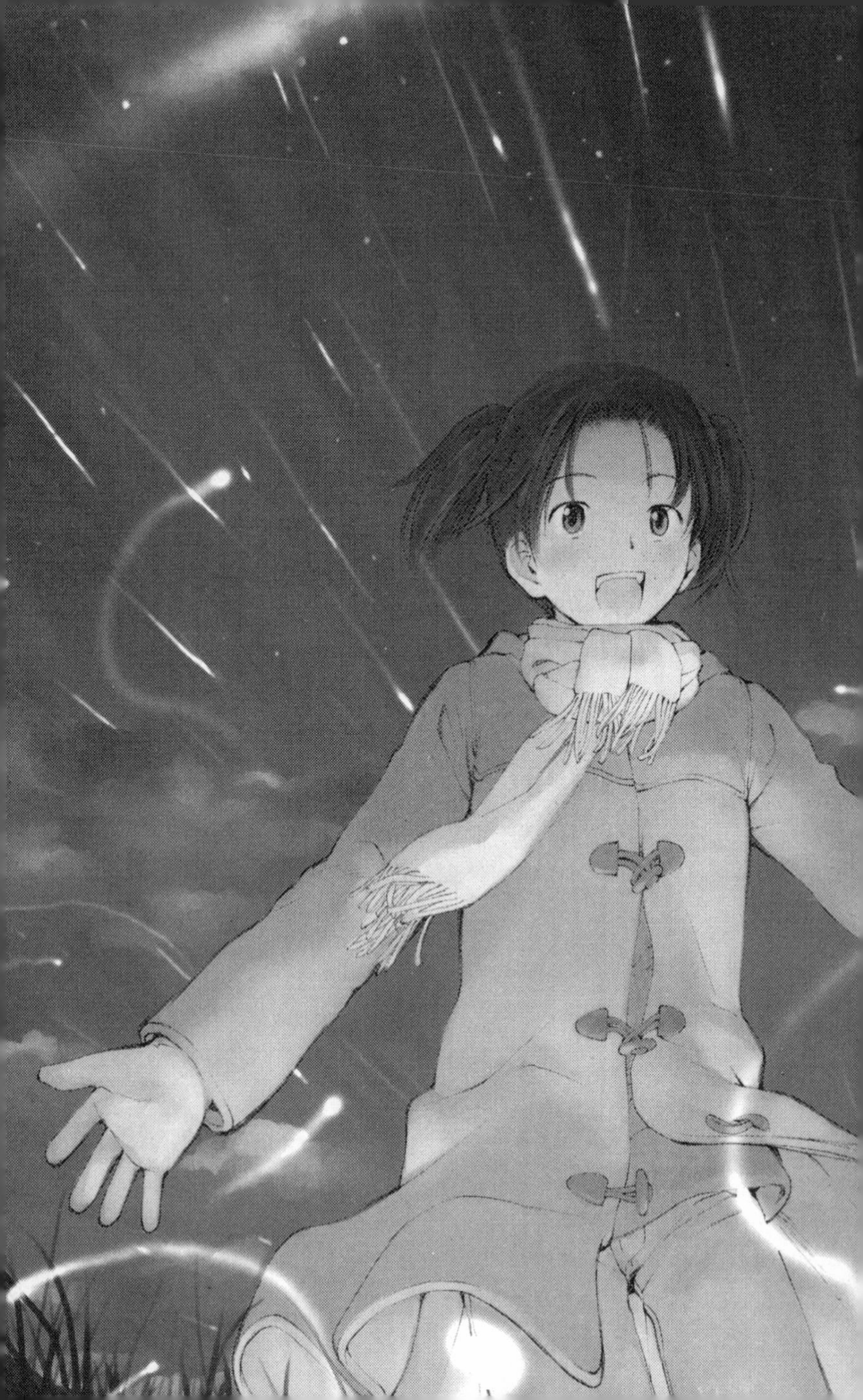

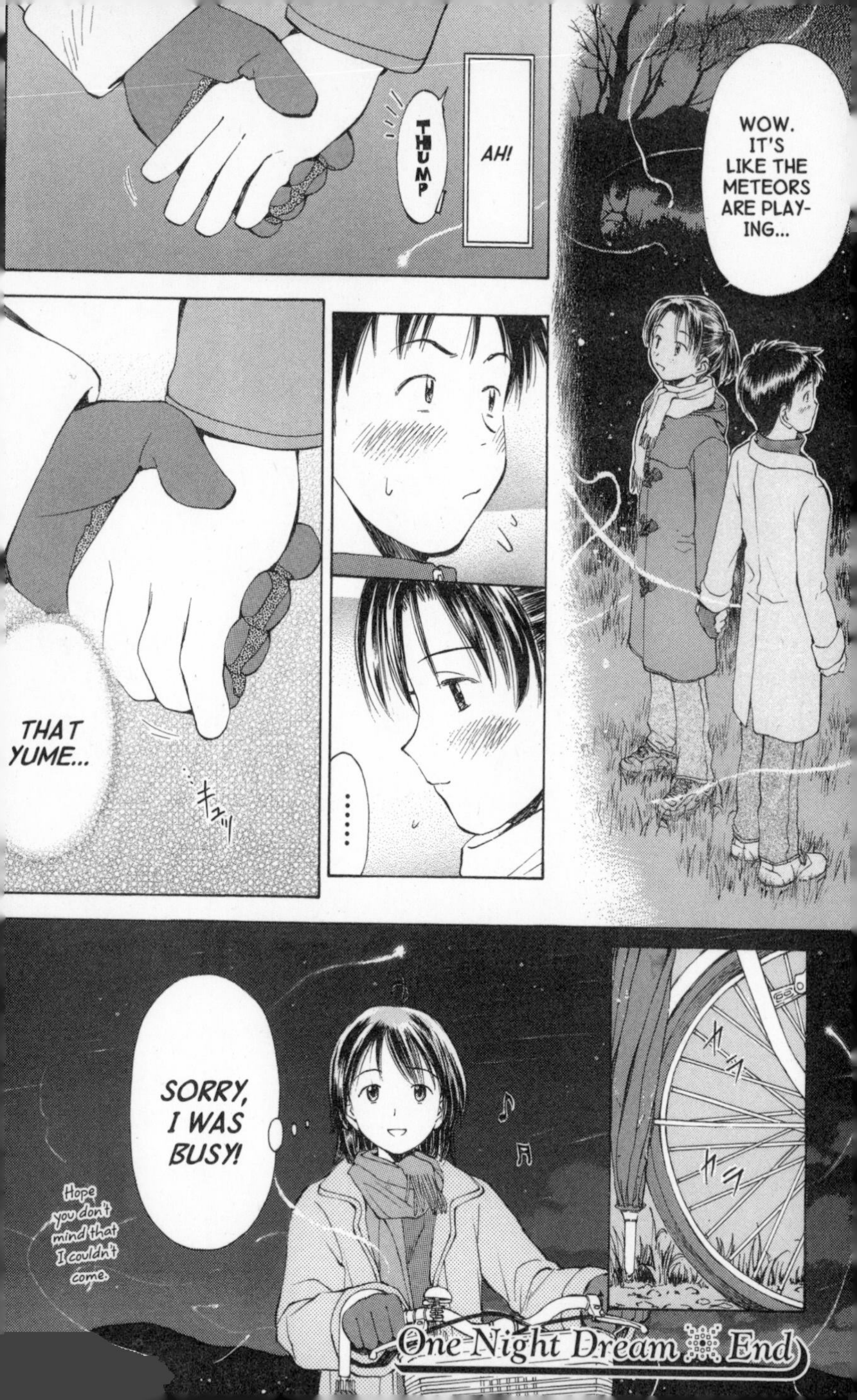

WOW. IT'S LIKE THE METEORS ARE PLAY-ING...
AH!
THUMP
......
THAT YUME...
キュッ
SORRY, I WAS BUSY!
Hope you don't mind that I couldn't come.
One Night Dream End

THE
UNIVERSE
IS INFINITE,
BUT WE LIVE
IN THE HERE
AND NOW.

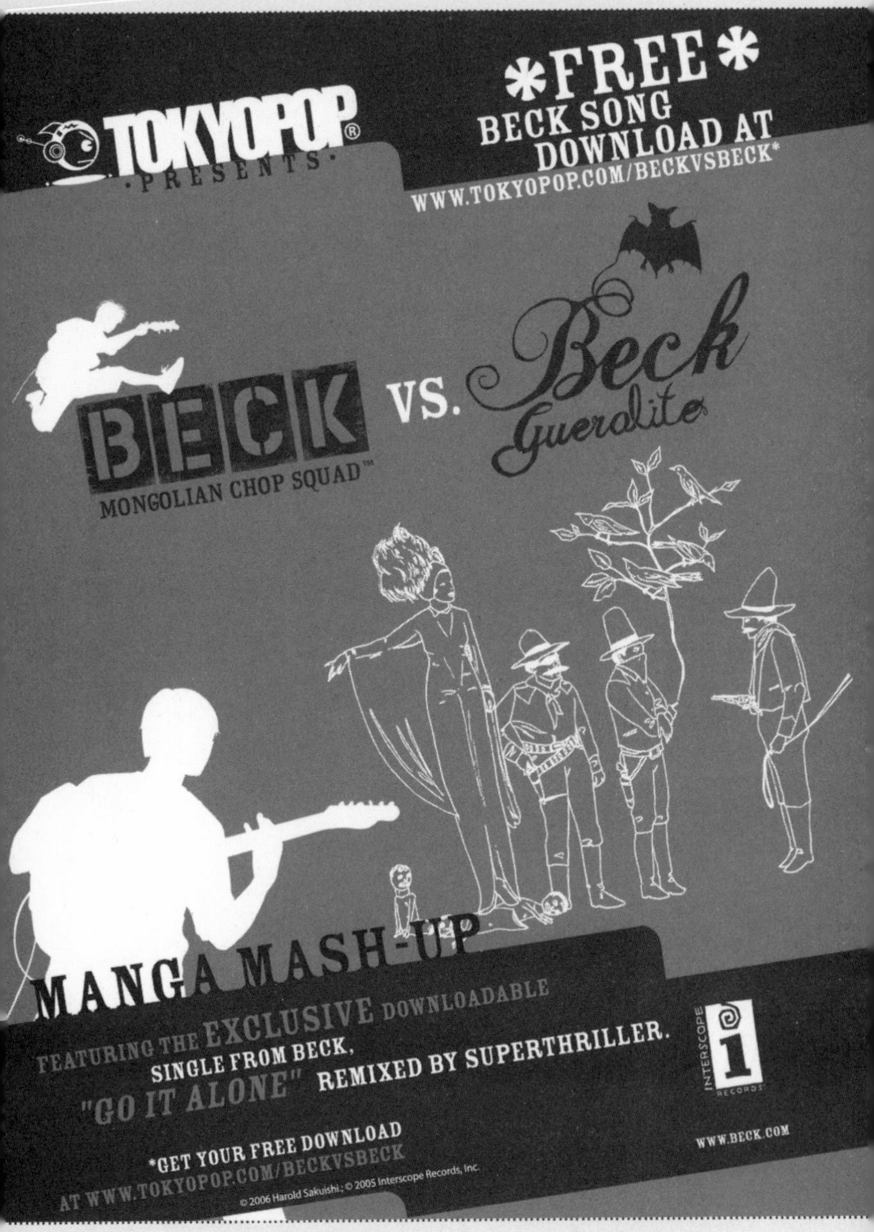
TOKYOPOP® PRESENTS
FREE
BECK SONG
DOWNLOAD AT
WWW.TOKYOPOP.COM/BECKVSBECK*
BECK
MONGOLIAN CHOP SQUAD™
VS.
Beck
Guerolito
MANGA MASH-UP
FEATURING THE EXCLUSIVE DOWNLOADABLE
SINGLE FROM BECK,
"GO IT ALONE" REMIXED BY SUPERTHRILLER.
INTERSCOPE RECORDS
*GET YOUR FREE DOWNLOAD
AT WWW.TOKYOPOP.COM/BECKVSBECK
WWW.BECK.COM
© 2006 Harold Sakuishi; © 2005 Interscope Records, Inc.

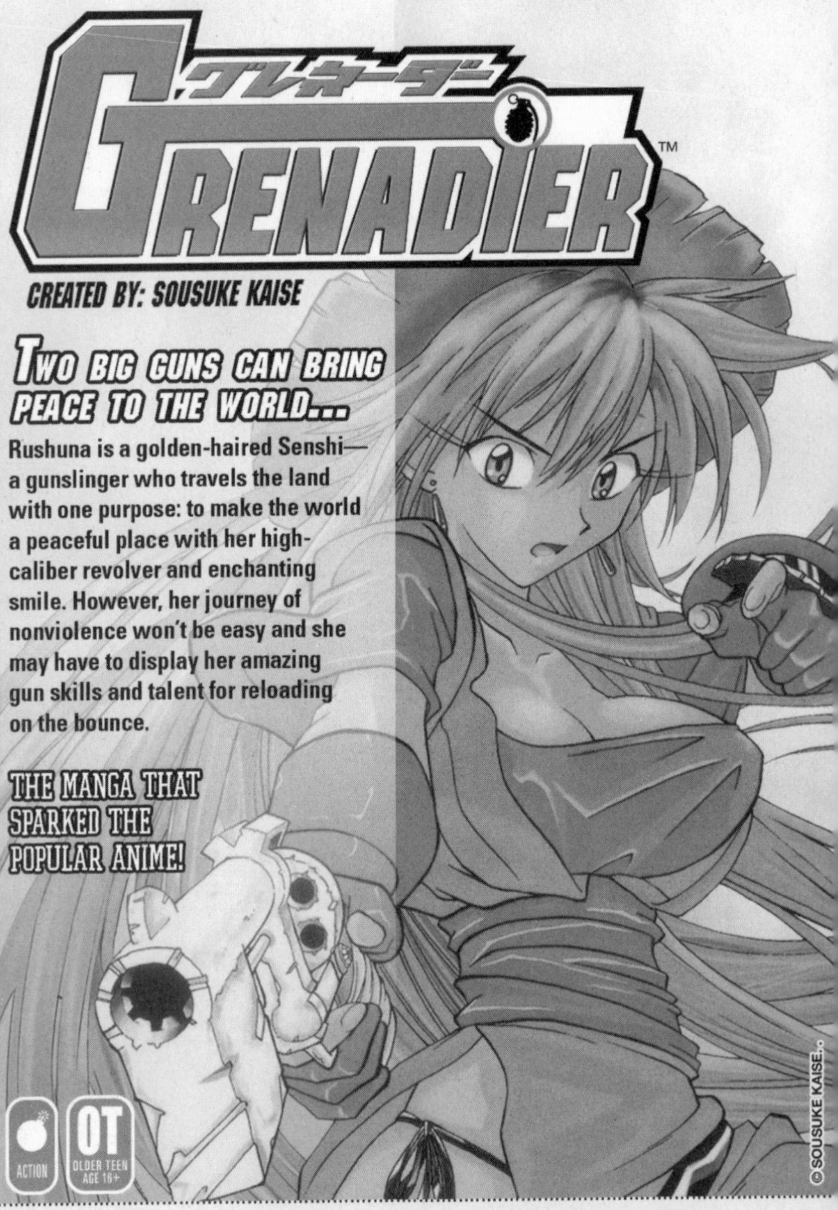
GRENADIER™
グレネーダー
CREATED BY: SOUSUKE KAISE
TWO BIG GUNS CAN BRING PEACE TO THE WORLD...
Rushuna is a golden-haired Senshi—a gunslinger who travels the land with one purpose: to make the world a peaceful place with her high-caliber revolver and enchanting smile. However, her journey of nonviolence won't be easy and she may have to display her amazing gun skills and talent for reloading on the bounce.
THE MANGA THAT SPARKED THE POPULAR ANIME!
ACTION
OT
OLDER TEEN AGE 16+
© SOUSUKE KAISE.